Nathan

Triumph of the king

I hope you have a great time
in University — work hard, play hard
and stay close to Him.

Take Care,
Rowland

Psalm 96:3

Triumph of the king

The message of 2 Samuel

Gordon J. Keddie

 EVANGELICAL PRESS

EVANGELICAL PRESS
12 Wooler Street, Darlington, Co. Durham, DL1 1RQ, England

© Evangelical Press 1990
First published 1990
Reprinted 2000

British Library Cataloguing in Publication Data available

ISBN 0-85234-272-1
Unless otherwise indicated, Scripture quotations in this publication are
from the Holy Bible, New International Version. Copyright © 1973, 1978,
1984 International Bible Society. Published by Hodder & Stoughton.

Printed in Great Britain by Cox & Wyman Ltd, Reading, Berkshire.

Contents

Part IV: Restoration — David's return

Part V: Reflection — David's prophecy of Messiah

Part VI: Recessional — David's last days

Preface

This volume continues the earlier exposition of 1 Samuel in the Welwyn Commentary Series, entitled *Dawn of a kingdom*. 'Continues' is the appropriate word because the division of the original Hebrew text of the one book of Samuel into two shorter portions is wholly artificial and not particularly helpful. Although the Greek (Septuagint) and Latin (Vulgate) translations divided up the text of Samuel and Kings from ancient times, the division of the original Hebrew text of Samuel was as recent as the sixteenth century A.D. and was a concession to what was then the new technology of the printing-press. It was perhaps the first, but certainly not the last, time that the convenience of a publisher made its impression on God's Word!

This unnatural division in the narrative must not be allowed to obscure the sweep and flow of the history which these Scriptures record. Still less must we subdivide it further into a series of 'Bible stories', some of which we teach, while sidestepping others. If we allow ourselves to do this, then instead of a line, we will be left with a collection of segments. The unfolding of God's mighty acts in and through his people over centuries will be minced into more or less disjointed episodes. And just as the eye that looks too closely at a painting loses something of the wider panorama of the artist's vision, so the dismemberment of the unified record of Scripture into bite-size portions will tend to diminish our sense of the majestic vista of redemptive history. We need the 'big picture' so as not to lose the true significance of the detail of which it is comprised. The whole is more than the sum of its parts, precisely because Scripture is not an anthology of pious stories, but a programme for history — the sufficient revelation of the eternal decree of the sovereign God for humanity from the creation 'in the beginning' to the new creation in the Lord Jesus Christ.

Furthermore, the Christ-centred focus of Scripture history in general must never be lost from our daily reading of shorter passages of the Word of God. In the case of the book(s) of Samuel, that focus comes explicitly to the fore in the latter part of 2 Samuel where, in chapter 22, David reflects upon the messianic King who was to come in a future day, and so puts in perspective the significance of his own reign and the unfolding drama of 1 and 2 Samuel as a whole. 1 Samuel brought us from the twilight of the Hebrew republic of the judges to the inception of the Davidic kingdom. 2 Samuel takes us from the triumph of David to the glory of the promised Messiah and the anticipation of the fulness of the gospel of Jesus Christ. This is the perspective which underlies the flow of Old Testament revelation and which ought to animate our reading of the older covenant. Otherwise, we will always wonder why we need to know all these things about often bizarre and always distant events. Jesus Christ really is 'the answer'! And you will see this clearly, just as long as you compare Scripture with Scripture and feast your eyes on the vast and splendid panorama of redemptive history which is the Scripture of the Old and New Testaments. May your study of 2 Samuel bring you closer to the only Redeemer of God's elect, the Lord Jesus Christ.

Gordon J. Keddie
State College, PA, USA.
February 1990

Introduction

History is far more than a bare record of the 'facts'. Inevitably, it is an interpretive process in which the significance of events is assessed and evaluated. It is what historians make of such 'facts' as they are able, or even willing, to observe. For this reason, 'history' depends to a very significant extent on who is writing it! Histories can tell us as much about the historian as about the events they purport to record 'objectively'!

In one sense, the Bible's history is no different from other historical accounts. Scripture is obviously no mere record of what happened. It is a carefully crafted account of the history of God's mighty acts and of the people he has called to be his own. The salient events of God's dealings with them are presented in such a way as to provide an interpretive framework for the proper understanding of both the origin and destiny of the human race. The difference between the biblical interpretation of history and all other histories is that it alone is truth revealed by the living God. Factual accuracy is selectively and interpretively, but infallibly, observed in order to bring out in the sharpest focus the purposes of God for the human race. Precisely because the Scriptures are the inspired, infallible and inerrant Word of God, they represent God's absolutely authoritative 'interpretation' of history. Needless to say, this is not the same as saying that the Bible is to be viewed as the divine theory of the meaning of history, as if, like some superior version of the academic historians of our universities, God were proposing a particularly weighty and sagacious opinion on things past, present and to come! Biblical history is certainly set in the contexts of specific peoples, locations and eras. Nevertheless, it is cosmic in scope in that it defines the essential form and direction of human history. As such it covers, in a broad sweep, the entire saga of the human race, from the creation to the as yet future consummation, when the Lord Jesus

Christ will return as promised to judge the living and the dead. It is that history, above all other histories, that we really need to know, precisely because it is neither theory nor speculation, but nothing less than the delineation of God's way of salvation against the background of the dark tapestry of human rebellion and the immanent and ever-active judgements of a holy God.

The flow of the text of the Word of God is therefore never a slavish catalogue of facts in which, with all the panache of the telephone directory, it delivers point by point a computer read-out of world chronology! Nothing will bury meaning faster than a deluge of mere 'facts'! God's Word never permits the trees to obscure our view of the wood! The chapters that straddle the two books of Samuel illustrate this point very well. 1 Samuel 28-31 and 2 Samuel 1 cover the two or three weeks in which Saul's reign ended and David's began. In the account of this period, however, the inspired writer does not follow a rigorous chronology. Two passages are conspicuously and deliberately out of correct chronological order. 1 Samuel 29 actually takes place in between 28:2 and 28:4. Then, to make things even more confusing, 28:3 has been brought out of the past, from 25:1! The true time-sequence is 28:3; 28:1-2; 29:1-11; 28:4-25; followed by chapters 30 and 31 (which may actually have happened simultaneously or in reverse order!). 2 Samuel 1 wraps it all up.

Why all this shuffling of chronology? The answer is 'history'! What is the writer telling us? Clearly he is not trying to change the facts. The information is all there to enable us to work out the actual sequence of events. So what is his purpose? Surely it is to highlight the way in which God was preserving and leading David through what could have been the most disastrous period in his whole life and career. On the one hand, the drama of Saul's sad end is heightened by placing the account of David's deliverance from having to fight for the Philistines (chapter 29) *between* Saul's meeting with the witch of Endor (chapter 28) and his death on Mount Gilboa (chapter 31), even though these last two events took place within a single period of twelve to eighteen hours! Furthermore, when David's victory over the Amalekites (chapter 30) — which was a mere border skirmish compared to the clash of armies on Mount Gilboa and, anyway, might well have taken place shortly after that great cataclysm — is put *before* Saul's defeat, then David's successes are given centre stage in the account and Saul becomes the background. Strict chronology would have had the opposite effect: David would have been marching to and fro around distant Ziklag with his 600 men, while Saul was engaged in a great, though disastrous, battle of national survival in the north. The careful rearrangement of the account gives us God's infallibly correct interpretation of the events. And what this amounts to is that David's local victory over the Amalekite brigands is ultimately more significant than the destruction of Saul and the army of the Lord at the hands of the Philistines! God was with David but he passed over Saul! The historian's art, under the inspiration of the Spirit of God, becomes the handmaid of God's revelation of truth! The real truth is rendered unmistakably obvious by the studied restructuring of bland chronology in such a way as to tease out the underlying threads of God's purposes for his people.

As the continuation of the narrative of 1 Samuel, the Second Book of Samuel further develops the three principal themes which were interwoven throughout the earlier book.[1]

1. *The development of the theocratic (Davidic) monarchy* continues to dominate the story-line. In 2 Samuel it comes into its own, not only because David's triumph is consummated in his establishment as king over all Israel, but because he is led by the Spirit of God to pen, in the eighteenth psalm (2 Samuel 22), a prophetic foretaste of the promised Messiah, in whom the deeper significance of the Davidic monarchy would be fulfilled. This messianic thrust is therefore central to any proper understanding of 2 Samuel. We are called by the text, as it unfolds, to look beyond the immediate context and its sometimes seemingly petty preoccupations, and see, rising above the horizon of divine revelation, the coming of the kingdom of God in the person and work of the Lord Jesus Christ. In his classic exposition of Psalm 18/2 Samuel 22, John Brown[2] argues persuasively that this psalm not only has a prophetic messianic component, but is as fully messianic as Psalms 2, 16, 22, 40 and 110.[3] 'The truth seems to be,' writes Brown, that 'David, full of pious gratitude to Jehovah for his goodness in his deliverance from his enemies, is visited with an impulse of the inspiring Spirit and rapt into future ages when his Son and Lord was to be delivered from deeper afflictions than his, and raised to higher honours.'[4] Referring to 2 Samuel 22 and 23:1-7, Graeme Goldsworthy observes that these 'last words of David sum up the theological

meaning of the covenant of 2 Samuel 7 and indeed of the whole reign of David. The covenant and reign of David are key elements in the messianic hope developing in the Old Testament. Both the man and his office are idealized here without the qualifications of the historic blemishes. As such they form an important link in the chain of Christological reference in the Bible.'[5] The apostle Peter declared in his great Pentecost sermon that David 'was a prophet and knew that God had promised him on oath that he would place one of his descendants on his throne'. And who was that descendant? Peter was clear that he is none other than the risen Christ: 'Seeing what was ahead, he [David] spoke of the resurrection of Christ...' (Acts 2:30-31). This is the most vital insight that can be brought to the understanding of 2 Samuel.

2. *The absolute sovereignty of God* again towers over the convoluted schemings of men. Perhaps particularly in the two great tragedies of David's reign — his sin with Bathsheba and the rebellion of his son, Absalom — we see the hand of God revealed in sovereign grace in the warfare between our sin and the claims of his righteousness. Even the failures of God's servant, David, ultimately serve the purpose of God. Sin is, in the end, the unwilling and uncomprehending tool of God's sovereign purpose. Try as it may to thwart the Lord, it only turns in upon itself to provide either an occasion of just judgement or an opportunity to produce a victory for redeeming love.

3. Inextricably interwined is *the certain triumph of the righteousness of God*. Were we to read daily events with the eye of faith instead of a jaundiced fascination with bad news, we should be far more aware of the fact that God is executing his justice in the movements of his providence (i.e., our history). His ways are most certainly not our ways. His timetable is quite different from ours. Nevertheless, the contours of divine justice are not so obscured by the effects of man's inhumanity to man as to be entirely invisible. The falls of empires have invariably been the just conclusions to their dark ascendancies; the rise of other nations, the harbinger and reward of divine righteousness in Christ. So Adolf Hitler justly perishes by his own hand and is ignominiously incinerated as if he were so much garbage. On the other hand, a generation and a continent away, once war-ravaged South Korea leaps to the forefront of world economic development and prosperity as God converts millions to Christ and makes that country, in practice if not in tradition, far

more of a Christian country than any in Western Europe. The hand of the Lord is there to be seen in the events of our times.

In the history of David — warts and all — all these elements are plainly discernible. They encourage us to look expectantly for the blessing of God in our own day — all the more so, since David's royal Son, the Lord Jesus Christ, is now enthroned in the glory of the Father's presence as the Mediator-King who rules over all things and will, in the fulness of his time, deliver up his consummated kingdom to his Father-God and ours (1 Corinthians 15:24). With the blessing of God, this is what we shall discover in the unfolding drama of 2 Samuel.

PART I
Revival — David the king

1.
The king is dead!

Please read 2 Samuel 1:1-27
'How the mighty have fallen!' (2 Samuel 1:19).

The Battle of Mount Gilboa and the virtual elimination of the house of Saul come as a kind of Hebrew *Gotterdämmerung* — an end of waiting for the inevitable and the beginning of a new order altogether. The 'turning-points' of history, however true from the perspective of historical and theological analysis, are never simple and painless transitions 'on the ground'. The fact that Saul's death heralded a giant leap for Israel in the right direction in no way meant that strife and confusion would be banished overnight. In point of fact, the interregnum following Gilboa lasted over seven years and saw civil war ravage the land, until David triumphed over the surviving son of Saul, Ish-Bosheth, and assumed the reins of power. The history of this period, as with the rest of 2 Samuel, places David at centre stage and so, not surprisingly, the account begins with the news of Saul's death coming to David's ears and his reaction to the demise of his enemy. The opening chapter consists of two parts: first, the account of the Amalekite's report to David of the death of Saul (1:1-16) and, secondly, the remarkable eulogy which David composed to lament the passing of Saul and Jonathan (1:17-27).

David hears of the death of Saul [1:1-16]

Most people would probably find it quite easy to gloat over the fall of their worst enemy. Not so David. His response is to mourn and lament — and to enshrine his sorrow for ever in a most remarkable and generous-spirited eulogy. The reason for this, observes D. F. Payne, lies in the reality that 'David was not Saul's enemy, not even

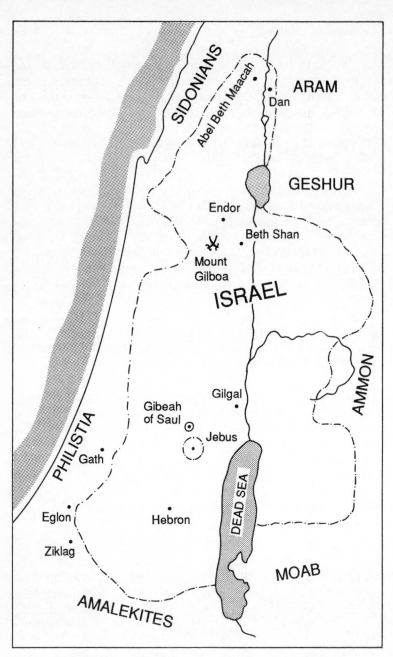

MAP 1 — The kingdom of Saul c.1025 B.C.

in his private thoughts.'[1] This points up the simple fact that it takes
two to make a fight. However much Saul was an enemy in his
actions towards David, David was under no obligation to think or
act with enmity towards Saul. It is a measure of the genuine
godliness of David that he grieved over Saul's attitude to him and
never once raised his hand against Saul. This is essential to any
understanding of David's reaction to the news of Saul's death.

Report from the battle: Saul and Jonathan are dead! (1:1-10)

This passage is heavy with ironies. David's defeat of the
Amalekites — really little more than a tribal skirmish — is in the
spotlight, while the mighty battle in the north is marked only by the
words **'after the death of Saul'** (1:1). The messenger from Gilboa
is an Amalekite — from the very tribe which had just felt the sharp
edge of David's punitive expedition from Ziklag. Furthermore,
Saul's death had been predicted by Samuel in his posthumous
appearance at Endor on the night before the battle and the reason
given was that Saul had not obeyed the Lord in carrying out his
'fierce wrath against the Amalekites' (1 Samuel 28:18).
    'On the third day' after David's return from the pursuit of the
Amalekites, a young man in the traditional garb of mourning — **'his
clothes torn and with dust on his head'** (1:2; cf. 1 Samuel 4:12)
— arrived at the camp. He had escaped, he said, from the Israelite
camp, having witnessed Israel's defeat and the death of Saul and
Jonathan. How did he know that Saul and Jonathan were dead,
asked David. The Amalekite's explanation (1:6-10) was that he
'happened to be' on the battlefield and came on Saul, all alone and
wounded, **'leaning on his spear'** with the Philistines **'almost upon
him'**. Spotting the young Amalekite, Saul called out to him and he
asked, **'What can I do?'** David must have smelt a rat, for he then
interjected a question as to who his informant was and discovered
him to be an Amalekite — a fact that could only have confirmed his
suspicion that all was not quite as it seemed (1:8). Why must this be
so? Simply because David knew Saul, the Israelite army and the
nature of battle. Young Amalekites did not serve in the Israelite
armies. Kings did not stand about alone on battlefields ready to
enlist the aid of wandering Amalekites who 'happened to be' there.
Even allowing that strange things can happen in the heat of a battle,

David would have been gripped by the improbability of the story. But the Amalekite continued: Saul had asked him to kill him and the young man duly obliged, pausing only to remove the crown and armlet so that he could take them to David. He had told his story. He could now only wait for David's response.

The explanation is so obviously a cock-and-bull story concocted by the Amalekite to ingratiate himself with David, who he surely believed was likely to be the next king of Israel. Apart from his claim that the king was dead and that he had removed his crown and armlet, all other details in 1:6-10 are self-serving fiction.[2] They are completely contradicted by the earlier matter-of-fact historical account of Saul's death in 1 Samuel 31, which is surely, as A. W. Pink observes, 'God's description of Saul's death,' while 'II Samuel 1 gives man's fabrication.'[3] David, of course, was hearing the news for the first time — and not the final version of the divinely inspired chronicler. In the account David heard, the Amalekite 'happened to be' on Mount Gilboa and happened to be the last able-bodied man around Saul, as the Philistine chariots happened to be closing in on him! After allegedly killing Saul, at the king's request, he then happened to be able to remove the crown and armlet from his body, in full view of the advancing Philistines, and escape in one piece to tell the tale! There was something wrong here. Things did not quite fit, even if the crown proved Saul's death and Israel's defeat. And it seems clear enough from David's question (1:8) and his subsequent actions (1:13-16) that he, while apparently taking at face value the young man's claim that he killed Saul, was not at all satisfied either by his rendition of the facts or his motives in coming to Ziklag.

One of the minor curiosities of modern Old Testament exegesis is the number of commentators who give credence to the Amalekite's account and see its reconciliation with 1 Samuel 31 as a problem. Some see it as a 'variant reading' — i.e., two contradictory accounts of events we may never be able to resolve with certainty. Others see them as complementary accounts which can be harmonized, thereby arriving at a workable theory about what happened. These views, it seems to me, arise from an underlying assumption that the entire account (1 Samuel 31 and 2 Samuel 1) cannot be regarded as a unitary, accurate and, not least, divinely inspired and infallible record of actual events, but rather are a collage of traditions, oral and written, cobbled together by editors, whose intentions are not readily discernible on the face of the text. The idea that someone can read this passage and discern that the Amalekite was a lying opportunist (2 Samuel 1), while the Lord's historian was setting down the facts (1 Samuel 31), seems to have been ruled out by these interpreters as even a possibility! Yet this is quite clearly the natural reading of the passage, for when the text is read for what it is — the inspired and infallible Word of God — questions of 'variant traditions' and speculations as to who is telling the truth (the Amalekite or the Spirit-led chronicler) do not arise. The text itself and its contextual relationship to the historical and theological connections of the whole history of God's dealings with his people (and the other nations of the region, including the Amalekites) does not suggest any problem. The quotations of the Amalekite are to be interpreted in the light of the historical framework set down by the chronicler under the inspiration of God. No one can possibly ascribe divinely inspired accuracy to the story of the Amalekite as if he were uttering sober history as well. The very thought that his tale is an equally valid historical source, which can be used as a basis for modifying or denying the accuracy of the sober historical record of Saul's death in 1 Samuel 31, rests on a practical denial of divine inspiration. As an accurately recorded part of the Word of God, the Amalekite's story does, of course, shed its own peculiar light on the proceedings. It shows us how opportunists work. More significantly still, it demonstrates the truly princely godliness of David as he responds to the death of Saul. It shows that his attitude to Saul in death, as in life, was one of genuine love for his person and reverence for his office. It shows also that above all he loved the Lord and law of the Lord.

Response to the news: mourning until evening (1:11-12)

No doubt the Amalekite expected David to rejoice that Saul was gone for ever. David's response, however, was to mourn for '**Saul and his son Jonathan, and for the army of the Lord and the house of Israel, because they had fallen by the sword'**. For the rest of that day, the outlaws of Ziklag grieved over the humiliation of the Lord's people at the hands of their enemies. The political advantage of the Gilboa defeat did not diminish their sorrow.

Rewarded opportunism: the execution of the Amalekite (1:13-16)

The mourning over, David turned to the Amalekite messenger, who no doubt felt he had a reward coming his way. David asked two questions. The first was to ask him from whence he came. The young man claimed to be **'the son of an alien, an Amalekite'** (1:13). An 'alien' was a foreigner resident in Israel, one who had certain privileges in the nation and who might well have been a believer. Whether this was true of the Amalekite, or just another part of his cover-story, we shall never know.[4] Suffice it to say that if this were true, it implied that he must have been acquainted with the contours of Israelite religion and society — in this specific instance, the status and role of the king as the Lord's anointed. He would have been aware of the particular honour with which the king's person and office were to be held by the people. Hence David's second question probed the ground for his subsequent condemnation as a murderer: **'Why were you not afraid to lift your hand to destroy the Lord's anointed?'** (1:14). This Amalekite was without excuse. It was not good enough to plead that Saul commanded it, or that it was suicide or even euthanasia. Still less could the man simply admit he murdered Saul to help David up onto his throne! He was trapped — condemned out of his own mouth! To confess to killing Saul was to admit to killing the man the Lord had anointed — the man whose death was in the hand of the Lord. The Amalekite 'had been guilty of murder and treason, and had usurped the prerogative of God himself' — something which David had refused to do, when he had been presented with the opportunity.[5]

David therefore ordered the Amalekite's execution (1:15-16). He was condemned by the witness of his own mouth and that of Saul's crown and armlet. For all we know, David may have wondered whether the Amalekite was a mercenary soldier who did play a part in Saul's death or merely a battlefield looter who took the crown and saw his chance for glory. But even if David suspected he was a liar and an opportunist, he was still obliged in all justice to act on the evidence. The man who so pointedly spared the life of Saul when he had it in his power to kill him could not permit a self-confessed regicide to go free, far less be rewarded and thus leave the implication that David not only approved of the regicide, but perhaps even arranged for it to take place. So perished the Amalekite.

David's eulogy — the lament of the bow [1:17-27]

'David took up [a] lament concerning Saul and his son Jonathan' (1:17). The *Qina*, or lament, was a chanted poem sung in
mourning for someone who had died, or even prophetically in the
prospect of death or destruction (cf. 2 Chronicles 35:25; Jeremiah
9:17; Ezekiel 2:10).[6] David composed this 'lament of the bow' as
a memorial of the house of Saul which would celebrate their
positive role in the national life of Israel, particularly their military
prowess — hence the mention of 'the bow'. It was to be taught to
the 'men of Judah' and was written in 'the Book of Jashar', which
is mentioned in Joshua 10:13 and is thought to have been an
anthology — added to over the years — of 'poems commemorating
great events in national life'.[7]

The lament is a great surge of anguish which, like a mighty sigh,
gradually fades into silent sadness. The structure appears to be as
follows:

    I. Theme: how the mighty have fallen! (1:19)
    II. Sorrow for the loss of mighty leaders (1:20-24)
    III. Sorrow for the loss of a dear friend (1:25-26)
    IV. Theme reiterated (1:27)

Theme: how the mighty have fallen! (1:19)

David was greatly wronged by Saul, but never once in Scripture is
there any record of him speaking abusively about the king. He
practises the ancient adage: *De mortuis nil nisi bonum* ('Of the
dead, say nothing but what is good'). Saul and Jonathan are
described as the 'glory' of Israel and 'the mighty' who have fallen
on the 'heights' of Gilboa. Saul's faults are laid aside and his status
as the warrior-king, who had unified and defended Israel through a
long reign by his military prowess, is lifted up before the sorrowing
nation. Whatever the defects of Saul's rule, it had many advantages
and blessings, which would be swept away now that he was no
longer there and Israel was exposed before the Philistine armies.

Sorrow for the loss of mighty leaders (1:20-24)

The disaster of Gilboa should be mourned on several counts. The loss of mighty leaders could only have profound and humiliating consequences for God's people.

1. **'Tell it not in Gath...'** (1:20). The celebration of the Philistines underlines the disgrace of the Lord's people and casts a shadow over the cause of God and his truth. When the failures of God's men and women are displayed before the world, the resultant shame calls for the deepest mourning. The triumph of God's enemies is the antithesis of redemption.

2. **'O mountains of Gilboa, may you have neither dew nor rain...'** (1:21-22). The very land of Israel — the site of the battle — must remember and mourn the terrible loss of her dead heroes. Saul and Jonathan died in defence of the land which God had given to his people as their inheritance. There **'the shield of the mighty was defiled'** — that is to say, it did not protect its bearer — but the weapons wielded by Jonathan and Saul did not **'turn back'** or **'return unsatisfied'**. The blood of the enemy mingled with that of the heroes.

3. **'Saul and Jonathan — in life they were loved and gracious...'** (1:23). The lives of father and son were intertwined in life and in death. Their relationship with one another is in view. David forbears to address the problems in his own relationship with the late king. This is no cover-up. Neither is it a historian's analysis of the man, his faith and his reign. It is a generous recognition of both the Saul who fought the wars of the Lord and the Jonathan who was loyal to him until his last breath.

4. **'O daughters of Israel, weep for Saul...'** (1:24). The reference to fine clothing indicates the fruits of the strong rule of Saul. He had been able, for the most part, to achieve the peace of Israel within secure frontiers — something which had largely eluded the fragmented nation of the period of the judges. Now they were at the mercy of the Philistines and so the women of Israel must weep, as surely as the daughters of the Philistines would be glad.

Sorrow for the loss of a dear friend (1:25-26)

David testifies to his personal loss in the death of Jonathan, his closest friend. Saul's name is conspicuously absent. The love he experienced from his friend, that was **'more wonderful than that of women'**, is not indicative of a homosexual relationship, as modern defenders of that perversion like to imagine.[8] This is that rich bond of affection and of covenant brotherhood which men share and which can indeed be 'wonderful'. The language is, of course, poetic and cannot be interpreted in a manner prejudicial to the biblical teaching on marriage and the love that is to exist between husband and wife. David speaks here of the cameraderie of youth and war, of the brotherhood of adventure and the risk of death, of the confidence of men in one another when their lives depend on the faithfulness and courage of the other. This is a joy that is as ineffable as it is thoroughly masculine.

The theme reiterated: how the mighty have fallen! (1:27)

The lament ends as it began, with the difference perhaps that the final words, **'The weapons of war have perished,'** leave us in the mud and carnage of the deserted battlefield to contemplate the aching loss which war inevitably carries in its train. There is nothing of the romanticized classical heroism so beloved of the Victorian era, when schoolboys were steeped in the glorification of patriotic death from the Latin classroom (where Horace taught them: *Dulce et decorum est pro patria mori* — 'It is sweet and honourable to die for your country') to the sports field (in which the poet Sir Henry Newbolt saw a model for fighting Britain's foreign wars!).[9] In contrast, the Bible never glorifies war or death, far less sees it as a kind of serious version of sport. Death is an enemy. Life is glory. When David says, 'Your glory, O Israel, lies slain on your heights,' he is not extolling glorious death, he is grieving for the waste of glorious life! Death and defeat are always humiliations. Humbling, not exultation, is the appropriate emotion. David begins his march to Israel's newly vacated throne in the deepest sorrow over the disaster that has come upon the Lord's people, but with a rising faith in the Lord who, in wrath as in mercy, does all things well for his believing people.

2.
Who will reign?

Please read 2 Samuel 2:1–4:12
'In the course of time, David enquired of the Lord' (2 Samuel 2:1).

The death of Saul on Mount Gilboa did not leave the way clear for David to ascend the throne as the Lord's anointed king, even if he had, in truth, been king since the prophet Samuel had so long ago chosen him from among the sons of Jesse. Although three sons of Saul had perished in battle, a fourth, named Ish-Bosheth, remained to polarize the loyalties of the surviving leadership of the nation and the tribes themselves. It was to be more than seven years before these rivalries would be resolved in favour of God's chosen king. For most of that time, civil war would wrack the body politic of Israel. And before it was over, treason and murder would become the very instruments of policy and ever after cast their shadow upon David's reign over the united kingdom.

The history of this turbulent period is recounted in 2 Samuel 2-4. David is certainly the dominating figure in the narrative, in that it is his rise to power which is its central focus. Most of the action, however, concerns four other men: Abner, the commander of Saul's army, who backed the losing side and lost his life as well; Joab, the son of David's sister, Zeruiah, and the future commander of David's army; and the murderous sons of Rimmon, Recab and Baanah, who repeated the mistake of the Amalekite who came to David at Ziklag and were justly executed for their crime.

The story is unfolded very straightforwardly in three parts, each in turn expanding our view of the events which transformed David from the exile of Ziklag to the unchallenged monarch of all Israel. We are first shown how there came to be *two kings* in Israel (2:1-11); then how this developed into *two sides* in a civil war (2:12–3:5);

and finally how that war ended in *two murders* and the triumph of David (3:6–4:12).

Two kings [2:1-11]

Any national disaster will leave a political vacuum in its wake. Saul's death was David's opportunity, but it also left the field clear for others to assert themselves. The test in such circumstances, for those who love the Lord, is to look to him for guidance rather than indulge self-centred opportunistic impulses. Two men immediately made their mark on the situation, although, as we shall see, in rather different ways. One was, of course, David. The other was Abner, the general of Saul's army. What these strong men now did was to shape the immediate destiny of Israel.

David becomes king in Hebron (2:1-7)

David was in no rush to claim his kingdom. Rather than leaning on his own understanding, he waited for the Lord to direct him (Proverbs 3:5-6). **'In the course of time, David enquired of the Lord'** and the Lord sent him **'to Hebron'** (2:1). 'We never lose anything by believing and patiently waiting upon God,' writes A. W. Pink, 'but we are always made to suffer when we take things into our own hands and rush blindly ahead.'[1] If Thomas Jefferson was wise enough to advocate counting to ten before acting on an impulse, how much more should God's children be content to put every decision before the Lord in patient prayer and meditation!

Careful diplomacy both preceded and succeeded David's anointing as king in Hebron (2:4).[2] Living for the Lord is a matter of *ora et labora* — of praying and working. The earlier cultivation of the people of Judah and the associated Jerahmeelites and Kenites (1 Samuel 30:26-31; cf. 27:8-12) created a climate of acceptance — indeed, a power base — in his own tribe of Judah. The first recorded act of his reign was to hold out an olive-branch to Jabesh Gilead, the heartland of support for the house of Saul. Commending them for their loyalty to Saul, he quietly invited their confirmation of his accession as king over Judah (2:4-7). The next time we see David, civil war had been in progress for **'a long time'** (3:1); six sons had

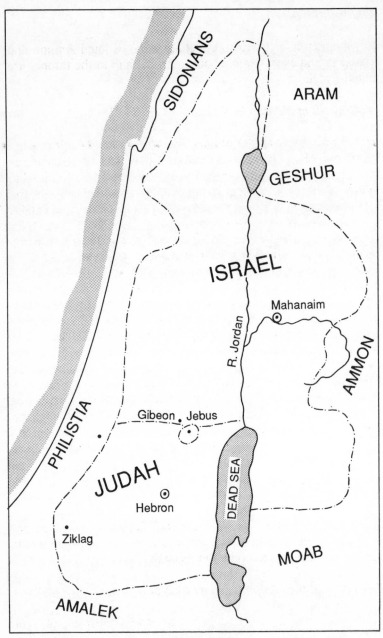

MAP 2 — The interim-kingdoms of David and
Ish-Bosheth c. 1005 B.C.

been born to him in Hebron, including the ill-fated Amnon and Absalom, and events were about to propel him to the throne of a united Israel.

Ish-Bosheth made king in Mahanaim (2:8-11)

In the meantime, Abner, Saul's army commander, carved out a kingdom in the north and west of Israel, ostensibly in the name of the house of Saul. He set up Saul's last son, Ish-Bosheth (literally, 'son of shame'), as a puppet-king in Mahanaim. We are told that Ish-Bosheth ruled for two years over Israel, while David reigned for seven and a half years in Judah (2:10-11). Since it appears from chapters 3-5 that Ish-Bosheth's two-year reign immediately preceded his death and the accession of David as king over Israel, these figures are best understood as indicating that Abner acted as a kind of war-lord for the first five and a half years. Then, having established his borders, especially against the Philistine incursions that must have followed the defeat at Gilboa, he felt it advisable to attempt to legitimize his power by placing Ish-Bosheth on the throne. There is some indication that until then, there was no strife between David and Abner and that war only broke out with the formal restoration of the house of Saul and the apparently provocative advance of Abner's army towards the Judean border (2:12). Only when Abner forced the issue with David did war erupt between their forces. David waited peacefully for the Lord to make him Israel's king in his good time.[3]

Two sides [2:12-3:5]

The principal instigators of the war itself appear to have been the generals, Abner and Joab — if Abner started the fire, Joab was to stir the pot that was to boil upon its coals.

The battle at the pool of Gibeon (2:12-17)

Abner with **'the men** [i.e., soldiers] **of Ish-Bosheth son of Saul, left Mahanaim and went to Gibeon'**. This brought Abner to the edge of Judean territory and was to prove the immediate cause of the war, for it obliged David to counter with the advance of his army,

under his nephew Joab. The armies watched one another nervously
across the pool of Gibeon (2:12-13).

At Abner's suggestion, it was apparently agreed to resolve the
issue by representative hand-to-hand combat between champions
of each side — twelve men apiece. This sanguinary conflict
produced twenty-four corpses and a draw (2:14-16), so a general
engagement between the armies ensued and **'Abner and the men
of Israel were defeated by David's men'** (2:17).

The death of Asahel (2:18-32)

As Abner and his men withdrew, Asahel, brother of Joab and
Abishai, decided that he would go for the 'big fish' — for Abner
himself. Fast enough to catch that doughty warrior, Asahel was
clearly no match for him in a fight. Abner knew this and twice
warned him to give up the chase. **'But Asahel refused to give up
the pursuit; so Abner thrust the butt of his spear into Asahel's
stomach.'** It must have been a powerful blow, for the spear butt (not
even the sharp spear-point!) **'came out through his back'** and,
needless to say, Asahel **'died on the spot'** (2:23).

Although the men had broken off the pursuit, Joab and Abishai
refused to allow Abner to make his escape and continued the
pursuit. Asahel had died, fair and square, in battle, but his brothers
'assume the role of avengers of blood, and Joab's fault will be that
he takes revenge on Abner after the hostilities have ended (3:27; cf.
1 Ki. 2:5)'.[4] By sunset, Joab had brought Abner to bay on a hilltop.
Abner, warning Joab about making the matter a vendetta and
emphasizing that they were pursuing their **'brothers'**, called for a
truce, to which Joab rather grudgingly agreed. With the 'butcher's
bill' 360-19 in his favour, Joab was the victor, but the death of his
over-confident brother, Asahel, left a deep scar of unhallowed resentment on his soul and, in any case, there are no winners in a civil
war (2:24-32).

David grew stronger and stronger (3:1-5)

From this point on, David's position improved, while Ish-
Bosheth's declined. This was no doubt because of David's victories
in the field, but perhaps also involved increasing disenchantment

among the people with the war and the rule of Abner and Ish-Bosheth.

The record of the birth of David's sons interposes a moment of domesticity. This reminds us that David was a polygamist and was also not above marrying for political purposes, having married Maacah, the Aramean princess of Geshur, a state on the north-east border of Ish-Bosheth's kingdom. With the hindsight of Scripture history, we know that three of these sons lived wickedly and died violently (Amnon, Absalom and Adonijah) — a sure indication that there is no automatic salvation for the children of believers. God's covenant blessings, even in the line of the generations of his believing people, must be appropriated through personal faith and obedience. The later apostasy of some children, however, must not obscure the fact that 'Sons are a heritage from the Lord, children a reward from him' (Psalm 127:3). That the heritage was squandered in particular instances only emphasizes that salvation is by the free grace of God.

Two murders [3:6-4:12]

The cracks in the foundations of Ish-Bosheth's regime were soon to bring down both the kingdom and her king. Two years had passed since the civil war started at the pool of Gibeon. The writing was on the wall for the house of Saul. And now, in quick succession, events would overtake what remained of the rule of Saul's line.

Abner's defection to David (3:6-21)

The fate of nations can turn on almost trivial events — in this case, an argument over a woman, one Rizpah, a concubine of Saul.[5] Whatever the truth of the matter, Ish-Bosheth accused Abner of having sexual relations with this lady and Abner took the greatest offence — not, one suspects, merely because he was caught *in flagrante delicto* with a woman who was not his wife (if that was indeed the case) — but because of the implicit charge of disloyalty associated with the common assumption of the time that to possess the concubines of a king was to claim the mantle of monarchy as well. Abner did not deny the charge itself, but hotly defended his loyalty to the house of Saul — only to declare, with ferocious indignation, that he would deliver the kingdom over to David! Not insignificantly, Abner recognized that 'the Lord promised him [David] on oath... Israel and Judah from Dan to Beersheba' (3:6-10). One wonders if Abner, far from wanting the throne for himself, saw that things were not going well and contrived the incident to provide an excuse for defecting to David and saving his own skin! We are not told if he sincerely believed that David was the Lord's anointed, or if he was just an opportunist who was bowing to realities. In any event, Ish-Bosheth was finished, and he knew it (3:11).

Abner wasted no time in acting on his threat. He began negotiations with David, who shrewdly made one condition — that his first wife, Michal, the daughter of Saul, be returned to him — thus emphasizing his consistent goodwill to the house of Saul and thereby demonstrating his desire for national unity and continuity of government (3:12-14).

In accordance with protocol and political sagacity, Abner successively persuaded Ish-Bosheth (who was no more than a cipher in any case), the elders of Israel and Saul's own tribe of Benjamin to fall in with his plan. He then went to Hebron and arranged with David the convocation of Israel which would mark the reunification of Israel (3:15-21).

Joab's assassination of Abner (3:22-27)

This was not at all to Joab's liking. Consumed with hatred for Abner, he could only reproach his royal uncle for treating with the man. Contriving to lure him back to Hebron, without David's knowledge, Joab took him aside 'as though to speak with him privately' and there 'stabbed him in the stomach, and he died'. Asahel, whom Abner had killed in battle after two warnings to desist and only in self-defence, had been 'avenged' by a murderous act of betrayal, made all the more heinous by the fact that Hebron was a designated 'city of refuge', where even a legitimate 'avenger of blood' (which Joab was not) could not take his revenge without a proper trial! (3:30; Joshua 20:7; Numbers 35:10-28).

David's lament for Abner (3:28-39)

When David heard of Abner's death, he was deeply disturbed. He denied complicity in the murder and invoked a curse upon Joab and his family which reminds us of the boy Samuel's prophecy against Eli's house (1 Samuel 2:31-36). He was, of course, calling upon God to bring justice upon Joab and Abishai (who was evidently implicated also, 3:30) — very probably because he realized that he could do nothing about it himself. It was no doubt one of these cases in which everyone knows what took place but no one can prove anything. Joab could plead self-defence in a quarrel and, in any case, Abner was 'the enemy'! He was 'a relative of David, and was too powerful a man to be treated as he deserved; his excesses did, in the end, catch up with him (1 Ki. 2:5f., 28-35)'.[6]

Public mourning for Abner was commanded by David — sincere, to be sure, but with an eye to the politics of *rapprochement* between Judah and Israel — and David sang a lament for Abner and fasted until sunset. The lament plaintively asks why Abner had to **'die as a fool dies... as one falls before the wicked'** (3:33-34, NASB).[7]

Privately, David lamented the fact that with friends like his nephews Joab and Abishai, he hardly needed enemies. Whereas Abner was **'a prince and a great man,'** the sons of Zeruiah were **'too strong'** — i.e., too hard or ruthless — for him. Beyond committing the matter to the Lord, he did nothing until many years later, on his deathbed, he charged Solomon not to let Joab's **'grey head go down to the grave in peace'** (1 Kings 2:5-6).

Ish-Bosheth's murder by the sons of Rimmon (4:1-12)

With Abner dead, Ish-Bosheth's precarious rule continued on borrowed time. He **'lost courage'** — literally, 'his hands dropped'. He was, as the Scots said in the thirteenth century A.D. of John Balliol (the puppet-king imposed on Scotland by Edward I of England), a 'toom tabard' — an 'empty gown'![8] He did not have long to wait. In a grisly echo of the Amalekite's story of his alleged despatch of Saul on Mount Gilboa, the two sons of Rimmon actually did murder Ish-Bosheth and took his head to David in confirmation of their deed. David made short shrift of their fantasies about being the Lord's instruments in ridding David of Saul's last son. He had them executed for their regicide and their mutilated corpses hung up by the pool in Hebron for all to see! This was an open and shut case, but it is striking to compare David's just severity here with his incapacity and/or unwillingness to deal with Joab. Ish-Bosheth's removal from the scene did, however, leave David with an open path to his accession to Israel's throne.

A slice of life

What are we to draw from this narrative? There are no great doctrinal truths stated here, no great moral principles. We do see David seeking guidance from God and waiting patiently for his direction. We see David rebuking sin. We see genuine humility and gracious generosity in his lament for Abner and his assessment of Ish-Bosheth as **'an innocent man'**.

This passage gives us a slice of life in the real world. We see people in their true colours: the petty, selfish, murderous, yet fiercely loyal, Joab; the war-lord Abner, honourable perhaps, but only when it suited him; the sad, incompetent Ish-Bosheth, 'alone and palely loitering' through his humdrum colourless life; and the miserable and vicious sons of Rimmon, who murdered Ish-Bosheth in his sleep. They all point us to the nature of sin. So tied up in the things of this world, they appear to care nothing for the next; so absorbed in themselves, there is no room for the Lord and both his righteousness and his blessings. They all warn us of our need for humility and self-knowledge before the measure of the Word of God. And there is David, the man after God's own heart, borne along to his regal calling on the tide of God's mighty providential acts. He was perhaps thirty years old. The work of God's grace in his heart shines forth in his words and actions. But he was bone of our bone and flesh of our flesh. And both his godliness and his weaknesses call us to that greater Son of David, the Lord Jesus Christ.

3.
King in Zion

Please read 2 Samuel 5:1-25

'And David knew that the Lord had established him as king over Israel' (2 Samuel 5:12).

With the death of Ish-Bosheth, all resistance to the Lord's anointed crumbled and the way was open for David to become king over all Israel. For over seven years he had waited in Hebron for God's moment and now it had come. The record of his accession, while a simple historical narrative and very matter-of-fact in tone, is nevertheless one of the most significant in the history of redemption, for it records the establishment of the Davidic kingdom, which in turn foreshadowed the coming of the kingdom of our Lord and Saviour Jesus Christ. That connection may be as much by way of contrast as of typology, for David's reign exhibits that mixture of 'theocratic ideal and human sinfulness' characteristic of all of salvation history.[1] And when the 'son of David', the Lord Jesus Christ, came in the fulness of God's time, he came as 'the Davidic king' and 'triumphed,' but 'not in the Davidic way'.[2] We should be careful to resist the temptation to find applications to Christ in every detail. And we should not conclude that David himself was conscious at this time of any symbolism or typological significance in his actions or in the sequence of events. All we may say is that as David becomes King of Israel, we, with New Testament hindsight and the perspective of the prophets, are led to meditate upon the ultimate goal of history and redemption — the enthronement of the risen Saviour, Jesus Christ, as the mediatorial King for his people.

The chapter may be divided into four distinct sections, giving a step-by-step account of how David was established as king: there is first a *coronation* (5:1-5); then a *capital* is chosen (5:6-10); the *consolidation* of the regime is effected (5:11-16); and, finally, the *conquest* of the kingdom's enemies is undertaken (5:17-25).

Coronation for God's king [1-5]

The elders of Israel came to David at Hebron and offered three
reasons for their desire that he be their king:

1. **'We are your own flesh and blood'** (5:1).

2. **'You...led Israel on their military campaigns'** (5:2)

3. **'The Lord said to you, "You shall shepherd my people
Israel"'** (5:2).

As a result of this embassy, David made a covenant with them
and was anointed king over Israel (5:3). The standard accession
announcement for a new king notes David's age and the length of
his reign (5:4-5). We should notice two points in particular in this
narrative.

The first is that **'They anointed David king over Israel'**
(5:3).This was David's third anointing. The first had been private,
the second partial, but the third was plenary, or complete — each
stage reflecting faithfully his actual progress, one step at a time,
towards the kingship. We are reminded of the way in which the
reality of Christ's kingdom is progressively unfolding in human
history. Matthew Henry points up the parallel with both the kingdom and the incarnation: 'For we see not yet all things put under
him, Heb. 2:8, but we shall see it, 1 Cor. 15:25. Thus Jesus became
our Brother, took upon him our nature, inhabited it that he might
become our Prince and Saviour: thus the humbled sinner takes
encouragement from the endearing relationship, applies for his
salvation, submits to his authority and craves his protection.' Do
you entertain doubts, because the promises of God remain in part to
be fulfilled? Do you despair because the 'big battalions' do not
seem to be on the Lord's side in this world? Then remember David's
three anointings and the years of delay and distress that intervened
before his triumph. Above all, remember Jesus Christ in his humiliation, waiting patiently for our sakes, before he should become
King of kings as the risen Saviour of his people! The day is yet
future when the kingdoms of this world will definitively and
eternally 'become the kingdom of our Lord and of his Christ'
(Revelation 11:15). But the Lord is now 'head over everything for
the church' (Ephesians 1:22). Therefore, be strong and of a good
courage!

A second point of interest concerns the three reasons given by
the elders for recognizing David as their king. These are arranged

in ascending order of importance, from personal relationship (5:1), to track record and finally to divine appointment (5:2). This is no different in principle from the way in which any man or woman receives and accepts the lordship of Jesus Christ. To believe in the Lord Jesus Christ and be saved means, among other things, being adopted as children of God through Christ (Ephesians 1:5) — that is, becoming by grace through faith fellow-heirs of Jesus in a personal relationship closer than any earthly consanguinity. It also means being profoundly aware, in heart-felt gratitude, of all that Christ has done to save sinners through his entire ministry, culminating in his death on the cross. Christians daily bless the Lord both for forgiveness of sin and for his gracious gifts in the course of daily living. But most of all, the Lord's people rejoice in the great fact of the gospel, that Jesus was the Son of God, sent in terms of an eternal decree of covenant love to take our flesh and appointed to die on the cross to pay for the sins of others, when he himself was sinless. He then must be our Lord, because he is the Shepherd who gave his life for us sheep — and all according to the grace of God. This is the joy, confidence and godly boast of everyone who loves the Lord.

A capital for God's people [5:6-10]

David needed a capital suitable for the theocratic king of all Israel. Both Hebron, his royal seat in Judah, and Gibeah, Saul's old capital in Benjamin, were too tribal and bound to be an offence to one or other of the main divisions of the new kingdom. Where was David to go for a capital on neutral territory, acceptable to all? The answer lay in the last remaining enclave of independent Canaanites — Jerusalem of the Jebusites, situated on its mountain called Zion between Judah and Benjamin. David had found his federal capital territory — his ancient original of Canberra, Australia and Washington D.C. It only remained for him to do what Israelite leaders from Joshua to Saul had failed to do — dislodge these stubborn Jebusites from their nigh-impregnable crag.[3] Herein lies the fundamental significance of David's decision to make Jerusalem his capital.

David 'marched to Jerusalem', was rebuffed contemptuously by the Jebusites, but apparently soon found a way to take the city — perhaps by a water-shaft or by cutting off the water-supply (the text is too obscure to be certain).[4] It is not clear what is meant by the comment: **'That is why they say, "The 'blind and the lame' will not enter the palace"'** (5:8). The 'palace' may well be the house of God (the temple) and it appears to have been a proverbial statement indicating the rejection of people, who like the Jebusites ('the blind and the lame') made a profession of resisting the living God. In any event, David destroyed the Jebusites and made Jerusalem his capital.

The meaning of it all is summed up in the words: '**And he** [David] **became more and more powerful, because the Lord God Almighty was with him**' (5:10). There is some tremendous teaching in this event: it is that the very fortress which the God-rejecting Canaanites thought to be impregnable was, in the end, taken easily and then transformed into the seat of God's king, David, and, most profoundly of all, the location of the tabernacle. When God's time comes, he does his will, opposition is subdued and what was once a monument to sin becomes a trophy of his grace! And as it was with Zion, so it is with human hearts. We may be exposed to the ministry of the gospel for long enough and resist the claims of Christ. But those whom God sovereignly purposes to save, he one day effectually calls. This is the call of irresistible grace, which is, as Paul says, 'according to his purpose' (Romans 8:28-30). This is the plunging fire of Christ's power to save as it penetrates the hardened defences of the unconverted soul. The citadel is stormed by free grace. Commenting on the steps by which God acts to save a sinner, John Murray notes that 'It is calling that is represented in Scripture as that act of God by which we are actually united to Christ (cf., 1 Cor. 1:9). And surely union with Christ is that which unites us to the inwardly operative grace of God. Regeneration is the beginning of inwardly operative saving grace.'[5] We may resist, but when God's final assault goes in, hard hearts melt and sins are blasted away! From that effectual call, to regeneration (subconscious new birth), to faith and repentance (conscious response in conversion to Christ), to justification, to adoption and on to sanctification (and in heaven, to glorification) God's powerful acts of grace transform his erstwhile enemies into new creations in Jesus Christ. The arm of the Lord is not shortened that it cannot save!

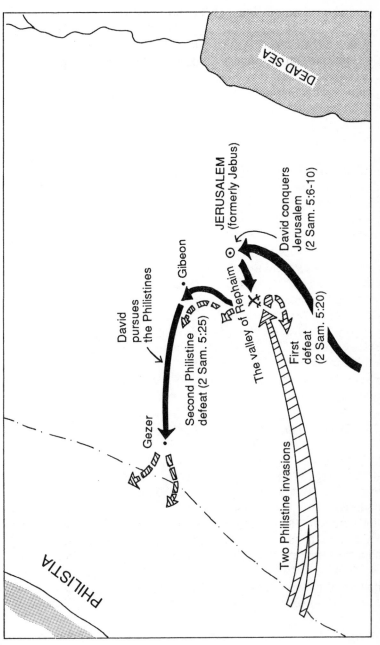

MAP 3 — David captures Jerusalem and defeats two Philistine invasions (2 Samuel 5).

The consolidation of the rule of God's king [5:11-16]

The new regime was recognized by the Phoenician king, Hiram of Tyre, who sent artisans and materials to build a palace for David — a circumstance that reminded Matthew Henry of the much later prophecy which speaks of the fact that the New Testament church will be blessed by the assistance of non-Christian governments: 'Foreigners will rebuild your walls, and their kings will serve you' (Isaiah 60:10).

The listing of the children born to David in Jerusalem (5:13-16) reminds us of something quite different and less encouraging: namely that, as we have already seen, David was a polygamist, in open contradiction of the law of God (Deuteronomy 17:17). This was no doubt in part a compromise with the surrounding polygamous cultures and the practice of taking wives to seal international treaties (1 Kings 11:1-3). But that is not the whole story. David had a wandering eye and a problem with unhallowed desire. It is clear that the acquisition of many wives did not make him more faithful to those he already had. As Matthew Henry puts it, 'Men that have once broken the fence will wander endlessly.'

Nevertheless, David was God's man. David was assured of this in his own heart (5:12). He also knew that God had not established his kingdom for David's sake, but **'for the sake of his people Israel'**. The Lord's purpose is redemptive, not merely political, and certainly not merely to exalt one man as a monarch. The prophetic element is never far away, for as 'David was established king, so is the Son of David, with all who through him are made to our God kings and priests'.[6] The love of God is always very particularly poured out upon his elect people. They are the apple of his eye. The church does not exist as a platform even for great evangelical preachers, still less for popes, but for the salvation of lost men and women.

The conquest of the Lord's enemies [5:17-25]

It was not in everyone's interest that there be a strong king in Israel. The Phoenicians' meat was the Philistines' poison. Much of David's kingdom was still largely occupied by the Philistines. To assert their supremacy they promptly advanced their forces up the valley of Rephaim, very close to Jerusalem. Twice they came, twice David enquired of the Lord and twice they were crushed by Israelite tactics dictated by the Lord. The abandoned idols of the Philistines were seized and burned (1 Chronicles 14:12). David gave the glory to the Lord and called the place Baal Perazim — **'As waters break out, the Lord has broken out against my enemies before me'** (5:20). He recognized that this was the Lord's battle and that the Lord's people were involved in a spiritual warfare that far transcended the parameters of one campaign.

Every success experienced by Christians ought to bring forth heart-felt praise to God. When Lord Hailsham was interviewed by a TV reporter on the steps on No. 10 Downing Street as the British Cabinet met to respond to news of the Argentine surrender in the Falklands War (14 June 1982), he simply and movingly answered with a quotation from Psalm 115: 'Not to us, O Lord, not to us but to your name be the glory...'[7] Every blessing that the Christian experiences must be laid in humble thanksgiving at the throne of grace.

The psalmist (in this case not David) gave expression to the true nature of the spiritual warfare between God and Satan and light and darkness, when he wrote,

'Be still, and know that I am God;
    I will be exalted among the nations,
    I will be exalted in the earth.
The Lord Almighty is with us;
    the God of Jacob is our fortress'

(Psalm 46:10-11).[8]

Believers will, as Paul has declared, 'be more than conquerors through him who loved us' (Romans 8:37).

4.
A false start

Please read 2 Samuel 6:1-11
'The Lord's anger burned against Uzzah because of his irreverent act' (2 Samuel 6:7).

'The noblest use of power,' observed Charles Simeon, 'is to exert it for God.'[1] As soon as David's throne was secure, his thoughts turned to the matter of true worship in his kingdom. Israel was, in itself, the visible manifestation on earth of the kingdom of God. It was a theocratic state (i.e., ruled by God), governed by a theonomic constitution (i.e. the law was given by God). In other words, God was the true King and his revealed will was the standard rule of law. David knew this and realized that God had the right to the central place in the life of the nation. This is why he thought about the ark of the covenant. This was the symbol of God's sovereign grace to Israel and the centre-piece of the worship of God's people. It was therefore David's plan to bring the ark to Jerusalem and revive the ancient pattern of worship, which had all but disappeared during the reign of Saul. 2 Samuel 6:1-11 records his first, abortive, attempt to do this. We shall discover that the account of what transpired is replete with vital lessons about the character of God and our relationship to him and to his Word.

The background to this incident is to be found in the neglect of the ark for perhaps half a century from the day it had returned from Philistia. The Philistines, you will recall, had seized it in the Second Battle of Aphek (1 Samuel 4:11), but subsequently discovered it to be a dangerous trophy (1 Samuel 5). The ark had come to Beth-Shemesh. The inhabitants treated it like a carnival curiosity and peered into it, totally disregarding the relevant provisions of the Mosaic law as to the way it should be handled. Some seventy men were struck dead by the Lord for their irreverence. The ark was sent away to Kiriath Jearim, to the house of Abinadab (1 Samuel 6:19-7:1).

Good intentions: bringing up the ark [6:1-2]

Accompanied by a large cavalcade, David marched in what must have been a glittering procession to **'Baalah of Judah'** (Kiriath Jearim). His understanding of the significance of the project is surely summed up in the description of the ark as **'the ark of God, which is called by the Name, the name of the Lord Almighty, who is enthroned between the cherubim that are on the ark'**. The ark was a chest of acacia wood encased in gold and with a covering, called the mercy-seat, which was made of gold and had a cherub on each end (Exodus 25:10-22).[2] W. H. Gispen notes that 'From the beginning the ark was... both the Lord's throne... and the repository for the Law.'[3] Here was the visible token of God's presence and communion with his people, where God was enthroned between the cherubim.

To neglect the ark was to neglect God himself. It was effectively to deny both the supremacy of truth and the covenant mercy of the Lord. While the ark was absent from the centre of Israel's worship, the nation was in a covenant-breaking condition. This is not to say there were not many true believers in the land. Just as churches today can have some real Christians in them, but still be apostate institutions, so Israel was backslidden while a remnant of her people were faithful to the Lord. That remnant was on the increase, revival was in the air and the return of the ark was a call to the covenant-breakers and the very institutions of the nation to embrace their Father-God, Yahweh, and show the heathen world around them that the living God was still enthroned between the cherubim and also in the hearts of those whom he had redeemed! As we shall see, this great and laudable goal was to be deferred by as yet hidden obstacles and David's good intentions were to dissolve in unholy frustration.

Uzzah lends a hand [6:3-7]

The goal was to move the ark of God to Jerusalem. The means

employed was **'a new cart'**, pulled by oxen and led by Uzzah and
Ahio, the sons of Abinadab, in whose house the ark had hitherto
rested. When they arrived at **'the threshing-floor of Nacon, Uzzah
reached out and took hold of the ark of God, because the oxen
stumbled'**. This, we are told, was an **'irreverent act'**. The Lord
was angry and **'struck [Uzzah] down and he died there beside the
ark of God'** (6:6-7). This remarkable incident poses some pretty
hard questions. Why was God so angry? Uzzah's sin — some might
say, 'if it was a sin' — seems so trivial. And God's reaction seems
so fierce. How can the penalty of death be justified? What does it
mean? What does it mean for us today, in the light of Jesus Christ?

Some background to the problem

When we set these events against the backdrop of Scripture as a
whole, certain features begin to stand out.

Firstly, there is no indication that David asked the Lord as to
whether, when or how he should move the ark to Jerusalem. Had he
done so, we could have expected at least an indication of the Lord's
encouragement, and perhaps even some mention of the law of
Moses and the involvement of Abiathar the priest. We have no
reason to doubt David's good intentions. We do have reason to
believe that he 'counted his chickens before they were hatched' and
that would imply that he never sought the Lord's will by the
appointed means.

Secondly, had the Scriptures been consulted, it would have
been discovered that the ark was to be covered by a curtain of badger
skins; that it was to be carried only on the shoulders of the Kohathite
priests, of the tribe of Levi, using poles run through the rings on its
sides; and that no one, not even a Levite, was to touch the ark!
(Numbers 4:5-15; 7:9). All this taught God's people about the
holiness of God, for just as the ark, the symbol of God's presence,
was not to be handled in a casual way, but with the utmost
reverence, so the Lord was to be approached with holy fear. Yet the
ark was put on a cart and Uzzah put his hand on it when the oxen
stumbled.

Thirdly, the idea of putting the ark on a cart came from the
Lord's enemies, the Philistines (1 Samuel 5:1-11; 6:3). The Philistines were not judged for that (they had enough in the way of
judgement to cope with anyway!). Israel, however, should have

known better, were without any excuse and therefore had to be corrected in such a way as to make clear that God is to be worshipped and served, in both spirit and letter, in the manner appropriate to his exalted character, everlasting covenant love and eternal majesty.

The Lord's anger burned against Uzzah

When we grasp this background, we can easily see that there is nothing merely arbitrary about the law and the judgements of God as they were applied in this case. What then is the meaning of Uzzah's death? Let me suggest two considerations.

Firstly, *God is just in all his ways.* Righteousness and justice are the foundation of his throne (Psalm 89:14). Even if we, with David, initially cannot see why Uzzah should have been struck down, our basic assumption must be that God not only knew what he was doing, but was wholly justified in his action. Eliphaz the Temanite was absolutely correct when he asked, 'Can a mortal be more righteous than God? Can a man be more pure than his maker?' (Job 4:17). God knew Uzzah's heart and the (to us) sudden application of his judgement only proves how little we see of the true provocations of human sin. The case of Ananias and Sapphira is very similar, with respect to summary judgement for something that looks outwardly trivial to us but was, in fact, inwardly the deepest contempt for God. This judgement, too, was designed to awaken the people to a realization that God is never to be trifled with (Acts 5:1-11).

Secondly, God is to be accorded all reverence and holy fear (Psalm 89:7). The goodness and severity of God are co-ordinate, not contradictory truths. His severity with Uzzah is a measure of Uzzah's violation of his standard of goodness. God cannot trample on his own holiness and he will not allow others to do that with impunity. In the last analysis, this is what true justice is: God's perfect vindication of absolutely everything that is holy by means of his perfect retributive judgement upon all that is opposed to his sovereignty and righteousness. This is, of course, why the atoning death of Christ is necessary[4] for sinners to be saved. Uzzah's death reminds us of the issues of life and death, concerning both time and eternity, and calls us to bow in humble submission before the Lord. 'Among those who approach me,' he says, 'I will show myself holy;

in the sight of all the people I will be honoured' (Leviticus 10:3).

The sufficiency of God's Word

The death of Uzzah also reminds us that we are called to be completely satisfied with straightforward, practical obedience to God's Word and are to resist the temptation to add to it or subtract from it. Where God has revealed his preceptive will on any matter, our proper response is to 'toe the line' with a joyful heart and we are neither to invent extra rules and acts of holiness which he never commanded (that is what 'pietism' is about), nor to devise evasions and modifications to get out from under what he has commanded us to do in plain language (that is 'antinomianism')! God has given a full and sufficient revelation of himself and his will and has expressly forbidden additions to and subtractions from the Word (Deuteronomy 12:32-13:4; 31:9-13; Joshua 1:7-8; Isaiah 8:20; Revelation 22:18-19). This is what is called 'the regulative principle' of Scripture and it says, simply and positively, that Scripture is sufficient as the rule of faith and life. Conversely, it follows that what God has not required of us in Scripture is not to be required or enjoined by men or, indeed, by the church. For any of us to go beyond, or aside from, what is commanded in Scripture is to presume to be wise above what God has written. This was the fundamental problem of both Uzzah and Israel. In the drive to a good goal they disregarded the Lord. Their method was wrong because it was not what God had set down in black and white. The problem was not a matter of technique — ox-carts certainly carry boxes more efficiently than human shoulders — but a matter of self-centred pride that did not care to submit itself to God. We are so prone to try improving on God's methods. We are attracted to building our own 'carts'. We may even call it 'creativity' and insist that it is honouring to the Lord. Think of the 'carts' that have been built for worship, fellowship, doctrine, evangelism, denominational distinctiveness, even church membership! How easily we clothe our own ideas and shibboleths with the borrowed mantle of divine authority and end up 'teaching for doctrines the commandments of men' (Matthew 15:9, AV). There is certainly scope to express obedience to the Lord with freshness and even ingenuity, but at no point are we warranted to set aside the plain teaching of Scripture, out of the presumptuous notion that the Lord's stated will may be enhanced or improved by our emendations. This is exactly why so much of that which calls itself 'Christian' and 'the church' today is little more than an empty husk of what was once truly biblical Christianity.

David takes offence [6:8-10]

David was offended by God's judgement upon Uzzah. We can certainly understand this very well. We might even protest: 'It's only a box, Lord! Uzzah meant well! David only wanted to reinstate your proper worship in the new capital city. He just wanted to get the nation back on an even spiritual keel! So why kill Uzzah and stop the ark going to Jerusalem?' What are we to say to this? The facts are actually very plain. God was not quibbling over trivial points. He was asserting nothing less than his absolute sovereignty over against the careless presumption of Uzzah and his ilk. When Uzzah put his hand on the ark, God moved to stop the rot! Uzzah became the example which would show all Israel what they were actually doing, how they were actually disregarding their Father-God, in their wilfully uninformed zeal for moving the ark. The spirit that took the ark from Shiloh to Aphek as a lucky charm to help win the battle still lurked in Israelite hearts. That is the point of Uzzah's death. That is the reality of God's check to David's otherwise laudable intentions.

But David would not see it. He was a bit like Hughes Mearns' 'Perfect Reactionary', who one day contemplated the non-existence of the chair upon which he was sitting:

As I was sitting on my chair
I *knew* the bottom wasn't there,
Nor legs nor back, but *I just sat*
Ignoring little things like that.[5]

David knew the Lord; he knew God's law; but he *chose* to do what he wanted to do; he decided to serve God on his own terms. His response at being called to account is very revealing — and very apropos the attitudes of each one of us, when we are rebuked and

brought face to face with home truths we do not particularly like!
We just do not want to be bothered by 'little things like that'! Notice
David's threefold response.

1. He wa*s angry and disbelieving* at the Lord's dealings with
Uzzah and himself (6:8). Instead of assuming as a matter of bedrock
faith that God is holy and just in every single one of his actions, he
made the mistake of judging God on the basis of his inability to see
how God could be so angry at something so apparently trivial.
David was taken by surprise as much as was poor Uzzah! And he
cried, 'Injustice!' when he should have reflected in the deepest
humility about God's possible reasons for doing what he did. We
are so good at pretending to be more just and fair than the Lord   —
and yet we can hardly read our own hearts, never mind the secret
purposes of God! Matthew Henry wisely counsels us: 'When we lie
under God's anger, we must keep under our own.' It is precisely
when we do not fathom the *providence* of God, that we must trust
in his *purposes* of grace towards his people in Christ.

2. Rash anger soon gave way, however, to the cold sweat of *the
fear of judgement* (6:9). David felt the withdrawal of the blessing of
God. He then began to speculate about the future and, as we all do
in similar circumstances, he feared the worst and descended into the
cauldron of self-pitying pessimism: **'How can the ark of the Lord
ever come to me?'**

3. This should have led David to find out why things had
happened as they had and then to go on to repent and begin again
to do God's will. Instead, *he was paralysed* into a kind of 'do-
nothingism': **'He was not willing to take the ark of the Lord to
be with him in the City of David'** (6:10). His confidence in the
Lord had evaporated. He just didn't seem to know what to do. What
this shows us is how easily self-generated zeal — call it the
enthusiasm of the flesh — soon turns to doubt and the spirit of
giving up. How often have you heard Christians promise to do all
sorts of things for the Lord, only to give up at the first set-back? Far
from accepting this as the Lord's disciplinary redirection of our
chosen course, we see it as the end altogether and lapse into sulking,
resentful inactivity. David was a better man than to be ensnared in
this way for long, but he should have devoted himself immediately
to a positive response to the Lord's leading. And so should we, at
every turn!

The blessing of Obed-Edom [6:10b-11]

What a strange irony that David should treat the ark like a 'hot potato', drop it in another man's lap and then see the Lord bless that man with the blessing that might, in the meantime, have been poured out upon himself and the whole nation![6] We are reminded that the gospel of Christ is both a 'fragrance of life' to those who are being saved and a 'smell of death' to those who are perishing (2 Corinthians 2:14-16). The same hand which judged the apostate Uzzah now blesses Obed-Edom. Obed-Edom is called a Gittite, which at first blush appears to identify him as a Philistine from Gath. He probably came from Gath-rimmon in Dan (Joshua 21:24).[7] For three months the ark remained in the Gittite's house **'and the Lord blessed him and his entire household'**. Matthew Henry, with all the inimitable sweetness of Puritan spirituality, urges us to seek such blessing from the Lord in our own families: 'Let us masters of families be encouraged to keep up religion in their families, and to serve God and the interests of his kingdom with their houses and estates, for that is a way to bring a blessing upon all they have... The ark is a guest by which none shall lose who bid it welcome... Piety is the best friend to prosperity. In wisdom's left hand are riches and honour. His [Obed-Edom's] household shared the blessing. It is good living in a family that entertains the ark, for all about it will fare the better for it.'[8]

Jesus Christ is our 'ark'. He who is priest, sacrifice, altar and temple is also Immanuel — God with us, the meaning of the ark of the covenant, the Saviour of all who trust in him. And so, David's false start ultimately points us to the Lord and finds him to be the one who, though he will by no means clear the unrepentantly guilty, is keeping his mercy for thousands upon thousands! 'Will any say that the Ark of Moses is no more?' asks Henry Law, 'True. When the Temple fell, this framework disappeared. But Christ the substance ever lives. In heaven the Throne of grace cannot be moved. The name is changed but the reality is one... And when you reach the stream of Jordan, Christ, the true Ark, will lead you onward, and parting waters will be your passage to the land of rest'.[9]

5.
Celebrate before the Lord!

Please read 2 Samuel 6:12-23 and 1 Chronicles 15:1-16:43
'Lift up your heads, O you gates... that the king of glory may come in' (Psalm 24:7).

After the anticlimax of his first attempt to bring the ark of God to Jerusalem, there could have been little joy in David's soul. When he left the ark at Obed-Edom's house, he was frustrated and fearful. God had delivered to Israel a sobering demonstration of his righteous power. Uzzah's death, now commemorated in the new name of the place of his death (Perez-Uzzah — literally, 'outbreak against Uzzah'), had so badly shaken David that he abandoned his scheme and returned to Jerusalem. And so for three months after the tragedy of Uzzah's sin, the ark of God remained in the house of Obed-Edom and the Lord blessed that good man and his entire household.

Two things happened during this time which persuaded David that all in fact was not lost and that God would bless Israel in the re-establishment of the ark at the centre of the nation's life. One was that David was told that **'The Lord has blessed the household of Obed-Edom and everything he has, because of the ark of God'** (6:12). The other factor was that David realized that he had not done things properly the first time and took steps to ensure that the Lord's revealed will be obeyed in future. 1 Chronicles 15 records in great detail how carefully David organized his second attempt to move the ark. It would be carried by Levites only, for their earlier mistake had been that they 'did not enquire of him about how to do it in the prescribed way' (1 Chronicles 15:2,13). The glory of God, rather than royal achievement, was wonderfully pre-eminent. 'Who is he, this king of glory?' asks David. 'The Lord Almighty — he is the king of glory,' comes the thunderous answer of exultant praise (Psalm 24:10).

2 Samuel 6:12-23 records the relevant public and private events

of the day of the ark's entry to Jerusalem. The first and public event is the triumphal procession of the ark to the capital (6:12-19). The second is private and concerns the response of Michal, Saul's daughter, to the whole proceedings — in particular, David's dancing before the ark (6:20-23). The juxtaposition of these two incidents sets up for us a contrast between the blessings of doing the Lord's will, on the one hand, and the curse of opposing the Lord's will, on the other.

Blessing — obeying the will of the Lord [6:12-19]

The narrative is simple and straightforward. David, influenced by the evidence of God's blessing upon Obed-Edom and repentant of his former sins in this matter (1 Chronicles 15:13), determined to bring the ark to Jerusalem and proceeded reverently and joyfully to do just that. After only six steps, David **'sacrificed a bull and a fattened calf'**, surely in thankfulness for a good beginning. The Chronicler refers to the Levites sacrificing 'seven bulls and seven rams' because 'God had helped the Levites who were carrying the ark of the covenant of the Lord,' (15:26) but this would be in thankfulness for the Lord's help at the end of the ten-mile journey. David, in token of a humble spirit, laid aside his finery for plain clothes — **'a linen ephod'** — and **'danced before the Lord with all his might'** (6:14). When they arrived at Jerusalem, David was still dancing. We are told that his wife Michal saw this and did not like it at all and **'despised him in her heart'** (6:16). But David was not yet aware of this and went on to instate the ark in the tabernacle he had prepared. Sacrifices were offered to the Lord and David distributed gifts of bread, dates and raisins to everyone present before they returned to their homes.[1]

God's blessing are open and public in nature

When Obed-Edom was blessed by God, it was noticed. We are not told what these blessings were, although there is a tradition recorded by Josephus that he had been poor and now became prosperous. In any event, the blessings of God are never a secret. They cannot be hidden. Whether they involve inner spiritual transformations — joy, peace, integrity, loving attitudes, etc. — or more outward blessings of prosperity, health or family stability, they are in the end observed publicly. When Paul told the Corinthians that they were letters read by all men (2 Corinthians 3:2), he was not talking so much about what they had consciously done to project themselves, but more about the fact that what we are comes through anyway, and people inevitably read, dissect and assess one another in normal social intercourse.

1. God's blessings are *real*. We experience the goodness of God. This is not a merely subjective feeling about ourselves or about life. There is hard evidence to support it: marriage, children, the love of God's people, kindnesses, career openings, recovery from illness, preservation from harm, daily bread — all sorts of tangible realities that point to the loving hand of our heavenly Father.

2. God's blessings are *noticed by others*. People could see the change in Obed-Edom's circumstances and perhaps even his character. When we see things going well for others, we are often profoundly affected. The apostle John rejoiced to find some of the children of a certain lady 'walking in the truth' (2 John 4). In contrast, Saul was jealous and fearful of David when he saw the evidence that the Lord was with David (1 Samuel 18:28-29).

3. God's blessings are *spoken about*. David was **'told'** about Obed-Edom. God can do his own evangelism through the grapevine of human amazement at his wonderful works of grace in people's lives. What we may *say* about the gospel is powerful enough, but what drives home the claims of Christ is often the visible proof of the truth of these claims in the evidence of what God has done for his people.

4. The *reason* for God's blessing *is apparent*. For Obed-Edom, it was the presence of the ark of God, answered by his faithful response to the calling God had given him. When Peter and John stood before the Jewish Sanhedrin and acquitted themselves with such courage, observers were astonished by their performance and 'realized that they were unschooled, ordinary men... and ... took note that these men had been with Jesus' (Acts 4:13). God does not hide himself when he does us good. When we rightly understand how he has blessed us, we cannot but give the glory to him. Others, likewise, will not make the mistake of attributing it to native ability or 'luck' or some such thing. People are sensitive in real measure to the presence of God in the lives of Christians.

God's blessings have an effect on those who observe them

We have already noted that there are two basic responses to others' experiences of the blessing of God. One is to desire to share that blessing, or at least to enjoy it for the sake of the one who receives it. The other is to recoil from it — to find it a cause of stumbling and a root of bitterness.

David is in the first category. See what happened to him in response to Obed-Edom's experience with the ark (cf. 6:14-15, 17-19; 1 Chronicles 15:2-3, 12-13). He praised the Lord, repented of past sin and made proper preparations to serve God aright. He put away his regal finery and wore a simple Levite tunic. He struck no kingly pose, but danced before the ark without any affectation. And his heart sang with joy as he contemplated the goodness of the Lord to his people. Psalms 24, 68 and 105 are thought to have been composed at this time, the first possibly for this very occasion. He had been restored by the Lord and stimulated to fresh obedience, through seeing the goodness of God to Obed-Edom.

Michal had quite the opposite reaction. David's 'meat' was Michal's 'poison'! She was embarrassed by his godly joy. She thought it demeaning for a king to act that way and there is more than a suggestion from what followed (6:20-23) that she despised the Lord as much as she despised her husband. In the New Testament era, Jesus Christ is similarly a stone of stumbling and a rock of offence to those who do not want to heed the call of the gospel. Yet to believers, he is the chief cornerstone! (1 Peter 2:6-8).

God's blessings are only experienced in practical obedience

David's attitude breathes the spirit of an enjoyed obedience. When he distributes gifts to everyone, it is surely because of his deep sense of having received great gifts and blessings from the Lord. He expresses his desire to serve the Lord in Psalm 132, a 'song of ascent' commemorating the restoration of the ark:

'I will not enter my house
or go to my bed...
till I find a place for the Lord,
a dwelling for the Mighty One of Jacob.

We heard it in Ephrathah,
    we came upon it in the fields of Jaar [Kiriath Jearim]:
"Let us go to his dwelling-place;
    let us worship at his footstool —
arise, O Lord, and come to your resting place,
    you and the ark of your might'

(Psalm 132:3, 5-8).

Do we want to know the Lord's blessing in our lives? Then we must realize that discipleship is not a spectator sport. Look at David's zeal — even when it is somewhat misguided it is a powerful rebuke to the modern Christians who say they want blessing, but whose enthusiasm stretches no further than one service a week and the odd church social. That suggests they want heaven on the cheap, and argues that they've missed the point that when heaven is really in your heart (i.e., by grace through faith in Christ), enthusiasm for the Lord flows in a Spirit-led stream which wells up to eternal life (John 7:37-39). Lukewarm water in the kettle argues that the flame is low — or out! David began with practical discipleship and went on to joyous fellowship with the Lord!

Curse — opposing the will of the Lord [6:20-23]

David went home **'to bless his household'** — i.e., to pray and worship God with them. When he got there, Michal, who earlier in the day had 'despised him in her heart' (6:16), berated him for his behaviour in dancing before the ark in simple dress. Why she should fly off the handle is not altogether clear, although, as Payne remarks, 'Obviously her outburst... was the tip of an iceberg.'[2] David replied with a rebuke which perhaps hints at something of the problem: **'It was before the Lord, who chose me rather than your father or anyone from his house when he appointed me ruler over the Lord's people Israel — I will celebrate before the Lord'** (6:21). Michal was really objecting, as we shall see, to the work of God in finally bringing David to his kingdom, largely over the dead bodies of the house of her father, Saul. The consequence was that she **'had no children to the day of her death'** (6:23). The prophecy against the house of Eli echoes in the judgement on the house of Saul: 'Those who honour me I will honour, but those who despise me will be disdained...' (1 Samuel 2:30).

Resisting the Lord's will has a cost

Michal demonstrates what a blight it is to go against the Lord. It is a curse to disobey the Lord's will and to reject his gracious acts. Perhaps you may think this is overstating the case, especially as applied to Michal. 'After all,' you might say, 'Michal only disagreed with David's piety. She only felt he was going over the top and being undignified before the common people. Surely that's understandable in the circumstances?' This leaves the problem, however, that David and, more importantly, the Lord, took her outburst very seriously indeed. What, we must ask, made the Lord displeased enough to afflict her with childlessness? I believe the answer lies along two lines.

Firstly, Michal's attack on David's enthusiastic devotion was in fact *an expression of hatred for all that God was doing in David's life*. We all know this phenomenon at first hand. A parent (who is a nominal 'Christian') resents her son leaving her (liberal) church to travel miles across the city to an evangelical congregation, noted in the community for its strong emphasis on believing the Bible, personal faith in Christ and vigorous discipleship. Any small event — being discovered reading the Bible or declining to watch a TV film on the Lord's Day — can trigger off a snide remark about being a 'holy Joe' or having a 'judgemental attitude'. This happens between generations, relatives, workmates and old friends, and it is very often indicative of deeper layers of resistance to the claims of God. The world of the unconverted feels reproached by the open-faced devotion of committed Christians. Nothing pricks consciences like honest holiness. And so the only way to 'suppress the truth' is by 'wickedness' (Romans 1:18). Hence the frequent resorting to ridicule and charges of 'extremism' in such cases.

Secondly, it was therefore expressive of *the personal rejection of the Lord himself*. David's reference to the passing over of Saul and his house as the kings of Israel was another way of saying that Michal partook of the spirit and attitude of her father. Michal's sin was no different from that of Saul! Her subsequent childlessness is directly related to this fact. The punishment is not childlessness *as such*, but rather the denial of an heir to the house of Saul. This is an important distinction, because childlessness itself, however sad a condition it may be, must not be assumed to be a judgement of God on each and every childless woman. Childlessness is, no doubt, one of the sorrows of life in a fallen world, just like every other illness and, indeed, death itself. But that is not to say it is *ipso facto* an act of divine justice towards the afflicted woman (the same can be said of male sterility). God's judgement on Michal related to his deter-mination to end the line of Saul and thus establish the house of David upon Israel's throne (1 Samuel 15:28; 24:20; 28:17-19).

There are costs to disregarding the Lord. To reject him and exclude him from your life is to commit yourself to a kind of spiritual dehydration; it is to shrivel into an existential cocoon which has no exit, no future and no joy beyond the passing pleasures of this life, such as they may be. Masses of people flee the sad realities of life without the living God into the fantasies of false religions, and in the West today, the escapism of New Age mysti-cism and the anaesthetism of drugs and alcohol. The viciousness and bitterness of modern societies is the self-generated fruit of mass commitment to godless unrighteousness. The only solution is salvation by the blood of Christ, as people come to Christ in repentance and faith, one by one, and the leaven of the gospel permeates society with life-giving power.

I will celebrate before the Lord

David was gently firm in his answer to Michal's rebuke. Christians are enjoined to 'gently instruct' those who oppose the Lord's servants, 'in the hope that God will grant them repentance leading them to a knowledge of the truth...' (2 Timothy 2:25). As long as we are standing on the bedrock of Scripture truth, we have every reason to stand fast, disregard criticism and ridicule, and give a clear answer for the hope that is in us. To be opposed or persecuted for the sake of righteousness is, in its own way, an encouragement to hold more firmly to our faith in the Lord. If we are to beware when all men speak well of us, we may take some heart from the hostile response of certain people. If 'the devil looks after his own', he also reserves his most powerful blows for those who love Jesus Christ. But the Lord is faithful and will not let his people be taken from him (1 Corinthians 10:13). As surely as David parried Michal's riposte and the Lord won his victory in David and for all the people of Israel, so he will surely sustain all believers in their personal faith and walk with him.

Christians, are, however, called to more than a dour defence of their faith. David celebrated the goodness of God. When there was occasion to rejoice, he did just that. And even though there are occasions when the people of God have cause to be solemn and reflective, or to be crying out to the Lord in brokenness of heart, the predominant theme of our personal devotion and public worship ought to be a rising sense of the joy of salvation. The psalms show us the way. Many a time, the psalmist begins in the depths of his troubles and sorrows. But as he worships the Lord and reflects on his grace to his people, his heart is lifted above the earth-bound horizon of his problems and, from the high ground of communion with the Lord, he sees everything in the perspective of the finished work of Christ: sin forgiven, the future secure, the Lord with him as the way, the truth and the life, and heaven opened as his everlasting inheritance in his beloved Saviour! (See, for example, Psalms 73, 77, 102, 120 and 130.)

The ark of the covenant arrived in Zion. God, whose presence was symbolized by the ark, was lifted up in the midst of his people. For the New Testament believer, this reminds us of the exaltation of the Lord Jesus Christ as a Prince and a Saviour. He is Immanuel — 'God with us'. He is exalted in heaven to the right hand of God but he sent forth the Holy Spirit at Pentecost to live within the hearts of all believers. What a privilege, that God should come to his creatures, renew their nature, convert them to a living personal faith and take up residence within them by the Holy Spirit! This is what it means for Jesus to have come into his kingdom as the king of glory. This is what we celebrate as we worship our Father-God, through our risen Lord and in the strength of the indwelling Spirit. Let us join daily with David in the joy of our Lord's victory:

'Lift up your heads, O you gates;
    be lifted up, you ancient doors,
    that the King of glory may come in.
Who is he, this king of glory?
    The Lord Almighty -
    he is the King of glory'

(Psalm 24:9-10).

6.
In covenant with God

Please read 2 Samuel 7:1-29
'With your blessing the house of your servant will be blessed for ever' (2 Samuel 7:29).

The idea of the covenant (i.e. God's) is inseparable from the flow of redemptive history. To say that God deals with mankind in terms of a covenant relationship is simply to say that we, whom God has made in his own image, are answerable to him in virtue of his eternal purpose to have a people in fellowship with himself. Had God merely made man and then left him to get on with his life, without either any revelation of the divine will or any intervention in human history, we could hardly be regarded as being in covenant with God. But God not only created us, he also revealed himself to us. Both the fact and the content of that revelation not only imply but determine the contours of a relationship. This is precisely what we find in God's dealings with Adam both before and after his fall into sin. God set forth Adam's calling in what has been called 'the covenant of works'. He promised Adam endless life (which is the positive promise implied by the penalty in Genesis 2:17: 'When you eat of [the tree of the knowledge of good and evil] you will surely die'). Adam failed the test and death came upon him and all his descendants (Romans 5:12, 18). God then revealed himself in terms of what is called 'the covenant of grace' when he cursed the serpent:

> 'And I will put emnity
>   between you and the woman,
>   and between your offspring and hers;
> he will crush your head
>   and you will strike his heel'

(Genesis 3:15).

It later becomes clear that the 'offspring' (or 'seed') of the woman is actually the Lord Jesus Christ! That is why Genesis 3:15 is called the *protevangelium* — the proto-gospel.[1] The idea of the 'seed' recurs throughout the Scriptures, most notably in the later unfoldings of the covenant of grace to Abraham (Genesis 12:1-3), to David (in our text) and finally in Jesus himself, whom Paul pointedly calls 'the seed of Abraham' (Acts 3:22-26; Galatians 3:14, 29). It is a covenant of *grace*, because the provision of salvation is a gift of God, not something that can be merited by man's best efforts (cf. Isaiah 46:10). It is a *covenant* because it is between two parties, God and man (in Christ, who alone perfectly fulfils the stipulations of the covenant in paying the penalty of sin as the substitute). God gives the covenant unilaterally; man responds in terms of the gospel of Jesus Christ. The covenant of grace receives its final and definitive publication as the prophesied 'new covenant' of Jeremiah 31, which has been fulfilled in Christ and the New Testament era.

Are you perhaps wondering what all this has to do with David and 2 Samuel 7? The answer is that our passage recounts the specific announcement of the covenant of grace to David — the so-called 'Davidic covenant'. We need to remember that 'The stability and prosperity achieved by David in finally removing the threat of Philistine incursion into the promised land and also in rooting out the last pockets of Canaanite influence represent fulfilment of the covenant promises. Now some substance is given to the covenant summary, "I will be your God and you will be my people".'[2] And it is at precisely this point that the Lord sends a new prophetic word through Nathan the prophet, which sets David's significance in redemptive history and gives an additional pointer to the as yet future fulfilment of that plan of salvation in Jesus Christ, the Son of God. We are given a brilliant glimpse of what it meant for David to live in covenant with God and what it must mean for us in the context of the New Testament age and the claims of Christ.

The ark of the covenant [7:1-3]

David was at last **'settled in his palace'** and enjoying **'rest from all his enemies around him'**. The nation was united and the ark of the covenant had been returned to its central place in the life of Israel. David's thoughts began to turn to the future and in particular to the matter of God's house. David noted that while he was **'living in a palace of cedar'**, the ark of God remained **'in a tent'**. The Lord seemed to suffer by the comparison and David was exercised in his heart about how best to honour the Lord. Nathan the prophet, with whom the king had shared this thought, was impressed by David's genuinely godly concern and simply encouraged him in general terms: **'Whatever you have in mind, go ahead and do it, for the Lord is with you.'** It is good to be meditating on ways to serve the Lord more perfectly. Notice three things.

1. *David was thinking in terms of God's covenant.* Unlike many a politician — or, sad to say, many a modern Christian — he was not concerned with his self-image, self-esteem or self-validation. Rather, he was absorbed by the desire to respond to his covenant Father-God so as to glorify him. His happiness and joy were not inward eddies of his soul, but heavenward effusions of covenant commitment. 'How can I repay the Lord for all his goodness to me?' (Psalm 116:12). God reached out first in covenant commitment: a believing response can only be expressed properly within the parameters of that union with the Lord which he effected by his sovereign grace.

2. *David took time to think on these things.* When we have some leisure time, we are more likely to evacuate our minds in front of the TV. The art of quiet meditation has been elbowed out of our lives. David could have diverted himself less profitably, even in a pre-electronic world. But he gave his mind to the Lord's work, pondering ways to glorify him. He sought to be more faithful by expanding his vision of God's kingdom through active, pious meditation.

3. *David was free to think of ways of serving the Lord, within the parameters of a commitment to doing the Lord's will.* Nathan had told him, 'The Lord is with you.' David was not an automaton, programmed by the mind of God, but a man made in the image of God and called to an intelligent discipleship. God calls us to think — to exercise renewed minds in a quest for renewed behaviour. Obedience to the Lord's revealed will integrates and shapes our thinking, but does not put it in a straight-jacket. God says 'No' as well as 'Yes' in answering prayers. Spiritual discernment is

thinking that is constantly and progressively being informed and reformed by the teaching of God's Word and the leading of the Holy Spirit.[3]

As it happened, David's thought about building a house for God was to be turned down gently by the Lord. David was wrong on this score. But it was a blessing to him to have given his mind to the ways he might glorify God. Why? Because it is in the nature of true communion with God that we learn his will through his 'No's and well as his 'Yes'es. God's believing people are, as Richard Ganz has put it, 'free to be [their] own person before God'.[4]

God's covenant with David [7:4-17]

David's vision for a future permanent temple for the Lord and the ark was a good one. But the Lord did not want David setting his heart on something he did not intend him to do. So he gave Nathan a word to convey to the king — thereby, incidentally, giving David a living example of the prophetic office in action and a tacit encouragement to regard his prophet highly and resort to him for guidance and counsel. Notice four principal points.

1. David was thinking of building a house for God, but *God had not commanded him to do so* (7:5-7). This is a very gentle correction indeed. God simply points out that he had commanded that the ark be kept in a tent and had never asked for **'a house of cedar'**. Here again is that 'regulative principle' of Scripture — that in the things of God we must be content to do his will as he has specifically revealed it and not add things, however good they may seem to us to be in themselves. Where God has stated his will, all other alternatives are prohibited, because they are either additions or subtractions from his perfect will.

2. God indicates that *one day a temple will be built,* but it will be at a time when Israel enjoys unhindered peace (7:8-11). To counter any discouragement that David may feel about this, God reminds him of all that he had done and would yet do for him. God would make his name **'great like the names of the greatest men of the earth'** and use him to establish the security of the nation on the international scene. So he will have blessing and to spare! For the

rest of us, whose names will not be so great, Matthew Henry encourages us that 'A man may pass through the world very obscurely and yet very comfortably.'[5]

3. God also says that *he will build a house for David* (7:11-13). This 'house' is not a building but a dynasty. From this dynasty, after David is gone, will arise the man who will build that other house — as it turns out, Solomon's Temple. Furthermore **'the throne of his kingdom'** will be established by the Lord **'for ever'**.

4. God further declares that *'David's son will be the personal embodiment of the people of God and is declared to be God's son'* (7:14).[6] The promises to Solomon appear also to be an intimation of the Christ who is to come. These promises also 'relate to Christ, who is often called "David" and "the Son of David", that Son of David to whom these promises pointed, and in whom they had their full accomplishment. He was of the seed of David, Acts 13:23. To him God gave the throne of his father David, Luke 1:32... That promise, "I will be his Father, and he shall be my Son," is expressly applied to Christ, Heb. 1:5. But the establishing of his house, and his throne, and his kingdom for ever, can be applied to no other than Christ and His kingdom.'[7]

God did nothing less than further reveal his covenant of grace, setting it in the context of the history of Israel, the calling of David and his descendants, the progressive unfolding of the plan of redemption and the coming fulfilment in the everlasting kingdom, whose King would be Jesus Christ, son of David, Son of God. God's goodness always transcends our limited anticipations of his blessings. He is 'able to do immeasurably more than all we can ask or imagine' (Ephesians 3:20). David begins to consider that he might have the blessing of building a temple for the Lord. The Lord answers by denying him that privilege but promising, first, that his son will be the builder; second, that he will have a dynasty of kings following him and, third, that the Davidic kingdom **'shall be established for ever'**.[8] The last declaration would surely have been understood by David as prophetic of the same Holy One of whom he speaks in Psalm 16:10 (cf. Acts 2:27) and the Lord (whom we know to be the Son of God) to whom God speaks in Psalm 110:1. These intimations of Christ were veiled from David, to be sure. His understanding was not that of the noonday light of the New Testament. But he knew when he was near to the Lord and being given to hear, or to speak, the words of inspiration from the Lord. And it filled his heart with inexpressible joy and a sense of the glory of the Lord.

Responding to God's covenant [7:18-29]

Noting that, whereas Nathan spoke prophetically to him on God's behalf and David replied directly in prayer to God, Matthew Henry suggests that when 'ministers deliver God's message to us, it is not to them but to God, that our hearts must reply; he understands the language of the heart, and to him we may come boldly'.[9] When David responds to the Lord in prayer, his original desire to build a house for the Lord has been entirely supplanted by his thankful wonderment that the Lord intends to build a 'house' (i.e., a dynasty) for him! This marvellous prayer, one of many in the Bible which provide models for our own spiritual exercises, is a window in the heart of a true child of God — a window through which we are permitted to gaze for a moment to see the fruit of God's grace in a human life. The prayer consists of five parts.

1. David went into the tabernacle — the tent he wished to replace with a permanent structure — and **'sat before the Lord'**. He begins to pray by confessing *the basis of his approach to the Lord.* This is that God is sovereign and full of grace. With a humility appropriate to the Lord's most recent dealings with him, he acknowledges the Lord's goodness to his family both with respect to the past and the future. He asks, **'Is this your usual way of dealing with man, O Sovereign Lord?'** What he means is that since we are by nature so deserving of divine judgement, then the blessings he is receiving are unutterably 'unusual', in that they are all of undeserved favour, i.e., free grace. They are above and beyond what we might normally expect! Notice how his prayer is current and based on his experience. It is no formal recitation of fine words, but the voice of the soul reflecting on all that God has been doing personally for him. Real prayer cannot be anything else, for it bears today's joys and sorrows, without delay, to the throne of grace (Hebrews 4:16).

2. The body of the prayer begins with *the praise of God* as the only Sovereign God (7:20-22). This is worship in its purest sense — the simple adoration of God for who he is. It is the worship, not of ritual mumblings and liturgical recitations, but of personal experience in the depths of the soul: **'There is no God but you, as we have heard with our own ears.'**

3. David then recalls *the covenant faithfulness of God* in his mighty acts on behalf of his people (2:23-24). God knows this, so why repeat it? Surely, in order to reinforce the memory and implications of these redemptive acts upon the heart of the one who prays, to stimulate faith and love towards the Lord! David reminds himself of, and in the process praises God for, his steadfast love towards Israel. This, in turn, is the heritage of the New Testament Christian, for it all points to Jesus Christ who came to save his people from sin, to unite believers to God by faith in him and to forge new lives of holiness in all believers.

4. David declares that his motive in seeking the Lord's blessing is not selfish, but *a holy desire for the glory of God* (7:25-27). He does not pray merely because he has a need, or because he wants something. He prays because he has a claim upon the promises of the covenant God has made. The promises of God are, as Charles Simeon has said, 'our warrant for asking' and 'our security for receiving'.[10] Everything comes together in the desire that God's glory might shine brightly before the world in the evident spiritual and temporal well-being of his believing people.

5. The prayer ends with *an expectant petition* that God would pour out the promised blessing (7:28-29). Here is hope, peace and contentment — all resting on the certainty of the covenant faithfulness of the Lord. This is the engine of confident prayer — if we have no promises, then, as the saying goes, we 'haven't a prayer'. We would only pray into the void. True prayer is always based on the covenant. Why? Because true prayer is to the God who (1) has revealed himself and (2) has promised to answer with his blessing (Hebrews 11:6). The self-revelation of God and the promise of salvation are the very heart of the divine covenant. He calls; we respond. We cannot, by searching, find him out (Job 11:7). God is the initiator and his call is covenant mercy to all who will, by his grace, hear and heed him. This was true for Adam, Noah, Abraham and Moses in time past and was now true for David. It was to be true in the ages to come.

Towards the end of the earthly Davidic kingdom of Judah, perhaps as late as the sixth century B.C., the psalmist (in this case, Ethan the Ezrahite) lamented the sorry state of the Lord's people and prayed for the Lord to revive them according to his gracious promises. In so doing, he invoked the Davidic covenant:

'O Lord, where is your former great love,
which in your faithfulness you swore to David?
Remember, Lord, how your servant has been mocked,
how I bear in my heart the taunts of all the nations,
the taunts with which your enemies have mocked, O Lord,
with which they have mocked every step of your anointed
one'

(Psalm 89:50-51).

But these verses not only look back to David but forward to Christ. 'The sacred songster,' writes J. G. Murphy, 'soars in this passage above the type, and celebrates the Antitype, who was pre-eminently despised and rejected of men, at the same time as he was bearing the sins of many, and making intercession for the transgressors. The guilt of man and the grace of God are combined in the affecting argument; and this is an appeal which cannot fail with Him whose tender mercies are over all his works.'[11]

This is the same covenant which is preached in the fulness of the gospel of Jesus Christ and promises new life, eternal life, through faith in Jesus Christ as Saviour and Lord. 'The promises of God,' said Thomas Scott, 'belong to all who believe in Jesus Christ, and plead them in His name. As far as we are conscious that this is our desire, experience and practice, we may find in our hearts to make our requests as large as the largest of God's promises; we shall not meet a refusal. If the blessings we have already received are vast and unmerited, what shall we say to the future? The eternal happiness God has promised to His people, and the gift of His Son to be the ransom for our souls.'[12] 'It is "in Christ alone",' as Charles Simeon reminds us, 'that they [God's covenant promises] "are all Yea, and Amen" (2 Cor. 1:20): and it is to those only who are in Christ by a living faith, that any of them are made... The Covenant of grace provides for us all that we can ever stand in need of. But we must "lay hold on that covenant" and on "Jesus the mediator of that covenant" before we can possess the blessings of it... Let us not suppose that we are to obtain mercy in ways of our own devising. We must come to God by Christ: we must plead what Christ has done and suffered... we must trust in him alone. There is "no access to God for any of us, but by Him" (John 14:6; Eph. 2:18): nor is there any name but His whereby any man can be saved [Acts 4:12]."'[13] This is life 'in covenant with God'.

7.
The victorious servant

Please read 2 Samuel 8:1-18
'The Lord gave David victory wherever he went' (2 Samuel 8:14).

David's period of rest and recuperation was over. His kingdom was secure but not without enemies — surely a parable of the kingdom of God upon earth before the Lord returns. So David embarked on a series of campaigns which, one after another, reduced the enemies of God's people to vassals and tributary peoples within an empire that stretched from the upper reaches of the Euphrates to the Gulf of Aqaba. It is tempting to interpret this in terms of the dominant notions of twentieth-century liberalism as so much monarchical self-aggrandizement and imperialist expansionism, typical of the time, and so on. But this is to miss the point, which is that David was acting as the servant of the Lord in establishing the rights of the covenant people of God to the Lord's gift of the land of promise. Israel's history, including her wars, is unique in that it charts the direct revelatory hand of God in the guidance of his people. We are observing the mighty acts of God in history as he unfolds his plan of redemption for a desperately troubled world. And this is not merely about the past, but points ahead to the triumph of the kingdom of God in the rule of the promised Messiah, the Lord Jesus Christ.

The chapter portrays David as the servant of God, who successively gains total victory over the Lord's enemies (8:1-8), dedicates the spoils of victory to the Lord (8:9-14) and executes his kingly calling in faithfulness to the Lord (8:15-18).

Victory [8:1-8]

David subdued the Philistines of 'Gath and its surrounding villages'

(8:1; 1 Chronicles 18:1).[1] He then turned west to make the Moabites his subjects, thereby fulfilling the prophecy of Balaam that 'a sceptre' would arise out of Israel to 'crush the foreheads of Moab' (8:2; Numbers 24:17). They were to remain in subjection until the death of Ahab (2 Kings 3:4-5). We might note in passing that Balaam's prophecy against Edom was later fulfilled when Abishai defeated the Edomites in the Valley of Salt (8:14; 1 Chronicles 18:12; cf. Numbers 24:19; 2 Chronicles 21:8). Finally, he moved north to dispose of the Syrian kingdoms of Zobah and Damascus (8:3-8). The key to all this success is mentioned in 8:6: '**The Lord gave David victory wherever he went.**'

It is obvious what this meant for David, but what does it say to us? All of Scripture, including the record of ancient battles, is God-breathed and designed, rightly understood, to be a blessing to God's people. Let me suggest three points of relevant application to Christians today.

The Christian warfare

We are reminded here about the Christian warfare. David was not just another Eastern potentate on the rise. He and his people were the church of God in the world! In fact, they constituted the revived church of the Old Testament going forth conquering and to conquer in the name of the Lord and in obedience to his perfect will! As such this illustrates some profound truths about the church throughout history, not least in these 'last days' — the New Testament period.

1. Most obvious, perhaps, is the truth that however low the church may sink under the pressure from a hostile world, *she will triumph over every effort to extinguish her.* The gates of hell will not prevail against the church. Apparently insuperable difficulties will neither delay nor prevent the victory of our Lord. We have this promise and it ought to generate a quietly trusting confidence in every Christian.

2. Less obvious is the truth that *the church is the instrument by which God judges the wicked.* Israel kills Philistines. This was God's justice applied to international relations. The apostle Paul almost chides us over this point when he asks, 'Do you not know that the saints will judge the world?' (1 Corinthians 6:2). We ought to know this very well! In New Testament terms this does not mean bearing the sword in order to execute the revealed sentences of God

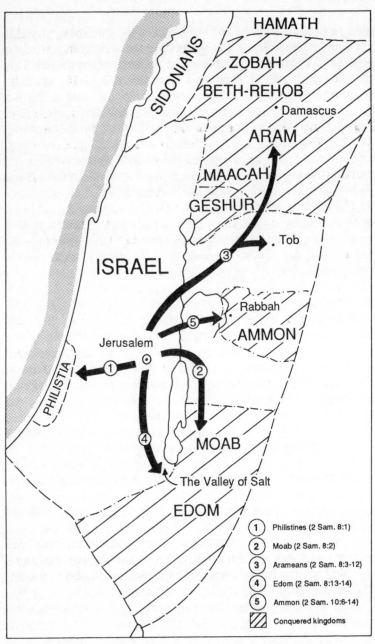

MAP 4 — David's campaigns (2 Samuel 8).

upon peoples and nations and claim real estate for God by force! It is rather the extension of a ministry of judgement by means of the gospel and in parallel with the saving message of the gospel! This is what Paul is talking about in 2 Corinthians 2:15-16, where he shows how the preaching of the gospel divides the hearers: 'For we are to God the aroma of Christ among those who are being saved and those who are perishing. To the one we are the smell of death; to the other, the fragrance of life.' The church's message of salvation can and does cast a shadow — a shadow of divine wrath against the rejection of the Lord — in other words, a ministry of condemnation. This is often overlooked but is an ever-present reality associated with all public preaching of, and personal witnessing to, Jesus Christ as the sin-bearing Saviour of the lost. To hear the gospel and not believe is a fearful and solemn event. And that is why God's ministers are so deeply saddened when their own ministry is rejected by some of those to whom they have held out the message of life in Jesus Christ. God is employing his servants not only as instruments of redemption in Christ, but as the ministers of his righteous judgement against the reprobate lost. This is just to say that the church's faithful ministry separates the saved from the lost. The lost are already lost, of course, so the church does not make anyone lost who was saved. But the fact remains that persistent rejection of Christ only happens when Christ is preached. In this sense it falls to 'the saints' to 'judge the world'.

3. Closely related to this is *the reality of the spiritual warfare within the life of the individual Christian.* Did David, when he conquered Gath, remember his times there and perhaps see his return and conquest as somehow symbolic of overcoming the temptations and backslidings of the past? Twice he had fled there, when it was sin to do so. And these were days of worldliness, compromise and apostasy for David, even though the Lord delivered him from his predicaments! When our 'right hand' causes us to sin, we are, as Jesus commanded, so to speak, to 'cut it off'. Sin must and will be cut out, for it will have no dominion over the Lord's discipled people. But this will not happen without a bit of a fight! (Matthew 5:29-30; Romans 6:14; Ephesians 6:10-20).

There is a real warfare for hearts and lives, for communities and nations, for created reality in its entirety. Of that struggle between light and darkness, God and Satan, the wars of the Lord's people are but a small illustration and indicator.

Our spiritual inheritance

We are also reminded that while the Lord calls us to make war on
sin and evil, this is not an end in itself, but a means of bringing us
to the spiritual inheritance he wants us to have. Struggle, even with
sin, is not the 'be-all and end-all' of Christian experience. Far from
it. We are encouraged to 'make it [our] ambition to lead a quiet life'
and to pray for 'peace at all times and in every way' (1
Thessalonians 4:11; 2 Thessalonians 3:16). Still we need to heed
Peter's stirring challenge at all times: 'Therefore, my brothers, be
all the more eager to make your calling and election sure. For if you
do these things, you will never fall, and you will receive a rich
welcome into the eternal kingdom of our Lord and Saviour Jesus
Christ' (2 Peter 1:10-11).

The victory of Christ

We are also pointed to Christ, of whom David is a foreshadowing
in certain respects. For 2000 years, the victory of Christ has been a
reality in the world — one which has been experienced with
glorious certainty by the redeemed on earth and in heaven, but also
as certainly by those who have died in their sins and now inhabit a
lost eternity. Jesus is the true Son of David, the Lion of Judah, who
must reign (in heaven) until his enemies are all put under his feet
(Luke 1:32-33; Revelation 5:5; 1 Corinthians 15:25). This reminds
us that *our* warfare is not what earns victory (Christ alone merits the
victory and salvation itself), but is the sharing in *his* triumph and one
of the means, in our experience, by which Jesus chooses to bring us
to the complete possession of all the blessings he sovereignly
bestows.

Dedication [8:9-14]

David reaped a considerable harvest from his conquests. The King
of Hamath, near the Euphrates, submitted willingly to David and
the borders of Israel were secured. Plunder also poured into David's
treasury and David dedicated all this new wealth to the Lord (8:11).

In this way, David secured for his son and successor both the peace and the wealth necessary to the successful building of a temple for the Lord. Psalm 60 was composed at this time, in prospect of battle with the Arameans and the Edomites, and it is quite clear from that song that David took nothing for granted. These were not 'easy' victories, but triumphs of divine power and human blood, sweat, toils and tears. The fruits were all the sweeter for that and the Lord all the closer as the object of his people's worship.

The bare narrative, while once again of great interest in itself, must be understood and applied in the context of the overall purpose of God for humanity. Two principles appear to suggest themselves as of particular relevance to our lives, irrespective of the time in which we live.

1. *The Lord's people are called to dedicate all their gifts and graces to the Lord.* The greatest privilege of the Christian, apart from his own experience of salvation and eternal life, is to be a channel of God's love towards others and a means of leading them to the Lord.

2. The Lord's people are reminded that, if like David they become **'famous'** (8:13), then *they are to take care to humble themselves and give the glory to the Lord.* 'It is through God we do valiantly,' notes Matthew Henry (cf. Psalm 60:11-12). 'To God be the glory, great things hath he done...!'

The theme, then, is *submission to the Lord* in, through and after victories over the enemies of the Lord and of our souls. This is most wonderfully illustrated in the mediatorial submission of the victorious and glorified Jesus, who having completed and perfected his kingly rule, with all his foes subdued and his people saved, subjects this kingdom *and himself* to 'him [God the Father] who put everything under him, so that God may be all in all' (1 Corinthians 15:20-28). With this willing submission, the risen Jesus signals to us the absolute primacy of the glory of God as embodied in our and his heavenly Father. We are led in our thinking to contemplate the consummation of the kingdom of God at the end of this world and so give ourselves to living in the light of the total victory of the Lord Jesus Christ. This is the perspective from which to approach the most immediate challenges in daily life! Christ's ultimate triumph steels us for today's trial and testing!

Service [8:15-18]

Foreign wars have been the ruin of many a nation. David was neither an adventurist nor a megalomaniac. He only waged the 'battles of the Lord' — those which the Lord commanded for the accomplishment of his covenant promises concerning the land of Israel (1 Samuel 18:17; 25:28). David did not neglect his government at home. He ruled impartially over **'all Israel'**, in other words, over every part of the kingdom, without prejudice to Judah over the rest. His was a **'just and right'** administration **'for all his people'**. And he delegated authority: military (Joab, 8:16), civil (Jehoshaphat, 8:16, and Seriah, 8:17), ecclesiastical (Zadok and Ahimelech, 8:17) and, startling to us in these days of the civil rights movement, that of minority peoples (Benaiah, 8:18). He also appointed his sons as advisers for his own executive role as king. All this was to provide for benevolent and efficient government.

In its veiled way, this points us to the rule of Christ over his church, for the theocratic state of Israel was the rule of God over his church in that phase of redemptive history. Power was exercised to honour God and bless his subjects. The institutions of spiritual order were directed to the end of doing God's will 'on earth as it is in heaven'. The organs of human government were ministers for good, which is to say, they were to be acting redemptively in their appropriate sphere of divine calling. This is indeed the calling of civil government under the New Testament, of course within its prescribed limits (Romans 13) and, needless to say, the mandate of church government within the body of Christ (e.g., Matthew 18; Acts 15; 1 Timothy 3; 1 Peter 5:1-5 etc.)

Faithful servanthood to the Lord is joyous discipleship, guided by the divine intelligence of the Holy Spirit in and through the Word. As David was the servant-king over God's people 3,000 years ago, Jesus is the one true and final king over all of God's people, now fully revealed in the New Testament. As our Mediator King, he not only rules over us and blesses us, but he calls us to serve him as ambassadors in the world. He calls us, in other words, to share in the fruits of his perfect atonement both with respect to our personal spiritual life through faith in him but also in claiming the ground of this world, so to speak, for his kingdom through the spreading of the gospel and the gathering in of new believers through conversions to Christ. This implies two basic facts for Christian experience and witness.

1. *Jesus sees the church as the apple of his eye* (Zechariah 2:8). He is with her always, even to the end of the world. He deals faithfully and lovingly with his followers. Furthermore, so exalted are they in his eyes, that the world is, in truth, their stage — the backdrop to their mission as the witnesses for their Saviour who are seeking the lost with the message of salvation. Holy confidence is the only consistent and God-honouring consequence of this truth as it applies to the Christian response to the discouragements afforded by the mass opposition to the gospel in the world — confidence in Christ's rule — assurance of his final triumph and our entrance into glory!

2. The church is called by Christ to reflect his threefold office of Prophet, Priest and King through practical discipleship in the world. We are made to our God kings and priests (Revelation 1:6). Elsewhere in Scripture we are told that Christ received gifts for men and that he distributes them within his body, the church, so that according to the proper working of each individual part, the growth of the body is brought about for the building up of itself in love (Ephesians 4:16). *Jesus calls his disciples to serve him with gladness.* In this service there will be victory!

8.
The quality of mercy

Please read 2 Samuel 9:1-13
'What is your servant, that you should notice a dead dog like me?'
(2 Samuel 9:8).

William Shakespeare, like every child of the English Reformation, was aware of good theology and this is occasionally reflected in characters in his plays. Portia, the advocate of the *Merchant of Venice,* speaks of 'mercy' as that which has the quality of not being forced but freely given: 'The quality of mercy is not strained.' 'It is,' she adds, 'twice blest; it blesseth him that gives and him that takes.' 'It is,' she says, 'an attribute to God himself.'

Few incidents in the Old Testament illustrate these truths with such fragrant generosity of spirit as David's treatment of the crippled son of his old friend Jonathan. The principal motives of godly kindness are all here.

1. There is the motive of *obedience towards God.* The Lord has commanded us to be merciful. This is simply the revealed will of God. Discipleship to the Lord commands outward practical obedience in this matter. It also requires a merciful attitude of heart which earnestly desires to be kind even to those who have wronged us. It is a matter of doing the will of the Lord.

2. Another motive is *gratitude to God* for his blessings. Those who have received the mercy of God want to show '**God's kindness'** to others (9:3). This is a spiritual fruit of the transforming and renewing grace of God. Any privilege received implies a duty to perform arising directly from the benefits of that privilege. That is why Jesus tells us, 'From everyone who has been given much, much will be demanded' (Luke 12:48). The reception of God's goodness impels joyous responsiveness, which shares that unmerited kindness with others. Knowing God's love and salvation is evidenced by the desire to do people some real good.

3. Yet another motive is *a desire for the rewards of faithfulness to the Lord*. Jesus says, 'Blessed are the merciful, for they will be shown mercy' (Matthew 5:7). It is not that our good works earn the blessing of God, for in our obedience we show 'we are God's workmanship, created in Christ Jesus to do good works, which God prepared in advance for us to do' (Ephesians 2:10). Good works *are* the blessing of God in themselves. But they are also the occasion of further growth in grace as the Holy Spirit advances his work of separating us more to the Lord (i.e., what theologians call 'progressive sanctification').

4. A further motive may arise, as in David's case, from a *personal commitment* towards the person who is the object of kindness. David was kind to Mephibosheth for **'Jonathan's sake'**. The Lord is witness of the promises we make and we ought never to take our own commitments to people less seriously than if they had been made directly to God.

In the account of David and Mephibosheth, we not only see these godly motives at work; we also see their fruit in the reaching out of one man to another. The facts of the incident are wonderful in themselves, but they reach into Christian experience today and teach us much about the love of Christ and how, as his disciples, we are to be gracious to one another.

A gracious initiative [9:1-3]

Having rested from his recent campaigns, David turned his thoughts to the family of Jonathan. From a former servant of Saul's, named Ziba, he discovered that there was indeed a surviving son of Jonathan, Mephibosheth, who had been five years old when his father and his grandfather, Saul had been killed at Mount Gilboa. He had been crippled in a fall, during his family's flight from David (4:4). By this time he must have been in his late teens or early twenties. But why did David even bother to ask about possible survivors of the house of Saul? What moved him to seek to trace the remnants of that sad family?

Some commentators today look for dark motives. D. F. Payne suggests that David wanted to make sure that he knew where any survivors were so he could keep an eye on them as potential rivals for the throne.[1] There is no support whatsoever in the text of

Scripture for attributing such unworthy ulterior motives to David and we are justified in asking how such an idea arose. The answer is that current critical scholarship theorizes that this is part of a so-called 'succession narrative' (comprising 2 Samuel 9-20 and 1 Kings 1-2) written many years later to justify for succeeding generations David's taking the throne of Israel for himself and his dynasty.[2] The assumption is that the Bible's history of David is too good to be true. To be believable it must be interpreted as basically a cover-story to sanitize the nasty mixed motives of the king! This presupposes a sceptical and unbelieving attitude to the text as it stands, puts a premium on elaborate speculations about what is *not* mentioned in Scripture over against what it actually says, and leaves no room for the divine inspiration of the Word of God.

The Word itself paints a beautiful picture of David reaching out in godly compassion to the son of Jonathan. It is clear that for David, this grew out of his love for Jonathan and the covenant that he had made with him many years before (1 Samuel 20:15-16). David had promised not to cut off his kindness from Jonathan's family, 'not even when the Lord has cut off every one of David's enemies from the face of the earth'. David was concerned to keep his word to Jonathan, but there was more to it than that. What is **'kindness for Jonathan's sake'** (9:1) is also **'God's kindness'** (9:3). The greater intensity of the latter indicates that David regards this as a matter of faithfulness to God and not just to a man. This is to say that our promises and covenants to people are to be regarded with no less seriousness than if they had been made to God himself. We are accountable to the Lord for all we have done in the past and for all our promises and future actions. Your word *ought to be* your bond. Your personal covenants, promises, vows, agreements and under-takings — whether to keep an appointment, pay a bill, do a job or, on a higher plane, your covenant relationship to the Lord as his disciple — are all to be regarded as matters of faithfulness to the Lord! The fact that all around us promises are easily made and more easily broken should not deflect us Christians from resolving to be as straight as a die in everything we say and do. And if we are ever ridiculed for being honest — as happens more often than you think, especially to conscientious Christian young people — then count it a blessing from the Lord. He is pleased with you, for it is his will that you are doing.

David's action is, however, more than keeping a promise — it is also an illustration of the grace of God.[3] The fact that David and Jonathan had made a covenant did not give Mephibosheth an automatic right to David's favour. It is still conceivable that Mephibosheth might be one of 'David's enemies' to be 'cut off... from the face of the earth'. Even if he were not — and indeed he was not — Mephibosheth did not seek any favour from David. David had to find him and reach out to him. The initiative was David's and it was freely taken. David was, so to speak, found by one who sought him not (9:5).

So it is with Christ and the covenant of grace. The fact that God has made a covenant to save a people for himself in Jesus Christ does not make salvation less of grace or the conversion of the sinner any less a unilateral sovereign initiative from the Lord. 'I revealed myself to those who did not ask for me; I was found by those who did not seek me' (Isaiah 65:1). The covenant promise is fulfilled in the initiative of grace, for the covenant itself is all of grace! God always makes the first move. Were he not to do so, we would remain as we are, dead in our sins and oblivious to the gospel.

The same principle may be applied to personal relationships. If you want to be of help to someone, if you want to befriend a neighbour, if you want someone to come under the sound of the gospel, you must be ready to take the initiative. You have no right to expect someone else to do it for you. This is what grace is about — reaching out to bless even your adversary's household, without your being asked, or their deserving it! David owed Mephibosheth nothing; Christ owes us nothing; but praise God that Jesus came to save sinners like us and that, by his grace, the Davids reach out in compassion to the Mephibosheths of this world.

A man in his need [9:4-8]

Mephibosheth cuts a sad picture in the pages of Scripture. Yet, as we shall see, he was a man with a humble heart and gracious spirit (9:8; 19:24-30). Even his name gives expression to his destitution, for Mephibosheth means 'a shameful thing'. The name of his home-town seems to echo the general tenor of his circumstances — Lo Debar means literally 'no pasture'. He was disabled as a result of a fall in his childhood (4:4) and had, of course, been dispossessed of his ancestral land, which must have been considerable (1 Samuel 9:1). This is a kind of parable of the helplessness and lostness of every child of Adam. Outside of a personal relationship of reconciled communion with God in Christ, man is rightly called 'shameful'. Like Mephibosheth, lost mankind was crippled by a fall and has since been fleeing the face of the Lord's Anointed. The world is a 'Lo-Debar' (no pasture) for the lost sinner, where he wanders with neither title nor possession, having no hope beyond his life 'under the sun' and the gloomy uncertainty of eternity looming beyond the grave.

If the summons to appear before David caused Mephibosheth some anxiety, David soon reassured him and, indeed, promised to be kind to him, to restore his land and to receive him into the fellowship of the royal table. David 'took him to be one of his family'.[4] We are reminded of the grace of Jesus Christ as he draws crushed and helpless folk to himself. He calls the blind, the halt and the maimed. He chooses the weak things of the word to confound the mighty. He comes to the sinner's weakness and makes it perfect in his strength. And as he wins men and women to himself, to repentance and faith in him as the only Saviour, he allays the fears of judgement with the promise of his blessings.

Mephibosheth responds with the conventional humility of the time, but is no less sincere for that: **'What is your servant, that you should notice a dead dog like me?'** (9:8; cf. 19:28; 2 Kings 8:13). Today's counsellors and psychiatrists would probably set this down as 'a poor self-image' or 'low self-esteem' induced by disability and deprivation. And perhaps there was an element of this in Mephibosheth's self-deprecatory remark. Nevertheless, it needs to be said that there are times when self-deprecation and low self-esteem are justified because they are a realistic assessment of our true condition before God. When Jesus, in the words of prophecy, described himself as 'a worm and not a man ' (Psalm 22:6), it was a vivid way of expressing the true nature of sin and its condemnation as this affects the humanity of man made in the image of God. Jesus took all the sin of all the people he would save out of the whole world and bore its just punishment in himself. He who knew no sin became sin for us (2 Corinthians 5:21). This was, in a sense, a 'dehumanizing' experience, if we may so use the term. Sin itself mars the calling and constitution of man as the image-bearer of God, because it is the negation of the knowledge, righteousness and holiness which are of the essence of that image.[5] Sin is the contradiction of God and therefore is the contradiction of true humanity as created by God. Jesus bore that contradiction in his substitutionary atonement and triumphed over it. We, on the other hand, would never recover from sin's effects on our own. And however 'nice' people we were in this life, without a saving knowledge of Christ, we would certainly not be 'nice' in hell, for sin in all its depravity clothes the 'second-death' existence of the lost, and the image of God is no more than a bitter memory of what was and might have been.

All who believe in the Lord Jesus come to do so out of a recognition of their own helplessness. They come with eyes opened by grace to the extent of their own depravity and to the breadth of the mercy of the Lord, and their awareness of being 'dead dogs' in terms of their lost condition before God is soon overwhelmed by the love of Christ as he reaches out to them:

'Twas the same grace that spread the feast
  That gently forced me in
Else I had still refused to taste
  And perished in my sin.

(John Newton)

Mercy bestowed [9:9-13]

The final section of the passage records how Ziba, Saul's servant, was appointed steward of Mephibosheth's land and how David took Mephibosheth into his household. Saul's grandson now lived in Jersualem in the style of a scion of nobility, restored to his inheritance and surrounded by the favour of the king. The transformation was complete. The free grace of God and the personal covenant with Jonathan came together in the adoption of Mephibosheth into the house of David.

The words of Robert Murray M'Cheyne's poem, 'Jehovah Tsidkenu' (the Lord our Righteousness), come to mind as perhaps the sweetest application of this theme to the experience of all whom the Lord has saved by his free grace:

I once was a stranger to grace and to God,
   I knew not my danger, and felt not my load.
Though friends spoke in rapture of Christ on the tree
   Jehovah Tsidkenu was nothing to me.

When free grace awoke me, by light from on high,
   Then legal fears shook me, I trembled to die;
No refuge, no safety in self could I see —
   Jehovah Tsidkenu my Saviour must be.

My terrors all vanished before the sweet name;
   My guilty fears banished, with boldness I came
To drink at the fountain, life-giving and free —
   Jehovah Tsidkenu is all things to me.[6]

9.
A kindness rejected

Please read 2 Samuel 10:1-19
'So Hanun seized David's men...and sent them away' (2 Samuel 10:4).

The present chapter stands out in sharp contrast to the account in the preceding one of David's kindness to Mephibosheth. They are parallel in that each records David's seeking to return a kindness to a son for the sake of a father — Mephibosheth because he was a scion of the house of Saul, and Hanun because he was the son of Nahash, late king of the Ammonites. They are in contrast because, whereas Mephibosheth responded with joy and humble gratitude, Hanun took offence and precipitated a war with Israel! This contrast is instructive in that it illustrates graphically both the way that God deals with men (i.e., he is slow to anger and rich in mercy) and the differing ways in which men respond to the Lord's dealings (i.e., acceptance versus rejection). Remembering also that David points us ahead to Christ, we shall discern here lessons of universal applicability to Christian experience.

There are three main points covered in the narrative: David's kindness towards Hanun (10:1 2); Hanun's rejection of the overture (10:3-4); and David's exaction of retribution for Hanun's insult (10:5-19).

Reaching out in love [10:1-2]

David decided to do some kindness to Hanun on account of his father Nahash, who had shown some unspecified kindness to David, possibly when the latter was on the run from Saul.[1] All we really know about this Nahash is that he was the cruel king of an unbelieving nation. The Ammonites were the descendants of Lot by his incest with his younger daughter (Genesis 19:38). Early in Saul's reign, Nahash had sought to conquer the Trans-Jordanic Israelite territory of Gilead and had only been prevented from doing so by Saul's infliction upon him of a crushing defeat under the walls of Jabesh-Gilead (1 Samuel 11:1-11). Some forty years or more on, Nahash was dead and **'his son Hanun succeeded him as king'** (10:1). It was to this man that David sent an embassy with condolences on the passing of his father.

As with his initiative to Mephibosheth, we might ask, 'Why? What was the purpose? What does this mean?' Arthur W. Pink has suggested that David's motives were purely political and that he had no business being nice to a nation which was not always exactly friendly to the Lord's people.[2] There is no evidence for such a view. It should be remembered that while the Lord had commanded the annihilation of the Canaanites, he expressly charged Israel to leave the Ammonites alone, on account of their descent from Lot (Deuteronomy 2:19). In any case there is no reason to assume that political motives are *ipso facto* duplicitous and insincere! A sound political instinct is a necessity for wise, stable government and there is every reason to believe that sincerity and solid principle will make for good politics. There is certainly no hint of insincerity on David's part. His action breathes a spirit of straightforward friendliness. David was prepared to 'do good to all people', even if he was aware that this was to be especially true within 'the family of believers' (see Galatians 6:10). Kindness, on the human plane, ought to know no frontiers! No good purpose can ever be served by deliberately fomenting discord and cementing prejudices and animosities. It is Jesus who tells us to love our enemies!

We may perhaps go further and see in David's approach to Hanun an illustration of the way in which the Lord's people ought to be reaching out to the people around them. Christ has called the church to preach the gospel to 'all nations' (Matthew 28:19). In the parable of the sower, the seed was sown on all sorts of ground (Matthew 13:1-23). In the story, the sower could see these different types of soil, but in reality the sowers of the gospel cannot 'read' the soil of the hearts of those to whom they proclaim Christ. That is why, very often, what looks like 'good soil' to us turns out to be resistant to Christ, and what looks like rocky ground is transformed by the power of the Holy Spirit into a beautiful Christian.[3] It is through the widest *outreach* that the Lord *gathers in* his church — the *ekklesia tou Theou* (literally, the 'called out of God').

Remembering that David often provides a foreshadowing of Jesus Christ, we have in his overture to Hanun certainly an indication as to how God's people should reach out with sympathy and kindness to a sorrowing world, and perhaps even a slight intimation of the shape of the doctrine of the free offer of the gospel. You and I, walking by sight rather than by faith (as we are sometimes prone to do), might well have defended David had he left Hanun well alone. But God reaches out even to the Hanuns of this world and he will make some of them his saints!

Wilful rejection [10:3-5]

The rejection of sincere kindness is one of the hardest experiences to swallow. Hanun rejects David's sympathy, on the suspicion of political intrigue. The Ammonite nobles had asked him, **'Do you think David is honouring your father by sending men to you...? Hasn't David sent them to you to explore the city and spy it out and overthrow it?'** (10:3). As a result, Hanun set aside any rules of diplomatic courtesy, seized David's men, humiliated them and sent them packing (10:4), thereby precipitating exactly what he (erroneously) feared David was planning. David reached out in peace; Hanun delivered up 'an unsought *casus belli* [i.e. an act precipitating war] and, in the end, an addition to [David's] empire'.[5] Matthew Henry observes wisely that 'False men are ready to think others as false as themselves; and those that bear ill-will to their neighbours are resolved not to believe that their neighbours bear any goodwill to them...Unfounded suspicion [indicates] a wicked mind. Bishop Patrick's[6] note on this is that "There is nothing so well meant but it may be ill interpreted, and is wont to be so by men who love nobody but themselves."'[7] Had David been the very soul of sinless perfection, there would have been someone to criticize him; the fact that he was a highly effective monarch with a somewhat imperfect reputation and a proven penchant for resolute action frightened the Ammonites, preyed on their suspicions and issued in their foolish rebuff of David's diplomacy.

Again, here is a parable of the way the Lord's disciples and their message will sometimes be received in the world.

1. Many an ambassador for Christ has been humiliated, persecuted and even killed for bringing the good news of the gospel to people who needed to hear the message of salvation. Just as some today will not, as Paul says, 'put up with sound doctrine' (2 Timothy 4:3), so many in Old Testament times despised the truth. This was true even of Israel itself. The destruction of the Davidic kingdom of Judah draws forth from Scripture this chilling epitaph: 'They mocked God's messengers, despised his words and scoffed at his prophets until the wrath of the Lord was aroused against his people and there was no remedy' (2 Chronicles 36:16).

2. Evangelism, although a single task, is made a selective process by the Holy Spirit. There is one gospel to preach, but two basic responses are the result. Where Mephibosheth's was positive, Hanun's was negative. By the same approach, God exalts the one and abases the other. And so the gospel is an 'aroma of Christ', which when it is sensed by those who receive Christ with joy is a 'fragrance of life' and when sensed by those who wilfully reject it is a 'smell of death' (2 Corinthians 2:15-16). This means that rejection may well be a mark of faithfulness on the part of the evangelist — in other words, 'results' do not in themselves indicate 'success' or 'failure', for our calling is simple faithfulness, irrespective of the blessing God may or may not add in his sovereign good purpose. This gives some real point to the Lord's injunction that we never 'tire of doing what is right' (2 Thessalonians 3:13). We need constantly to pray for grace to overcome temptations to discouragement in the face of the coldness of many to the message of the gospel and even to our personal kindnesses offered in the name of Christ. If we plough faithfully, the Lord will have his harvest. Even the crop failures must become an encouragement to persevere. The Lord is sifting men and women by his Word and when he has gathered in all he intends to redeem, his glory will be exalted in the earth.

Before David's men could be further shamed by having to pass through the towns and villages of Israel on their way to the capital, David sent messengers to tell them to rest up in Jericho until their half-shorn beards had grown. Beards were grown long among the Israelites and David's concern for the men shows his sensitivity to their proper dignity and self-esteem.

Judgement [10:6-19]

In the affairs of nations, the most terrible disasters often arise from the most apparently insignificant events. The Falklands War of 1982 is perhaps the most recent example of this in the history of the United Kingdom. The seizure of a group of barren islands 8,000 miles away, involving fewer than 2,000 British citizens and with no fatalities among them, precipitated a war which galvanized the nation into action, recaptured the islands at considerable loss to life and property and precipitated the replacement of the Argentine dictatorship with a democratic government. Hanun must have known that his abuse of David's men would not be ignored. He apparently thought he would get away with it, for it is with a note of surprise that we read, **'When the Ammonites realized that they had become an offence to David's nostrils...'** (10:6). Hanun had sailed too close to the wind! We might be inclined to ask whether David needed to treat the matter with such seriousness. Is the preservation of something like 'national honour' worth a war and a great deal of death and destruction? Whatever the specific rights and wrongs in such situations, it is undeniable that these little incidents of besmirching the integrity of another nation — like shaving beards and clipping clothes — are not merely acts of petty vandalism. The acts themselves may look ridiculously trivial, but are in fact profoundly significant. Even if they seem on the face of things to be more like practical jokes, the reality is that in terms of international relations they are tantamount to acts of war, because they deliberately set out both to humiliate another nation before the world and to violate its integrity in some way — perhaps by paving the way for later moves which will be aimed at more tangible goals such as territory or tribute. Think of how Hitler gobbled up Czechoslovakia a piece at a time in the late 1930s until it was completely subjugated. 'National honour' is actually a conventional frontier, erected by a nation to provide a buffer zone within which international relations can be regulated and where negotiation can function without the necessity of open conflict. When that frontier is crossed, it is only a short distance to the real border and a real conflict. 'Good manners' between nations and individuals indicate a degree of mutual respect and goodwill. Take them away, begin a war of insults, and pretty soon it all dissolves in violence. Even if one side 'turns the other cheek', our experience of human nature indicates that sooner or later that side will have to defend itself. The line has to be held at some point. Hanun's folly only added to Israel's long-standing impression (correct, it must be said) that Ammon was an inveterate enemy of the Lord's people. David was not about to permit such contemptuous lawlessness from any petty king along his border.

The passage details the preparations for, and the execution of, the war with Ammon. It was to be later in this year-long conflict that David would fall into his sin with Bathsheba and contrive the death of her husband, Uriah, before the walls of the Ammonite capital (11:1-12: 31).

1. The Ammonites, realizing themselves to be facing an un-equal contest, secured the services of some 43,000 soldiers from four other states, Beth-Rehob, Zobah, Maacah and Tob — all Arameans from the north and west of Israelite territory (10:6).

2. The Israelites under Joab advanced into Ammonite territory and discovered that the forces of the Ammonites and the Arameans had not united — the former remained outside Rabbah, their capital, and the latter were camped at Medeba, a little to the south (10:7-8; 1 Chronicles 19:7). This was the enemy's second mistake (the first was getting into a war with Israel), for it is a basic rule of warfare never to divide one's forces in the face of a potentially superior enemy.

3. Joab made no such elementary mistake.[8] He knew that he had to fight both armies at once, so he divided his forces, taking the best troops under his command to face the Arameans and leaving Abishai with the rest of the army to pin down the Ammonites before Rabbah. Depending on how the battle went, they could reinforce one another (10:9-11).

4. Joab issued a stirring order of the day (10:12): **'Be strong and let us fight bravely for our people and the cities of our God. The Lord will do what is good in his sight'** (10:12).[9] The 'cities of our God' is probably a reference to the trans-Jordanic territories of Israel, through which the Arameans must have passed on their way to Ammon, and which might well be lost to Israel should they lose the battle.

5. Joab's division routed the Arameans, and the Ammonites, duly persuaded by their allies' reverse that discretion is the better part of valour, retreated into the fastness of their city. Joab was

apparently unprepared for a siege and marched the army home to Israel (10:13-14). The conclusion of the war was to wait for another year (11:1; 12:29-31).

6. The war did not, however, go away (10:15-19). The Arameans, under Hadadezer, gathered at Helam, near Tob, to fight Israel, presumably in an attempt to revenge their earlier defeats (8:3-8). The result was another defeat, their subjection to Israel and the isolation of the Ammonites. 'It is dangerous,' remarks Matthew Henry, 'helping those that have God against them; for, when they fall, their helpers will fall with them.'[10] On this occasion, however, the helpers fell first and this paved the way for the final defeat of the Ammonites.

The significance of these events must be seen in the context of the flow of redemptive history and not merely in terms of the fleeting political situation in a corner of the Near East 3,000 years ago. The events of history are the visible manifestations of the decree of God. He is working his purpose out as year succeeds to year. History illustrates theology. The victories of Israel are the vindication of the Lord's cause and kingdom against the presumptions and rebellions of his enemies. This robust doctrine is integral to all of Scripture. The judgements of the Lord, which are altogether righteous and just, are repeatedly bursting forth across the face of human events. Israel's defeat of Ammon and the Arameans indicates the Lord's intention to preserve the honour of his name and the integrity of his people. He notes when his disciples are abused. And the same unjust persecution and affliction which achieves in the believer 'an eternal glory that far outweighs them all' (2 Corinthians 4:17) may well rebound upon the wicked and the oppressor as a very weighty eternal judgement unless, of course, there is repentance and turning to the Lord in saving faith. Outside of Christ, the godless will sit besieged in their own Rabbahs of the Ammonites, fearful of the pending judgement but unwilling to change their ways. The fall of the Ammonites presages the ultimate victory of the Lord and calls for a response to the gospel *now*. Now is the day of salvation, the day of the Lord's kindness, the day in which Jesus Christ calls to you to come to him, that you might have eternal life.

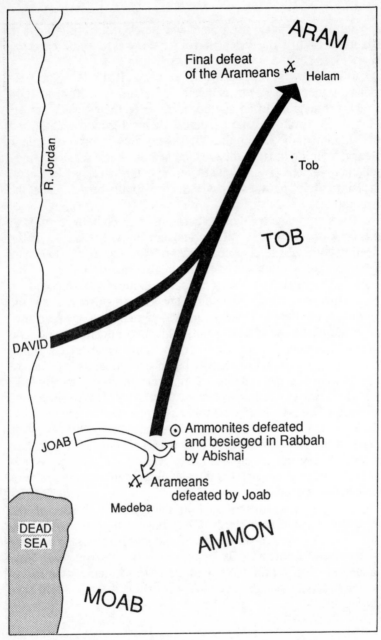

MAP 5 — Joab's victory over Ammon

PART II
Retrogression — David and Bathsheba

10.
The seduction of Bathsheba

Please read 2 Samuel 11:1-5
'David sent someone to find out about her' (2 Samuel 11:3).

Robert Murray M'Cheyne, the saintly pastor of St Peter's Church in Dundee, once told his congregation that if all the secret thoughts of everyone present that day were instantly exposed to public view, the house of God would look more like the gate of hell than the gate of heaven! He stated what is only obvious to every true Christian: namely that we all have a great deal in the way of sin to which we still need to die, and a great deal of gospel holiness still to attain. M'Cheyne was never one to dwell on the dark side of things, as all who read his sermons can readily attest. He was not trying to depress anyone. He was merely stating a truth that we all, one by one, could soberly confess to be true of ourselves.

It is just as well that all the sins that lurk in human minds are not exposed to public view! There is no great blessing in knowing how wicked people could be if they were not restrained by an unseen hand. Nevertheless, God has determined to record in Scripture several accounts of the sins of some of his choicest saints, in order that we should glean from their experiences spiritual lessons to keep us from the same errors and draw us into a deeper relationship with the Lord. In 2 Samuel 11-20, we have an extended account of some such failings. David's palmy days as the new, young and successful King of Israel gave way to a period of troubles which emanated from one terrible sin, the consequences of which were to hound the house of David for generations to come. The Lord, through the prophetic ministry of Nathan, passed sentence on the sins of the man after his own heart, when he said, 'The sword shall never depart from your house, because you despised me and took the wife of Uriah the Hittite to be your own' (12:10).

Here, then, we are to see the Lord's anointed, the sweet psalmist of Israel, commit a series of the vilest and most disastrous sins which were to rise, with a desperate air of inevitability, to a crescendo of horror and misery for himself, his family, those he wronged and ultimately for the whole tenor of his reign over God's covenant nation! David becomes 'a man under judgement'.[1] It goes without saying that in these distressing matters David is no 'type' or foreshadowing of the coming Messiah, the Lord Jesus Christ, but rather is an example of how vulnerable the greatest saints can be under the blandishments of temptation and sin and therefore of just how much we sinners are in need of Jesus Christ as our Saviour.

The conception of lust [11:1-3]

Our's Lord's brother, James, records in his letter to the Jewish Christians that 'Each one is tempted when, by his own evil desire, he is dragged away and enticed. Then, after desire has conceived, it gives birth to sin; and sin, when it is full-grown, gives birth to death' (James 1:14-15). James had earlier shown that temptation and sin are not to be blamed on God. Indeed, we may say unequivocally that although God permits sin to occur and Satan positively encourages it, no one can absolve himself of his personal responsibility and say, 'God made me do it,' or 'The devil made me do it!' Lust is always conceived in our hearts, with uncoerced willingness and personal responsibility before God. This is eloquently illustrated in the sad case of David's desire for Bathsheba. He allowed himself to be 'dragged away and enticed' by his own unmortified lust. The text suggests three elements which contributed to his fall.

Neglect of known duty (11:1)

It was the spring, when we are told, **'kings go off to war'**. This might seem at first glance to be no more than a literary flourish. In Scripture, as in all well-crafted writing, the flourishes are carefully chosen and often loaded with weighty implications. The point being made here is that when David should have been campaigning with his army, he **'remained in Jerusalem'**. He was neglecting his duty. It is not as if David was merely 'on hold', in a kind of behavioural neutral zone, in which he might or might not — however he chose

— get into trouble. He was already in trouble, just because he had stayed at home. 'When we are out of the way of our duty, we are in temptation.'[2] When we leave the post the Lord has assigned to us, we in some degree forsake his protection. He calls us back to honouring our commitments to him. A. W. Pink makes the point that this is what Jesus was teaching when he resisted Satan's temptation to fling himself from the pinnacle of the temple (Matthew 4:5). The Lord knew his calling — and it did not involve jumping from towers or doing tricks for Satan![3] When David stayed at home and let the army go off to do his fighting for him, he was in every way taking off the 'armour of God' (Ephesians 6:11). He was to pay a bitter price for his carelessness!

The love of ease (11:2)

We all know the truth of the proverbial saying, 'The devil finds work for idle hands to do.' Matthew Henry observes that 'Standing waters gather filth. The bed of sloth often proves the bed of lust.'[4] David had been lolling in his bed in the early evening. He **'got up from his bed and walked around on the roof of the palace'**. David's as yet unborn successor discerned the problem clearly: 'Diligent hands will rule, but laziness ends in slave labour' (Proverbs 12:24). Later he observed,

> 'I went past the field of the sluggard,
>   past the vineyard of the man who lacks judgement;
> thorns had come up everywhere,
>   the ground was covered with weeds,
>   and the stone wall was in ruins.
> I applied my heart to what I observed
>   and learned a lesson from what I saw...'
>
> (Proverbs 24:30).

The implications are not just for economics and agriculture, but for the very heart of the believer's spirituality and walk with God. Jesus says, 'Make every effort ['Strive', AV] to enter through the narrow door' (Luke 13:24). At the very least, spiritual laziness is backsliding. Christian diligence is the prerequisite of personal godliness: 'Watch and pray so that you will not fall into temptation. The spirit is willing, but the body is weak' (Matthew 26:41).

A wandering eye (11:2-3)

From the roof, David **'saw a woman bathing'** — that is, taking a purificatory bath after menstruation' (11:4).[5] The inspired historian tells it all with devastating simplicity: **'The woman was very beautiful, and David sent someone to find out about her.'** He was duly informed that she was the wife of Uriah the Hittite, one of David's élite formation, 'the Thirty' (23:39), then serving in the army fighting the Ammonites. Instead of turning his eyes away from 'beholding vanity' (Psalm 119:37, AV), David savoured every moment and no doubt hatched his plans for a future dalliance with Bathsheba. The 'royal voyeur', as R. P. Gordon correctly if unflatteringly calls him, had already committed adultery with her in his heart (Matthew 5:28).[6] We are reminded, by way of contrast, of the godly example of Job who 'made a covenant with [his] eyes not to look lustfully at a girl' (Job 31:1). This ought to be a working motto in every man's daily life, and for two reasons implicit in the text itself. The first is that visual input is so powerful that to control it requires the most serious, solemn and steadfast spiritual concentration and self-control. The second is that this requires a consistent modesty of dress and deportment in both men and women, in which they are discerningly conscious of the way they look, so as to avoid any provocation to lust in members of the other sex. This presupposes an inward commitment to resisting any feeding of their own lusts by 'a wandering eye'[7] — the periscope, so to speak, of the lurking submarine of a secretly sinful attitude that is looking for an occasion to sink the Lord's moral standards and get away with it unscathed!

The birth of sin [11:4]

God did not leave David without a check to his conscience. His servant noted that Bathsheba was a married woman. Single or married, Bathsheba was out of bounds from the standpoint of God's law. This had not prevented David from the polygamous accumulation of wives. Had Bathsheba been unmarried, David would probably have added her to his household. But the mention of a husband imposed a very obvious restraint. It represented a frontier

David had never crossed before. It challenged his moral fibre. God was offering him an opportunity to turn back.

David did no such thing, for he **'sent messengers to get her. She came to him, and he slept with her... Then she went back home.'** David has his one-night stand. Her husband need never know. How true are the words of James, the brother of Jesus, when he said that 'Each one is tempted when, by his own evil desire, he is dragged away and enticed. Then, after desire has conceived, *it gives birth to sin'*! (James 1:14-15, my emphasis). The sin started in the heart, while David was up on the roof. It became the sin of his hand in the adulterous tryst that followed. The seventh commandment was swept away. 'You shall not commit adultery' cast the shadow of its holy condemnation across the life of David, as a man, a head of a family, and the Lord's anointed king over the covenant people of God. Every trouble that followed in the remaining two decades or so of his life was to flow directly from what modern libertines would off-handedly trivialize as 'one little fling'! Sins have consequences. Because we try to minimize our sins, we are always surprised by what seems to be the vastly disproportionate complications that flow from them. 'Why should *one* indiscretion bear such a train of bad fruit?' we complain. The answer is that the 'one' indiscretion is in fact the breaching of the dam of ethics, trust and faithfulness. It therefore inevitably leads to multiplied and magnified repercussions, few of which are faced up to at the time of the sin itself.

One interesting sidelight in the text is that the parenthesis, **'(She had purified herself from her uncleanness),'** indicates that she had had her period and performed the ceremonial cleansing required in Leviticus 15:19-24. This proves that David was the father of her child, since she was obviously not pregnant before she went to David and her husband was miles away beyond the Jordan. The inspired historian leaves no ambiguity to muddy our interpretation of the event!

It is worth noticing that there is no hint that Bathsheba put up any resistance to the seduction. This may conceivably be a measure of her helplessness before the power of the king. Throughout the entire story she remains a passive participant. The focus of blame is entirely upon David, which in view of his position is entirely reasonable. It would, however, be quite wrong to conclude that she was an 'innocent victim'. True holiness may have a cost, but it never

has a price. That Bathsheba is portrayed as a kind of pawn may well
be a comment on her attitude to marital fidelity.

The birth of death [11:5]

David probably thought little of his sin as that spring turned towards
summer. Not, at least, until he heard Bathsheba's news: **'The
woman conceived and sent word to David, saying, "I am
pregnant."'** Now other factors would come into play and it would
affect the lives (and deaths) of others and the very life of the nation.
David's sin, now 'full-grown', gave birth to death (James 1:15). It
is one of the ironies of sin that what begins in secret, with the
promise of remaining hidden, sooner or later breaks out into the
open. These consequences are what gives sin its teeth — they bite
into the souls and rend the flesh of all involved. The hidden sin
becomes the public scandal. The fleeting pleasure of the flesh
becomes the blight of generations and nations.

We never fully foresee the tragic results of our sinful actions.
What for David was at the time no more than a moment of passion
was to have the most profound repercussions.

1. David's sin compromised *Bathsheba* as a wife bound in a
marriage covenant to her husband according to God's holy ordi-
nance. No sin is without a victim, in the end. The covenant David
broke in his thoughts when he saw and lusted after Bathsheba was
the precursor of a blow against the personal integrity and personal
relationships of those whom his sin would touch. The contagion of
sin can only be contained by a combination of immunization
(salvation by grace through faith in Christ) and quarantine (God-
honouring separation to living the Christian life of righteousness in
Christ).

2. David's sin issued in the birth of *a child* outside the family
structure that God had ordained for the nurture of a godly seed and
the establishment of a stable society. We reap as we sow, and in
adultery the harvest is all the more bitter for the fact that it is the only
sin that produces new life, which it blights from the start. The
wisdom of God in instituting the family and guarding it with the
seventh commandment could not be clearer. Sexual purity and
marital faithfulness are absolutely basic to the blessing of men,
women, children, societies and nations. Much more is needed, of

course, to provide for happy family relationships, but without this fundamental commitment to faithfulness only moral and social breakdown can result. The amorality and sexual 'freedom' of the second half of the twentieth century are as powerful a proof of this as history has so far provided. The future, including the children, is sacrificed on the altar of the present with its existential lust for gratification. Today, the children of such illicit liaisons are defined as 'unwanted' and end up in the abortion clinic rubbish-bin! Will God not judge this unspeakable horror?

3. David's sin was a great wrong against *Uriah the Hittite*, who was faithful as a husband to Bathsheba, a soldier to David and a convert to faith in the God of Israel. We shall see more of the implications of this in connection with Nathan's rebuke of David (12:1-12). Suffice it to say that Uriah, who was faithful at every point in which David sinned, had to suffer the injustices of being deprived of his wife, his family, his future in this world and his very life and limb! Uriah was a major victim of David's lust.

4. David's sin contravened *the law of God,* which he was bound to keep as a man and to uphold as the God-appointed king. This was to have consequences for the blessing of both his family and the nation as a whole. To walk away from the Lord is to say, 'No', to the goodness and the gifts of God and incurs the withdrawal of the Lord's blessing. When the rejection of the Lord's will pervades the leadership and government of any people, there cannot but be both a widespread moral decline and clear evidences in society of the bitter harvest of sin. It should be noted that the penalty of God's law for adultery in the Old Testament was death (Leviticus 20:10; Deuteronomy 22:22). The reason for this, together with prohibitions on pre-marital sex and prostitution, was undoubtedly to create and sustain what R. J. Rushdoony has called 'a familistic society', in which the central social offence was to strike at the life of the family. Adultery was placed on a level with murder because it was 'a murderous act against the central social institution of any healthy culture'.[8] David had, in a real sense, attacked his own kingdom — more, he had attacked God's kingdom.

5. David's sin broke *his own covenant with God.* He chose to go against the Lord and the way of blessing. He denied the Lord who had saved him and brought him through many trials. He had plunged himself into the way of spiritual death and it would not be long before this blighted his life. The sword was never to depart

from his house because of this sin with Bathsheba (12:10). He would repent and be forgiven by the Lord, but he would have to live with the hard consequences of his actions (12:13-14).

This is a very solemn passage in David's life. It teaches us about the sinfulness of sin. We are reminded of the powerful relevance of our Lord's command that we 'watch and pray so that [we] will not fall into temptation'. We are to do so precisely because 'The spirit is willing, but the body is weak' (Mark 14:38). May the Lord keep us by his mighty power and deliver us from evil in all its forms!

11.
The death of Uriah

Please read 2 Samuel 11:6-27
'Put Uriah in the front line where the fighting is fiercest' (2 Samuel 11:15).

There is something unutterably sad in the spectacle of a middle-aged man of God falling into gross sin. The moral failure of good men and women continues to dog the progress of the church, generation after generation, and serves to remind us of the realities of human frailty and the continuing necessity for the sustaining hand of God to be upon even the very choicest of believers. If there is any spiritual sensitivity and true self-knowledge in us, we will not fail to be touched by David's predicament. Far from justifying a self-righteous attitude towards the man, this must serve to bring us closer to him and, more importantly, closer to his greater Son, who alone is able to save us from our own foolishness. If we are inclined to any degree of self-confidence in our discipleship to the Lord, we should remember David, forsake our proud self-sufficiency and look, in a spirit of unconditional trust, to the Lord Jesus Christ.

David stands not only as a warning, but as a comforting testimony to the readiness of the Lord to receive the truly repentant to himself. We are not glad that David failed as he did. But we can readily identify with the fact that he failed. He is bone of our bone and flesh of our flesh. He is no pristine super-hero who floats across the ground in effortless triumph over the world, the flesh and the devil. If he is saved, it is God who saves him by pure grace. If he makes the right decisions, it is God who has instructed his heart and mind. If he repents and is forgiven and restored to fellowship with the Lord, it is all of God's grace at every point. This distinguishes the actual believers we read about in Scripture history from the pretty Pollyannas of too many Christian biographies. The David of the Bible is as real as the David that actually lived. And we are thankful for the stark honesty of the Word of God, because the experience of the real David meshes with the realities of our lives and speaks to us with power about the God who is love and who delights in being merciful to sinners.

We still have, however, some way to go before David is brought to repentance for his sin. For the best part of a year, David succeeded in hiding his sin. He also continued to be unrepentant over his adultery until God sent his prophet, Nathan, to rebuke David to his face. Our passage (11:6-27) records David's attempts to cover up his sin. This he does with such ferocious desperation that he ends up engineering the death of Uriah the Hittite, the soldier husband of Bathsheba and one of his own 'mighty men' (23:39).

First attempts at a cover-up [11:6-13)

It is surely a startling paradox that it is often the sinner's desire for a righteous reputation that drives him on to commit even more aggravated sins. Very few people in this world behave with such utter abandon as never to care what anybody thinks about them. Most people desire at least to *appear* straight and honourable. When the good, expensive wallpaper becomes hopelessly stained and torn, isn't it easier just to cover it up with layers of paint instead of making the effort to strip it down to the plaster? But as layer covers up layer over the years, the need of more basic renovation becomes more obvious. The very 'cleanness' of the thirteenth layer of latex paint protests too much! It obviously merely covers up a deeper problem of basic maintenance. The same may be said of human efforts to cover up sin. In the attempt to maintain a sanitized facade and avoid public exposure (not to mention repentance), the guilty are prepared to add sin to sin, layer upon layer, and so become ever more deeply enslaved to their wickedness.

This, in turn, involves another sad paradox: that more attention and effort are needed in order to hide sin than were required to resist it in the first place. It is certainly true that the initial fall into some sin can seem like being overwhelmed by an irresistible urge. We reason very easily that we could not help ourselves and that no effort could have held us back. If we are honest, however, I believe we will admit that we dallied wilfully with the temptation and savoured that future sin in our mind, until it was as easy to throw ourselves into it as it is to spin through a revolving door at the rush hour! Candid sinners know that their sins are planned one way or another and that such resistance as is offered by their consciences is eroded by successive acts of will that explain away the morality of the case in favour of the thrill of the forbidden fruit! On the other hand, the vigour and determination that might have turned away our eyes from beholding vanity soon becomes mightily evident as a factor in the rebellion itself! Now there is no easy readiness to repent and be humbled in the face of the disastrous consequences of our folly; now every sinew is strained and every muscle flexed to find ways of covering our tracks and laundering our public reputation!

Faced with Bathsheba's pregnancy and knowing that it would be obvious to all that Uriah could not be the father if he was across the Jordan with the army, David moved swiftly to cover up his sin. The deception unfolds a descending spiral of deceit. David sent word to Joab, who was busy besieging Rabbah of the Ammonites, to send Uriah up to Jerusalem (11:6), The plan was simply to provide Uriah with a conjugal visit to his wife and so deceive the poor man a second time by leading him to conclude that he was the father of the baby for which David knew himself to be responsible.

1. **'Then David said to Uriah, "Go down to your house and wash your feet"'** (11:8-9). David made it as easy as he could for Uriah to go to Bathsheba. The invitation to go home and 'wash [his] feet' was a warmly-delivered encouragement (possibly even a euphemistic innuendo?[1]) for Uriah to relieve himself of the sexual abstinence customarily required of soldiers while on a campaign (1 Samuel 21:5).[2] David also sent a gift after him. But to no avail. Uriah did not go home! He slept **'at the entrance to the palace with all his master's servants'**.

2. **'When David was told... he asked him, "Haven't you just come from a distance? Why didn't you go home?"'** (11:10-12). Whatever shock David felt when he heard his plan had come to nothing was well concealed in his second attempt to nudge Uriah down the path to home and Bathsheba. It is as if he good-naturedly clapped Uriah's shoulder and, with a knowing smile, said, 'C'mon, old friend, you're a long way from the army now. Don't take the rules so seriously. She is your wife, after all!' Uriah's response must have seemed to David like a clap of doom: how could he, Uriah expostulated, go home **'to eat and drink and lie with [his] wife'**

(he had not missed the drift of David's suggestion), when the army of Israel was camped in the fields?[3] This was, as Matthew Henry puts it, a 'very noble' reason for what the commentator calls 'this strange instance of self-denial'.[4] And, in the providence of God, it had a twofold effect: it completely destroyed David's cover-up scheme and, although we can be sure this was not in Uriah's mind as he spoke, it carried an implicit rebuke of David's indolent dallying in his palace, while his soldiers faced death in battle on a foreign field.

3. **'David made him drunk'** (11:12-13). Gentle persuasion had failed, so David plied Uriah with drink in the hope he might forget his high principles and go home to his wife. This too failed, but David had chalked up another gross sin to his discredit (Habakkuk 2:15-16). His attempts to cover his sin had come to nothing but a mounting sense of desperation at the inevitable consequences of the exposure of his seduction of another man's wife.

What are we being taught in this sad story? Perhaps the first and most obvious lesson is that the 'fun' of sinning never lasts. David was beginning to discover in practice that the 'pleasures of sin' only last 'a short time' (Hebrews 11:25) and that a time comes when our sin will find us out (Numbers 32:23). David knew these truths. We know them well ourselves. But is that formal knowledge itself enough to stop us? The truth is that the pallid righteousness of half-persuaded minds falls rather easily before the overwhelming force of unhallowed desires and passions. Always and exclusively, it is a humble, prayerful and faithful dependence upon the Lord and his power to sustain us which will see us through to victory over the powerful seductiveness of temptations and unholy desires.

Secondly, if your first concern in response to 'getting caught' is to try and launder your 'good name' and preserve your reputation before the public, then you will find, as David did, that you have doomed yourself to keep on trying, by hook or by crook, to whitewash your sin and avoid detection. This is the evil fruit of what Scripture calls 'the pride of life' (1John 2:16, AV).

Thirdly, unwillingness to confess means enslavement to deception and disinformation. You are living a lie. An unrepentant attitude weakens the conscience and opens the door to all sorts of self-serving schemes and stratagems that otherwise might never have entered your head. David had a guilty conscience, but he acted against it instead of upon it. He refused to turn to the Lord in sincere repentance. Indeed, so fixed was he upon covering his tracks that he was about to resort to nothing less than the sin of murder!

Finally and positively, we must learn from David the lesson that was, for him, still in the future. We must be ready to confess our sins to the One who is faithful and just and will forgive us our sins and purify us from all unrighteousness' (1 John 1:9). And where our sins have entailed the hurt of others, we must make the proper restitution. And we must be resolved to change our ways. Better still, 'The beginnings of sin are... to be dreaded; for who knows where they will end?'[5]

Anatomy of a murder [11:14-27]

The overthrow of David's carefully hatched plan only served to generate a more desperate scheme to hide his adultery with Uriah's wife. If Uriah would not oblige by sleeping with his wife and so becoming the 'father' of David's child, then, reasoned David, the mother of David's child must become the wife of David. At all costs, David's public image as an upstanding family man must be maintained. The cost of course, could only be the elimination of the innocent, upright and apparently oblivious Uriah!

Accordingly, David penned Joab a letter, instructing him to put Uriah in the front line and contrive to expose his position **'so that he will be struck down and die'** (11:14-15). By any judicial standard, this constitutes premeditated murder — and Joab, himself well practised in the art of disposing of people who got in his way, became David's willing accomplice.

In due course, the arrangements were made, Uriah was conveniently despatched by the Ammonites and Joab sent his report to David (11:16-21). The wily Joab did not want uncomfortable questions asked about how one man was put in a position where he was sure to be killed, so he arranged for a whole unit to be sacrificed, in that way dressing the incident up as a minor military error of judgement. He also needed a subtle way of conveying the news of Uarih's death to David. Knowing that any news of a skirmish lost would upset the king, possibly reminding him of Abimelech's fatal mistake under the walls of Thebez in the days of the judges (Judges 9:50-57), Joab ensured that the name of Uriah the Hittite was dropped, almost as an aside. David would 'get the message'. It would be too bad that so many men were killed but, after all, such are the fortunes of war!

David had no opportunity to flare up, because the messenger mentioned Uriah directly (11:22-24). His cool, calculated and callous reply was to dismiss the casualty list and encourage Joab to see the war through to its conclusion (11:25). Meanwhile, the remaining pieces of David's domestic cover-up were put in place. After a suitable period of mourning, Bathsheba moved into the palace as David's latest wife and the baby was born. As far as David knew, his tracks were covered. Dead men tell no tales! In fact one problem did remain, for '**The thing David had done displeased the Lord**' (11:26-27). And that, as we shall see in the next chapter, meant that the case was far from closed.

Facing up to the power of sin

This teaches us so clearly that there is no end of sinning until there is conviction by the Word of God. This is properly the subject of the next chapter, but it is important to note it here when we have before our eyes the picture of David's chain of sin. From the first conception of lust on that evening walk on the palace roof, to the death warrant delivered to Joab before the walls of Rabbah, there is progressive descent into spiritual darkness on David's part. What is significant is that he did not appear to have the resources in himself to stem that downward acceleration. Once started there is no stopping, short of repentance or death — and repentance requires the grace of God in an act of faith that casts itself upon the mercy of the God who is holy.

This, as we have already noted, is all the more reason for taking temptation and sin very seriously and taking the greatest care to 'avoid every kind of evil' (1 Thessalonians 5:22). It also highlights the role of opportunity in the commission of sin. David had the power to murder Uriah by setting up a local defeat for his army. He had the power and opportunity to acquire Bathsheba. Few people have quite the opportunities he had to do what he did. Those who can talk with horror about the gross sins of others, as if to suggest they could never do 'things like that', should reflect on the fact that 'There, but for the grace of God, go they', and that one vehicle of that restraining grace was a simple lack of opportunity! Money, power and fame, for example, can provide opportunities that may well make certain sins relatively easy to commit. This is one reason for the sixth petition of the Lord's prayer: 'And lead us not into temptation...' (Matthew 6:13).

Why did God not keep David from being led into temptation? Why did God permit him to sin so grievously? Why was David allowed to slide so deeply into such dreadful wickedness? At least three answers suggest themselves as powerfully applicable to all our lives.

1. We are shown *the sinfulness of sin*. Sin kills people. Sin kills for all eternity. Sin is not to be shrugged off as if it were no more than somebody else's pet dislikes, or the arbitrary standard of some 'puritanical' moralists; still less a mythical category which has evolved in man's religious thought to help him cope with the pressures and necessities of life in society. Sin is the contradiction of God, his will and his righteousness. Its wages are physical and spiritual death, with all that that means for time and eternity.

2. We are taught that, in matters of discipleship to the Lord, *past obedience is no guarantee of present and future faithfulness*. We cannot rest on our laurels, such as they may be, as if once being faithful was a ticket to heaven, irrespective of ongoing personal commitment to practical godliness.

3. We are also pointed to *the glory of the grace of God in Jesus Christ* towards sinners like ourselves. This answers the question: 'Are true Christians capable of committing such sins?' On the other hand, God's Word is clear that anyone committed to sin as his or her way of life — whether drunkenness, adultery, fraud, violence, murder, gossip, hoarding or whatever — shall not inherit the kingdom of God (Galatians 5:21). But Jesus Christ will save sinners like this (i.e., like us!) from their sins. And he will not let backsliding believers go. He will reclaim them. He has said that they shall 'never perish', for no one can pluck them from his Father's hand (John 10:28-29).

In this we see *the sovereignty of grace*. David was not saved because he was a great fellow by nature and, let us say, 'didn't really mean to do it'. He was saved by free, unmerited grace — the same mercy of God which would be purchased by the Lord Jesus Christ on Calvary's cross. God freely chose to save him and did so in order that he would be a very eminent servant of God.

In the spectacle of the returning and repentant backslider — the believer who has fallen into gross sin and is truly torn apart inside by the contradiction — we see *the perseverance of grace*. David had no right to think of himself as 'right with God'. God was not in his thoughts while he planned and executed his dalliance with Bath-sheba and his cover-up murder of Uriah, except perhaps in the distant nagging of his bruised and battered conscience. For all the peace and comfort he had, he might as well have been lost. But God did not leave him to himself. He reclaimed him. He restored him. And, as with the father who received the returning prodigal son from the far country, he fully intended to slay the fattened calf of his blessings in David's future. And this is the promise to all who believe in Christ as their Saviour. His love is the love that will not let us go.

12.
You are the man!

Please read 2 Samuel 12:1-14 and Psalm 51
'Then Nathan said to David, "You are the man!"' (2 Samuel 12:7)

Months, perhaps a whole year, had gone by since David had, with apparent success, covered up his adultery with Bathsheba by arranging the death of her husband Uriah. The son of that illicit union was rocking in his cradle and it is chilling to think that David may have felt comfortable within himself by this time — so at ease with his sins, perhaps, that he rarely spared them a thought. On the other hand, he may well have had a bad conscience. Indeed, it is difficult to imagine him not being aware that he had broken covenant with his God and was in a backslidden state. He was a true believer, most certainly saved by the grace of God. It is possible, although it cannot be proved, that Psalm 32:3-4 recalls David's experience during this time:

'When I kept silent,
    my bones wasted away
    through my groaning all day long.
For night and day
    your hand was heavy upon me;
my strength was sapped
    as in the heat of summer.'

Certainly, if David had any peace of mind, it was entirely illusory. He was deeply bogged down in a practical spiritual deadness brought about by living in unrepented sin, unreconciled to the Lord and therefore without that living awareness of union and communion with the Lord that is alone the fruit of a practical discipleship that does the will of the Lord from the deepest commitment of heart and mind. Accordingly, the king was in desperate need of recovery and restoration to the holiness of life to which he was called and committed, both by God and his own past confession. There is, as the saying goes, none so blind as those that will not see, and it is clear from the transition between chapters 11 and 12 that seeking forgiveness of God was not prominent in David's immediate plans.

The Lord purposed, as he always does sooner or later with all of us who become entangled in spiritual turpitude of one sort or another, to confront David with the nature and consequences of his sinful actions. Accordingly, the time came when 'the Lord sent Nathan to David' (12:1). Nathan was to be the instrument of the king's humbling. Hard though the prophet's task and, not least, his words, would be, and hard though David's experience under the chastening of God's rebuke would be, it ought to be noted that the purpose of such difficult ministry is one of grace and restoration and not one of wrath and naked punishment. The prophet with his message is the shepherd with his crook who has come to seek and save the sheep who has lost his way.

The passage unfolds in terms of three steps to David's restoration: conviction (12:1-12); repentance (12:13) and forgiveness (12:13-14).

Conviction of sin [12:1-12]

There is nothing of the flavour of a royal audience about the encounter between David and the prophet. There is no formality, no sense of rank, no standing on ceremony. The king is just another human being, about to be addressed by God through his sent messenger, the prophet. It was Nathan who had brought David the revelation of God's covenant with him and his house, that his 'throne [would] be established for ever' (7:4-17). He was no doubt a friend and counsellor to the king and, having access to the royal ear, was well placed to be a pastor to David.

Nathan's parable (12:1-4)

Nathan proposed a hypothetical case for David's adjudication. He 'fetched a compass with a parable', says Matthew Henry, to indicate that the purpose of the story was to point to truth as the compass needle points to the north.[1] There were two men: one rich with many sheep and cattle, and the other poor, possessing **'one little ewe lamb,'** which was **'like a daughter to him'**. When a traveller visited the rich man, the latter provided him with a meal, but instead of slaughtering one of his many animals, he took the poor man's ewe lamb and served it to his guest. 'What was to be done about this?' was the question posed for David.

The approach Nathan took is itself very instructive. It was indirect. He did not go straight up to David and read the Riot Act. He just told a story and solicited an opinion. Why this method? Clearly, it was designed, as far as was possible, to prevent David from flaring up in the kind of violent defensiveness that often results from direct confrontation. This protected Nathan from having to face the king's wrath and also had the effect of dealing with the issue when David's guard was down. This is not to say that direct confrontation is to be avoided on all occasions. It just means that, given prayerful and thoughtful preparation, we can trust the Lord to give us the right words to say at the right time and in the right way. Gentleness and wisdom are inseparable and a wise approach to the most difficult of problems will always be clothed in a spirit of meekness and sensitivity.

David's response (12:5-6)

He **'burned with anger against the man'** and invoked the fourfold restitution prescribed by the law (Exodus 22:1; cf. Luke 19:8).[2] He also went beyond the law in declaring the man worthy of death. It did not occur to him that his own behaviour deserved the more severe of these penalties and he was completely unaware of the fact that he had delivered himself into Nathan's hands for the rebuke which the Lord had given the prophet to deliver.

God's sentence (12:7-12)

With devastating simplicity, the sword of divine conviction transfixed the king as he revelled in the full flight of his righteous zeal against the robber of the poor man's ewe lamb. The trenchant words, **'You are the man!'** (12:7) turned his righteous anger in upon himself. He was naked before God and the righteous judgement of the law! He was the 'rich man', Bathsheba was the 'little ewe lamb' and Uriah was the 'poor man'! He was condemned out of his own mouth. He stood dumbfounded before the bar of heaven, his battered conscience surrounded by the shattered fragments of his hypocrite's mask.

Without pause, Nathan proclaimed the findings of the Judge. The prophet emphasized that this was **'what the Lord, the God of Israel, says'** (12:7). Beginning with a similar formula to that which prefaced Samuel's declaration of God's rejection of Saul, **'I anointed you king over Israel'** (1 Samuel 15:17), he set out a three-point indictment against the errant king.

Firstly, he reminded David that God had done great things for him in bringing him to the kingship and had promised even greater things in the future (12:7-8).

Secondly, he rebuked his despising of the word of the Lord in killing Uriah with the sword of the Ammonites and taking Bathsheba for his wife (12:9).

Thirdly, he pronounced a twofold sentence, in which the punishments fit the crimes (12:10-12). In answer to his murder of Uriah, **'the sword shall never depart'** from his house. 'Historically this may be seen,' remarks R. P. Gordon, 'as a comment on the deaths of three of David's sons but could be extended to include other traumas of the Davidic dynasty, for example its attempted liquidation by Athaliah (2 Ki. 11:1).'[3] In retribution for his taking of Uriah's wife, his own wives will be taken from him and **'one who is close'** to him will **'lie with [his] wives in broad daylight'** — doing in public what he did in secret. This was to be fulfilled to the letter during the rebellion of Absalom (16:22).

In assessing the manner in which the Lord convicted David of his sin, we should notice that it illustrates a general principle of all conviction of sin: namely that to be truly convicted of sin, we must actually convict ourselves. In David's case this is strikingly apparent, in that he unwittingly pronounced sentence upon himself through the mediation of the scenario in the parable. This set him up for Nathan's *coup de grâce*: 'You are the man!' Conviction of sin is, of course, sorrowful admission of guilt. Sometimes when someone has told us that we have done wrong and this has been exposed to public view, we may only feel sorry because we have been caught and put to public shame. Deep down we bitterly resent being brought to account and are more angry than contrite. This is not true conviction of sin, for a true sorrow is not accompanied by resentment and anger, but rather accepts the justice of our condemnation. It cries *'Mea culpa'* ('I am guilty') with profound sincerity of heart. Our own consciences tell us we trangressed and, wonder of wonders and work of God's grace, we freely cast ourselves on the mercy of the Lord, willing to accept his most just judgement! It is right there, at the point at which we are inwardly convinced of our sin and submissive to God's verdict, that we are ready to experience the truth of the gospel and that 'Where sin increased, grace increased all the more' (Romans 5:20).

One further point: spare a thought for pastors and elders who have to shepherd the members of their churches and must, more often than people often realize, confront professing Christians over their sins. It is not only a difficult task, but one that is also terrifying. We shrink from such confrontations. How much easier to let it go on, hoping that it will all somehow go away. How costly it is to rebuke from God's Word and to work lovingly for the repentance and restoration of the wayward! This is, of course, of the essence of pastoral oversight — applying the disciplines of the Word of God in the lives of the people of God. Nathan is, in this respect, an example of what it means to be a pastor who watches over his people as one who must give an account to the Lord (Hebrews 13:17).

Repentance [12:13; Psalm 51]

How rare it is for any sinner unreservedly to accept rebuke! The more usual response, even in the few cases where culpability is admitted, is to reserve a portion of blame for someone else, or else offer mitigating factors to reduce the degree of guilt. 'Well, you have a point, but...,' we stammer, 'I didn't intend things to work out that way...' The historian does not record all that David said on the subject, but the account must convey with absolute accuracy the substance of his response: **'I have sinned against the Lord.'**

This was certainly a *sincere* confession. In these days of corrupt TV evangelists and adulterous preachers, we have perhaps become somewhat cynical about the tear-stained confessions beamed into our homes via satellite. Inevitably, the sincerity of any confession has to be attested by evidence other than the mere words (or even tears) that flow from the unmasked sinner. This is as true for David

as it is for anyone else. And the evidence is that David was utterly
humbled before the Lord by Nathan's rebuke. The fact that he was
forgiven (see 12:14) is proof positive of the reality of his repentance. The Lord took away his sin. The Lord pardoned him of the
death penalty for his adultery![4] The Lord declared, says Matthew
Henry, 'Thy iniquity shall not be thy everlasting ruin... Though
thou shalt all thy days be chastened of the Lord, yet thou shalt not
be condemned with the world' and adds by way of commentary,
'See how ready God is to forgive sin.'[5]

It was also a *comprehensive* confession. The evidence of Psalm
51 — a song known definitely to refer to this incident — makes it
impossible to 'doubt the reality, the sincerity, [and] the depth of
David's repentance and broken-hearted contrition.'[6] Appealing to
God's 'unfailing love' and 'great compassion', David calls out for
mercy and the blotting out of his 'transgressions... iniquity and...
sin' (vv. 1-2). He acknowledges that his sin is first and foremost
against God (v.4) and is an essentially inward problem (v.5).
Consequently, his need is for comprehensive renewal — 'Create in
me a pure heart, O God, and renew a steadfast spirit within me'
(v.10) — and the restoration of the sense of the Holy Spirit's
indwelling presence and the joy of salvation (vv.11-12), rising to
sacrifices of praise to the Lord (vv.14-19). In a very real sense,
Psalm 51 is the prayer of every Christian who has been overtaken
by his failings and who, having plumbed the depths of his backsliding, has returned to the Lord with 'the sacrifices of God', 'a broken
and a contrite heart', which the Lord 'will not despise' (v.17).

Forgiveness [12:13-14]

Seeing that David was truly repentant, Nathan was able to assure
him that his sin was forgiven: **'The Lord has taken away your sin.
You are not going to die'** (12:13). The penalty of the law of
adultery in Leviticus 20:10 would not be applied. This indicates that
in terms of the ultimate issues of death and eternity, David's
forgiveness was complete. The wages of sin is death, but David
would live (cf. Romans 6:23).

This has led many to conclude that complete forgiveness means
the complete removal of all consequences of repented sin. There are
cases of convicted criminals who have become Christians in prison

and argued for the commuting of their sentences on the grounds that God has forgiven them and, therefore, so should the judicial authorities. Many people, whether Christians or not, think that being sorry ought to relieve them of all the consequences of their actions and restore them to the *status quo ante*. This has no support in Scripture, as David's case amply demonstrates. Certain disabilities were to flow from David's sin (12:11-12). One more is now detailed: **'The son born to you will die'** (12:13). Why did God do this? The child, after all, was hardly the guilty party. The answer is that David had by his sin **'made the enemies of the Lord show utter contempt'** (12:14). To put it another way, we may say that God took the child to himself 'in order to vindicate His reputation for righteousness among the nations'.[7] Any questions we may have as to the eternal destiny of the child are fully answered by the truth that God is love and may be depended upon to be perfectly just in all his ways.

It is very humbling (and so it is designed to be) to have some of the consequences of our sins leave their marks upon our lives, to stare us in the face as long as we live. Perhaps it is the ravages of earlier excess — smoking, drugs, alcohol, violence, sexual sin — adversely affecting our health, even our life expectancy. Or it may be the economic results of wasted opportunities or resources squandered by foolish business deals or an addiction to gambling. Again it may be the sadness of broken relationships resulting from attitudes that prevailed prior to our becoming Christians. Though covered by the grace of God and overshadowed by the hope of heaven, these are aspects of life which are often not reversible on this side of eternity. Like death itself, they await the fulness of redemption that yet remains to be completed in the glory that is to come for every believer in Christ. In the meantime, they are designed to draw us closer to our Redeemer and to help us both to understand, and to grasp in our experience, the fulness and freedom of God's saving grace in Jesus Christ. For he will save us from *all* the consequences of sin when he raises his people from the dead in the great day of his coming again at the end of the age.

13.
Reconciled to God

Please read 2 Samuel 12:15-31
'Then David... went into the house of the Lord and worshipped' (2 Samuel 12:20).

His task completed, Nathan went home.[1] His message to David had been a very hard one indeed and it is worth noting in passing that, notwithstanding that fact, this difficult encounter did their personal relationship no harm. Speaking for God is a tough job. Erstwhile friends and supporters can soon become enemies when they are faced with the necessary challenges of God's Word. Every minister of the gospel knows that if he places cordial relationships with those to whom he ministers before faithful proclamation of the Word, he is in effect denying the Lord and rendering his ministry worthless. It was not easy for Nathan to confront David. His faith had to overcome his dread anticipation of the potential cost of calling the king to account before the Lord. On this occasion, we have every reason to believe that David thanked God for Nathan's loving him enough — and, more than that, loving God enough — to tell him the home truths he needed to hear. That a later child of David and Bath-sheba was to be named Nathan — he was, incidentally, to be the son through whom the line of descent from David to Jesus Christ was traced — is indicative of the regard in which David held that excellent prophet (5:14; 1 Chronicles 3:5; 14:4; Luke 3:31, cf. Zechariah 12:12). Nathan had served the Lord unflinchingly. God honoured his faithfulness and has given him a place in the history of the Lord's people exemplifying the devotion which should characterize all of God's servants in every generation.

The final act in the drama of David and Bathsheba now unfolded and it was to be the most poignant of all. When David was first tempted, we felt able to understand him because we know what lust is in our own experience. When David covered up his sin with the death of Uriah, we were somewhat depressed by the vileness of it all. Then when he was confronted by Nathan, was personally convicted of his sin, freely confessed and was forgiven, we were encouraged by the sovereign mercy of God. But now, as we read of the death of the child of David's illicit union with Bathsheba, we are led to ponder quietly the continuing consequences of human folly and the wisdom of God's dealings with us.

What is brought out most clearly is the distinction, already referred to in the previous chapter, between *forgiveness of sin* and *relief from the consequences of sin*. The former does not guarantee the latter on this side of eternity. Nevertheless, Christians have frequently found it difficult to cope with the consequences of sin after they have been persuaded that the Lord has forgiven their sin. Their assumption appears to be that if God has forgiven them, all physical, providential and spiritual consequences ought to vanish without trace. The fact is that saved, forgiven Christians will not escape physical death itself (unless the Lord returns in their life-time). In a fallen and finite world, their frailties almost inevitably leave their marks and 'thorns in the flesh', so that only heaven and the resurrection of the body can erase them. The Word of God does not promise full and final redemption in this world. Sanctification is not glorification and the hope of heaven is not eternity itself. Grasping these truths will spare us a great deal of grief and enable us to grasp with biblical realism what the Lord is doing in our lives over the long haul.

Forgiveness and chastening [12:15]

The Scriptures are replete with instances of God punishing or correcting the sins of men and women. This is as basic a premise of God's providential dealings with the human race, as is the universal proclamation of the gospel message of salvation in Jesus Christ. Indeed, human history is unintelligible apart from the truth that 'His judgements are in all the earth' (Psalm 105:7). The experimental side of this is encapsulated in Paul's warning: 'Do not be deceived: God cannot be mocked. A man reaps what he sows' (Galatians 6:7). Scripture abounds in vivid examples of this truth. The 'burning lusts'[2] of Sodom are answered by the fire and brimstone of God's judgement (Genesis 19:24); Jacob deceives his father, and in his turn, is deceived by Laban and by his sons (Genesis 29:23-26; 37:31); Pharaoh kills the Israelite infants by drowning only to see later on the slaying of Egypt's first-born and the drowning of his army (Exodus 1:22; 12:29-30; 14:28); Nadab and Abihu offer 'strange fire' to the Lord and are consumed by fire from heaven (Leviticus 10:1-2); Adoni-Bezek amputates the thumbs and toes of seventy kings and in time suffers the same punishment (Judges 1:6-7); Agag's sword made women childless and, in just punishment, Samuel's sword made Agag's mother childless (1 Samuel 15:33). A pointed New Testament example is 1 Corinthians 11:30, where the abuse of the Lord's Supper in Corinth resulted in sickness and death in the membership of the church in that place. In these exceptionally clear cases, God establishes the principle that sin will be judged appropriately. In the general flow of his providence, his judgements may be less open to the public view, but they are nevertheless there, dogging the sinful actions of godless humanity. And this is no capricious vindictiveness; it is the just and necessary restraint and retribution of out-and-out wickedness. God is simply not prepared to be mocked!

What is the just punishment of the Judge in the case of the unrepentant unbeliever becomes the loving discipline of a heavenly Father in the life of the believer. Believers know that the Lord has not treated them as their sins deserve or repaid them according to their iniquities (Psalm 103:10). They simultaneously experience both the forgiveness of sin and the divine chastening. Even the hardest discipline in the lives of Christians life falls far short of their just deserts. Why? Because that discipline is not strictly judgement: it is not designed to cancel sin, to atone for the transgression, but to correct, straighten and guide our path in the future. For the Christian, the Lord Jesus Christ has already borne the ultimate judgement and has thereby wiped away all sin. He has atoned for the sins of those he has saved by his sacrificial and substitutionary death. He has taken the retribution; but we still need the rehabilitation. 'But why,' you may ask, 'does God even chastise those who love and serve him — and often in a way that is clearly in response to a particular sin?' This is the question raised by what was happening to David: **'The Lord struck the child that Uriah's wife had borne to David, and he became ill'** (12:15). And the answer is the same for us as it was for David. He was forgiven. Forgiveness looks to the removal of the eternal consequences of sin and redirects the course of this life heavenwards. Chastening involves something of the continuing consequences of sin in this life as a means of correction, guidance and rededication to the Lord. So it was with David: the child of his own sin must die. In reality it was David's sin that was dying, for we may be confident that the child was in the gracious hands of God. To be deprived of this life, at the call of God, is not to lose the 'be-all and end-all' of human existence. Those who criticize God for taking the baby from this world are affecting a (false) wisdom 'beyond what is written' (1 Corinthians 4:6). We must bow before the true wisdom — the wisdom of God.

Responding to God's dealings [12:16-31]

More often than not, sad to say, we are inclined to complain at the way 'life' (i.e., God in his providence) treats us, as opposed to humbling ourselves before God in acceptance of his holy and just interaction with our conduct. David's response to God's dealings is therefore a most instructive example of how a believer ought to handle the loving, though not pleasant at the time, discipline of his Father-God. The passage details five elements in this response: prayer (v. 16); open acknowledgement of sin (v. 17); a genuine submission to God's will (vv. 18-23); a readiness to seek blessing from the Lord afresh (vv. 24-25); and a rejection of past error through new obedience (vv. 26-31).

Prayer (12:16)

David **'pleaded with God for the child'**. He did not assume that the Lord's declaration that the child would die was so cast in stone as to be received with utter resignation. He knew that the Lord often proclaimed judgement in order all the more to show his compassion to those who call on him and plead for him to answer in terms of his mercy. No matter how inevitable some future eventuality may seem, we are never prohibited from praying that the Lord would arrest it and return a blessing. Prayer does not alter the eternal decree of God, but it does integrally relate to the application of his decree in his dealings with us in our changeability. He is the hearer of prayer.

Open acknowledgement of sin (12:17)

David did not hide himself from those around him, or for that matter
from the nation as a whole. How different from unmasked sinners
in today's church! We hide and refuse to face the very people and
ministry the Lord designed and purposed for our help, support and
restoration. David's elders were helpful to him. David was initially
absorbed in his sorrow and prayer, but the point is that he humbled
himself before the Lord and the Lord's people. It was not 'business
as usual'. He admitted his sin.

Submission to God's will (12:18-23)

When the child died, David responded with a remarkable quietness
of spirit. Mourning is often a mixture of sorrow over the departed
and anger that God should have allowed it to happen. David had
seven days of the former and none of the latter. His mourning — all
prior to the actual death of the child, although in prospect of that
prophesied eventuality — issued in a peaceable acceptance of the
reality of the death. This is the function of mourning and funerals.
Nevertheless, it is becoming fashionable in some circles today to
regard funerals as 'celebrations' — the pastor's opening words in
a funeral I attended recently were 'We have not come here to mourn,
but to celebrate.' Such people protest too much: their tears betray
their inability to 'celebrate' in the proper sense of the term. Death
is always an enemy. Redemption and resurrection are the only
answer to it. Weeping must come first and be exhausted before it
gives way to rejoicing (Psalm 30:5). The longer we have to
anticipate a bereavement, the sooner we will cease to mourn after
it happens. So David wept and fasted for a week and rejoined
normal daily life the day the child died. His explanation is solemn
and practical: while the child was alive he prayed, but after the child
died, there was no praying for the dead, no turning back the clock,
no reviving of the corpse. Death is a one-way street: **'I will go to
him, but he will not return to me'** (v.23).[3]

4. Seeking new blessing (12:24-25)

Life goes on. And going on with life implies a hope of better things,
certainly for the believer. David comforted Bathsheba. In due

course, the Lord gave them another child, who is none other than Solomon — **'Jedidiah,'** which means 'loved by the Lord'. In this way, the Lord transformed a relationship that was conceived in lust and established by murder into one which bore fruit in the person of David's illustrious successor, Solomon, and Jesus' ancestor, Nathan (Luke 3:31)! Life does not merely 'go on'! It goes on to a God-ordained goal that overflows with blessing for those he is saving from sin to be his own people! We have the promise of God's goodness as the reward of true faith. Forgiveness cancels past sin, promises future blessing and opens the gate of heaven.

New obedience (12:26-31)

We now return to where we began — to the reason David was on the palace roof the night he first set eyes on Bathsheba. The war with Ammon was already in progress, but David had not led the army personally. He had lolled in his palace, while others did the work. Now he must retrace his steps and do what ought to have been done from the start — he must join his troops. It still took Joab's timely encouragement to stir the king to this expression of new obedience to the Lord (12:26-28). David then **'mustered the entire army and went to Rabbah, and attacked and captured it'**. The Ammonites were subjugated and peace came upon the land (12:29-31). Forgiveness of sin and reconciliation to God not only imply, but produce, new obedience. Holy living is the immediate purpose of the Christian salvation in daily life. 'Go and sin no more!' is the first practical directive for the penitent believer.

Love that will not let us go

There is an amazing symmetry to the way in which God deals with those whom he loves. He tracks our lives with his grace. He follows the events of our lives and very often he unravels the tangles of our falterings and failings. This symmetry can be seen in the entire section recording the affair of David and Bathsheba. This may be seen as a regress and a progress, of backsliding and revival, as David descends into sin and God in his grace reverses the process one step at a time, to bring his servant back to a godly obedience to the divine will. It may be set out as follows:

A. War with Ammon begins — David stays home (11:1).
  B. Adultery with Bathsheba — a child is conceived (11:2-5).
    C. The death of Uriah — the cover-up of a sin (11:6-27).
      D. Confrontation with sin and its consequences (12:1-12).
      D. Conviction of sin and its consequences (12:13-14).
    C. The death of the child — removal of sin's fruit (12:15-23).
  B. A child conceived with Bathsheba — Solomon born (12:24-25).
A. War with Ammon ends — David takes the field (12:26-31).

This is a parable of salvation in its ultimate sense. The Lord, in his great love and mercy, undoes all that we have done against him. He reverses the entire direction and destiny of sin-blighted lives and embraces us in the everlasting arms of his free grace in Jesus Christ. His is a love that will not let us go:

> O Love that will not let me go,
>   I rest my weary soul in thee:
> I give thee back the life I owe,
> That in thine ocean depths its flow
>   May richer, fuller be.
>
> (George Matheson).

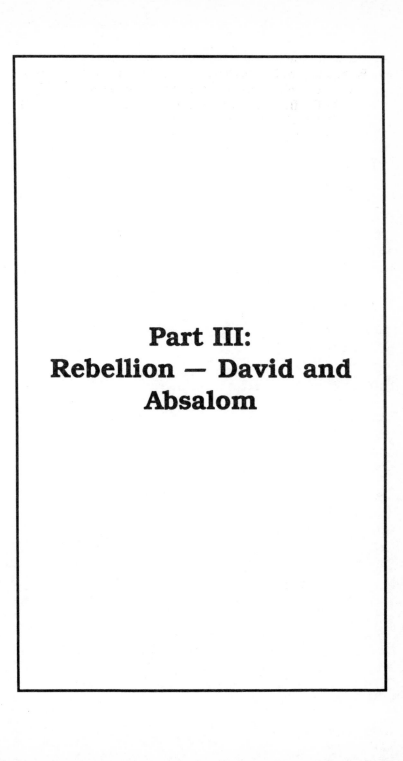

Part III:
Rebellion — David and Absalom

14.
False love

Please read 2 Samuel 13:1-39
'Amnon son of David fell in love with Tamar, the beautiful sister of Absalom son of David' (2 Samuel 13:1).

No one ever fully anticipates the consequences of his mistakes. Our actions, like nuclear explosions, have a kind of 'fall-out', which may continue for some time and even impose permanent effects. This is true of both good and bad actions. They produce fruit in keeping with their nature — the one for blessing, the other for curse. We have no problem with the former, needless to say: it is with sin and its aftermath that we experience the difficulties.

God had told David, through Nathan the prophet, that 'calamity' would come upon him from within his own family. This would be the chastisement of God and the direct result of David's sin with Bathsheba and the 'cover-up' murder of her husband Uriah (12:11-12). This solemn prediction was soon to be fulfilled: first in the incestuous rape of Tamar (13:11-14) and in the subsequent murder of the rapist Amnon (13:38-39); and then in Absalom's public seizure of David's harem (16:22) and the death of Absalom at the hand of Joab (18:15).

These events involved the wickedness of a number of David's children. Throughout this period, David was passive. The initiative always seems to be in the hands of others, especially his son Absalom. This, however, should not blind us to the fact that David is still the central figure in the drama. It is David's responses to events — whether in faith or in faithlessness — which carry the principal lessons for God's people. We must always bear in mind (no easy task in view of his often pathetic behaviour) that David is God's king and the man after God's own heart. He is the man who, as to his office, foreshadows the messianic king, Jesus Christ. David's failings do not, of course, foreshadow the actions of our

Lord. But they do remind us powerfully that in Christ 'the Davidic king has triumphed, but not in the Davidic way'.[1] The over-arching theme is still the redemptive-historical one: God is unfolding his purpose of salvation for his people and it will come to decisive fruition in the Son of David, of whom David the king is a pale and faltering foreshadowing.

If there is a specific theme in the thirteenth chapter of 2 Samuel, it is that of false love: the false love of Amnon for Tamar, which issues in her violation and disgrace; the equally false love of Absalom for his sister, which was expressed in two years of silence followed by an explosion of naked vengeance; and the false love of David for his sons Amnon and Absalom, which led him to fail to exercise justice in the face of their wickedness and thus spawned a legion of miseries that would eventually engulf the entire nation in civil war.

Amnon: unbridled passion [13:1-20]

The incestuous rape of Tamar by her half-brother Amnon is one of the most sordid and monstrous crimes recorded in Scripture. Amnon was David's son by Ahinoam of Jezreel (3:2), while Tamar and Absalom were his children by Maacah, the daughter of the King of Geshur (3:3). Amnon was the older of the two sons and, although strict primogeniture did not automatically determine the succession at that time, it may well be that he was regarded as the heir apparent. Absalom, as second in line of succession, might well have been already a man with a ready-made motive for the removal of his older half-brother.

Tamar was **'beautiful'** and, we are told, Amnon **'fell in love'** with her. The nature of this 'love' can be gauged from the fact that he was **'frustrated to the point of illness'** because **'it seemed impossible for him to do anything to her'** (13:1-2). The ingredients of a genuine love are altogether lacking: there is no self-giving commitment, no seeking of the other's highest good, no sensitive devotion, not even a hint of romance; there is only naked physical lust and an utterly self-centred disregard for Tamar's personal integrity, welfare and blessedness. Amnon is consumed, not by what he could do *for* her, but by what he wanted desperately to do *to* her. He wanted sex — it was as simple as that! Tamar was merely the intended victim of his obsessive desires. Amnon not only did not love her, he in effect hated her, for he was willing to violate her, body and soul, to gain his wicked goal. This is, of course, why he so contemptuously discarded her when the moment of his high passion was past (13:15-17). This is always the case when sexual desire jumps the rails of God's plan for personal sexual fulfilment. Self-giving love, commitment and faithfulness, marriage for life and of one woman to one man, family life and the raising of children as a godly seed, even social stability and peace, free from the immorality of sexual violations of all sorts — all are set aside in pursuit of what is actually an enslavement to self-gratification. All so-called 'love' without these profound moral and spiritual dimensions, which are so clearly set forth in God's Word as essential to our blessing as individuals, families and societies, is no more than a self-centred lust. And all lust is a kind of rape, whether of mind or body or both, for such pseudo-love can only consume the objects of its grasping attentions. This is why Jesus emphasized that lust, even in our thoughts, is the committing of adultery. The act of rape or adultery requires opportunity and occasion; the condition of being a rapist or adulterer is a matter of the heart and the inner life and requires no more than an inclination to sin.

Amnon had **'a friend'** — his cousin Jonadab, **'a very shrewd man'** — who, noticing that something was upsetting him, enquired what the problem was and came up with a proposed solution: Amnon should pretend to be ill and ask for Tamar to come and prepare something for him to eat. Then they would be alone and he could have his way with her (13:4-5). Clever or not, the Jonadabs of this world are not friends, but enemies, to those they aid and abet. Just as bookmakers never gamble, they would never actually perpetrate the evils they apparently enjoy arranging for others to do. They get their thrills setting up the sins of others. Their interest is essentially voyeuristic.

The account of the rape of Tamar makes the most depressing reading. Suffice it to say that everything went according to Jonadab's disgusting plot and Tamar was raped by her half-brother, only to be rejected mercilessly (13:6-17). Tamar's despairing attempt to restrain him was to no avail.[2] And when he was finished he added atrocity to outrage by turning her out to public shame, as if she and not he were the sinner. 'Nothing', observed Matthew Henry of this melancholy incident, 'could have been done more barbarous or ill-natured, or more disgraceful to her.'[3] And why did Amnon hate her so much as to treat her this way? Because, as with all sexual violators, the one thing he wanted even more than sex itself was for her to want to give herself to him, freely and willingly. The rapist hates his victim because in the very act of his self-gratification he knows the most profound frustration of all: the humiliation of rejection. Without brute force, he would have nothing at all. And this sense of inadequacy and frustration is all that he has left, after his fleeting passion has subsided. Sins 'sweet in the commission, afterwards become odious and painful, and the sinner's own conscience makes them so to himself'[4] — and all the more so when the victim will not take the blame by consenting to the deed.

Tamar was crushed by 'her humiliation and loss of virginity'.[5] She tore her virginal robe, put ashes on her head and **'went away, weeping aloud as she went'** (13:18-19), to live in the house of her brother, Absalom, **'a desolate woman'** (13:20). There she lived in 'virtual widowhood... a perpetual reminder to her brother of her unavenged violation'.[6] Modern rape victims will surely identify with the misery and pain which flooded Tamar's soul. She was, of course, innocent and needed to feel no reproach for her own actions. But such is the nature of injustice, that it is the innocent who feel the defilement most and who, as Matthew Henry so sympathetically puts it, go 'crying for another's sins'.[7]

Absalom: murderous revenge [13:21-29]

Justice is ultimately the prerogative of God. In his twin institutions of church and state, however, God has ordained the means by which justice may be done on this side of eternity, in terms of an administration in accord with the principles and precepts of his revealed Word. In Israel, what we recognize as the separate institutions of church and state were united in the theocratic kingdom of Israel. In fine detail, the law of the land was identical to the law of God. The violation of Tamar called for that law to be applied faithfully in vindication of the innocent and punishment of the guilty. When the latter is none other than the heir to the throne, the question might well be asked: 'Will justice take its course?' Will the king prosecute his son? Will God's law be applied to a prince of the blood? God's law was quite explicit: the penalty for incest was to be 'cut off' from the people (Leviticus 20:11, 12, 14, 17) — either by execution (Leviticus 20:3) or some other form of 'premature death' (cf. Leviticus 20:4-5).[8]

David was angry but did nothing (13:21)

As the king, David was responsible for law and order and the protection of his people, but for whatever reason — we are not told — he merely fumed and fizzed. His son remained unpunished. Why did David fail to carry out his duty? Did he perhaps feel compromised by his own behaviour with Bathsheba? Could he, who escaped a capital sentence, condemn another — especially his own flesh? Was David paralysed by the awful thought that his own sins were being repeated, only to worse effect, in his son? One thing at least is clear from this incident and the later activities of Absalom, namely, that David sinned the sin of Eli, in that he had an inordinate love for his children — the kind of love that does not help them, because it invites the kind of bitterness and vengefulness to which Absalom resorted. When the 'hands of the law' fail to pursue justice, the aggrieved will take the law into their own hands and perpetrate even greater injustice in the name of justice itself.

Absalom quietly plotted his revenge (13:22-29)

Absalom was furious but, in the face of his father's inaction, could do little about the situation. He merely comforted his sister and bided his time. He might have invoked the law and (who knows?) David might have been stirred up to dispense some justice. But Absalom is the classic example of a man with a vengeful spirit. He no doubt despised David for not dealing with Amnon, but it was not from any regard for the rule of law. He wanted revenge and more! He planned to repay Amnon's breach of the seventh commandment with his own breach of the sixth! Far from exhausting the legal remedies upon which he might have insisted, he nursed his wrath to keep it warm and quietly laid his plans for the punishment of his sister's violator.

Two years passed before the reckoning arrived. During that time, Absalom had given no hint to Amnon of harbouring any grudge and this served to remove any suspicions he might have entertained about possible reprisals for his treatment of Tamar

(13:22). When Absalom was ready to settle his account with Amnon, he devised a plan which was a macabre echo of that by which Amnon had trapped his sister. The occasion was the sheep-shearing on his estate at Baal-Hazor, perhaps some five miles north-east of Bethel (13:23).[9] He invited the king, his officials and all of the king's sons to attend his feast, evidently anticipating that David would decline. Anxious that Amnon be numbered among those who came, Absalom made a point of asking for him, and David, only momentarily intrigued as to why he should be singled out, gave his approval. And so Amnon's fate was sealed by the king's unwitting consent just as surely as Tamar's had been two years before (13:24-27). For the second time David had been totally deceived by one of his sons. The plan was carried out to the letter (13:28-29). Amnon was plied with drink and once he was well and truly **'in high spirits'** (i.e., drunk), Absalom's men did their master's dirty work and put him to death, incidentally ensuring their future loyalty as accomplices to murder. The remainder of the king's sons fled the scene with the utmost despatch.

The obvious parallels of these events with David's plot against Uriah the Hittite (the pretext for a meeting, the plying of the victim with alcohol, the killing by third parties) and Amnon's plot against Tamar (the pretext and the duping of her father) are not mere coincidences. Neither are they merely the standard components of murder regarded as a sociological phenomenon. God was dealing with David according to his word through the prophet Nathan (12:10). And his chastening of David's house was not through fire from heaven or miraculous interventions of divine judgement, but through the natural unfolding of day-to-day events, involving, as they always do, the choices and actions of people like us. It is in these personal attitudes and choices that we can discern the chastenings of God in our own lives. Choices have consequences which are often very predictable. Had Amnon loved the Lord and obeyed his Word, had Jonadab been a wise and good counsellor, had David been more discerning with his children — not to mention more holy in his own life — then how different would the history of his family have been! The final cataclysms of murder, rebellion and civil war did not come out of the blue, but were the culmination of a myriad of petty — and not so petty — decisions made by free agents, who had committed their way to everything but the way of the Lord. Earthquakes happen and we cannot control them, but we build our houses on the fault lines and fudge on the building standards which would minimize the disaster when it happens! Our dealings with ourselves and each other are, rightly understood, also the vehicle by which the Lord deals with us and instructs us about his will and the consequences of either following or rejecting him.

David: evading the real issues [13:30-39]

David soon heard the news of Amnon's murder (13:30-36). At first he thought that all of his sons had been killed. This provided Jonadab with the opportunity to assuage the king's grief and his fears that murder on such a scale could only indicate a bid for the throne by assuring him that **'only Amnon'** was dead. It was, he said, linked to **'Absalom's expressed intention'** since Amnon raped his sister and was, by implication, only a personal matter. That Jonadab could wait until this moment to reveal what he had known all along — that Amnon was a marked man — tells us what sort of a man he was. He was looking after number one: he had no care for Amnon either when he helped him rape Tamar or when he could have counselled him (or his father) not to put himself within reach of Absalom's vengeance. Jonadab was a consummate politician. He knew how to advance himself without being unduly encumbered by matters of principle or righteous obligation! The arrival, post-haste, of the king's sons no doubt raised Jonadab's prestige with David in proportion to the relief that only one of them had died. If David paused to regret his inaction over Amnon's crime, we are not told. He could not but blame himself, quite justly, had he reflected on the principal cause of the tragedy.

Absalom meanwhile fled to his grandfather, Talmai, the King of Geshur, in Trans-Jordan, where he was to remain in exile for some three years (13:37-39). David again sinned the sin of Eli and, after mourning for Amnon, **'longed to go to Absalom, for he was consoled concerning Amnon's death'**. In other words, as in the aftermath of Tamar's rape, he did nothing to see that the criminal was brought to justice, so in the matter of Amnon's death justice was set aside in favour of an inordinate love for his son. It is almost taken for granted that we should be so generous to our own as to shield them from the results of their folly. It was not the generosity or, indeed, the sorrow of godliness that moved David to pass over his son's sins. It was a false love that put a narrow personal interest before the righteousness of God. No doubt we would all rather have the evils of the past merely annulled, so that we should never have to face the consequences. No doubt we especially wish that the excesses of our loved ones never took place, so that they might not suffer personal loss and so that we might never suffer a breach in our relationship with them. David put off dealing justly with his sons and reaped a harvest more bitter than he could ever have anticipated. He simply evaded the real issues. Small wonder that things did not get better. Indeed, his bad example could only have issued in progressive degeneration among his own family. 'We do not find,' wrote Matthew Henry, 'that David's children imitated him in his devotion; but his false steps they trod in, and in those did much worse, and repented not. Parents know not how fatal the consequences may be if in any instance they give their children bad examples.'[10] Children are far more likely to do what their parents *do*, whatever they may *say*. This is the most practical way in which the sins of the fathers become the sins of their children. The history of David and his sons points clearly to the necessity of applying a single-minded faith in the Lord to every aspect of family life. David reaped something of what he sowed, but was saved by the Lord in whom he truly believed and trusted and towards whom he would repent in heart-felt sorrow for his sins. His reprobate sons neither believed nor repented and are still reaping the evil fruit of their sins in a lost eternity! This is the sombre, but none the less fundamental issue which this sad passage of Scripture history places before our hearts and consciences.

15.
False reconciliation

Please read 2 Samuel 14:1-33
'And the king kissed Absalom' (2 Samuel 14:33).

Three years had passed since Absalom murdered Amnon and fled to exile in Geshur — five years since Amnon raped Tamar — and we are told that **'Joab son of Zeruiah knew that the king's heart longed for Absalom'** (14:1). Thus was set in motion the chain of events that would not only end Absalom's exile but would, two years further on, see him restored to David's favour — the reconciliation marked with the chapter's last statement: **'And the king kissed Absalom'** (14:33).

As in the previous chapter (13), much of the narrative is populated by supporting actors — Joab, the woman of Tekoa and Absalom — while the central figure, David, appears merely to react to their initiatives and influence. This impression is not only an accurate assessment of the facts but also a deliberate emphasis on the part of the inspired historian. We are to bear in mind that David was the King of Israel, the Lord's anointed, type and shadow of the promised Messiah, and yet still a man in need of the grace, forgiveness and enabling strength of God to cope with life and gain the victory over his failings. He was in fact a man under the chastening hand of the Lord — the direct consequence of his adultery with Bathsheba and the contrivance of her husband's death (12:9-10). The way in which he is manipulated by Joab, who in turn is driven by Absalom — all to effect the latter's official reconciliation to his father — demonstrates the humiliating effects of sin as its ongoing effects compromise the happy normality of life as we would wish it to be, and as indeed the life of faith is when lived in dependence upon the Lord. David still refused to do what ought to have been done — namely, bring his son to justice, even if he was his son and the heir to the throne. And he had a bad conscience. In his heart he loved the Lord. He was a real believer. But he was torn between his knowledge of the Lord's will, on the one hand, and a grim unwillingness to do it. He was therefore very vulnerable to unprincipled and self-seeking counsellors and was almost bound to fall deeper into the pit of estrangement from the leading and blessing of God. The false reconciliation about to be consummated with his son was only the precursor of the rebellion which would all but cost him his kingdom and would cost the lives of Absalom and many of his people.

Recall [14:1-20]

It is not for nothing that **'the hand of Joab'** is a byword for pragmatic scheming of the most insidious kind. Joab was a loyal lieutenant to David, albeit one who invariably acted 'in the best interests of the kingdom as he happened to conceive of them'.[1] This, needless to say, usually coincided with his personal interests. So, when Joab saw that David wanted to be able to recall his exiled son, he realized that the man who could give him the encouragement, if not the excuse, to bring Absalom back, would be all the more appreciated by a grateful monarch.

Joab's plan (14:2-3)

Joab's approach was indirect. He suborned a woman from Tekoa to tell a tale to David so as to lay the groundwork for a decision on Absalom's return. She is described as a **'wise woman'** — an indication of her reputation as a kind of seer rather than a marker of her character, but the reason why she would readily gain the attention of the king. Joab carefully prepared her for her role as a mourning widow and fed her the story she would tell. This story, in unintentional (or was it intentional?) imitation of Nathan's approach to David over Bathsheba, was actually a parable in the guise of petition. A.W. Pink, pointing out that this was the devil's work where Nathan's was the Lord's, succinctly describes it as 'a poor parody' of the prophet's parable.[2]

The trap is set (14:4-11)

The woman played her part brilliantly. Her story told a touching tale of a widow with two sons, one of whom had killed the other in a quarrel, leaving one son under threat of execution (Exodus 21:12; Leviticus 24:17) and opening the possibility that the family might be extinguished altogether — an eventuality regarded as so desperate that the law of God provided the rather drastic remedy of levirate marriage (Deuteronomy 25:5-10).[3] The king, duly moved by her plight, declared a willingness to **'issue an order in [her] behalf'** preventing the execution of the remaining son (14:8). This was not enough for the woman, who recognized that she must extract an oath-bound commitment to reprieve the fictitious murderer-son, for the king to be boxed in to the position of applying the same principle to Absalom. And with nerveless aplomb, this is precisely what she achieved, for she successfully induced the king to **'invoke the Lord his God'. '"As surely as the Lord lives," he said, "not one hair of your son's head will fall to the ground"'** (14:11). If the sob-story was the hook, then this oath to reprieve the killer was the landing of the fish. Although he was not yet aware of it, David had committed himself to a rationale for recalling his son — no, more, to an inward obligation to recall his son. The true basis for this was the triumph of sentiment over the law of God, but the wheedling of the 'widow' had clothed it all in the sanctity of an oath before God!

The woman was then ready to deliver the *coup de grâce!* David was about to pay the bill for his ill-considered oath! To grasp the full import of her final argument (14:12-17), we must note how her earlier parable meshed with Absalom's situation. Notice the line of argument.

1. She had first suggested that her son (in the story) was guilty of manslaughter rather than premeditated murder (14:6) — a veiled encouragement to David to think later that Absalom's crime might be similarly less aggravated.

2. She claimed the son was persecuted by his family (14:7). This was not true in Absalom's case, but might it not have a certain appeal to a man who wanted his son back so much that he would rather admit to a persecuting spirit than keep him in exile for fear of just retribution for his crime?

3. She told of a son who was her only heir (14:7). This was not true of Absalom, but the thought of estrangement from his heir apparent might be made to tug at the king's heart-strings as much as if he were indeed an only son. David's later grief over the dead Absalom indicates an emotional attachment to him of an intensity that almost implies that the king's other sons hardly mattered to him. This may perhaps be an overstatement, but where is the evidence of some proportion in David's affection for his sons?

4. When she explicitly appealed for Absalom's recall, she invoked public opinion and the national interest (14:13). No mention is made of justice and the rule of law, far less the will of God himself! Indeed, she charged the king with sin! Had he not made a commitment to be merciful to her son? Why then could he not show mercy to his own son, who was also the next king of the people of God?

5. She went even further and reminded David of the grace of God, who **'devises ways so that a banished person may not remain estranged from him'** (14:14). She referred both to the patience of the God who does not immediately execute judgement every time his law is broken and to the provision of mercy that God makes through atoning sacrifice. The woman's argument in effect appealed to biblical teaching on God and redemption. The only problem was that there had been no repentance and sacrifice on Absalom's part — he was in fact an unrepentant reprobate — and, in any case, there was a civil charge to answer, in which the penalty of the law was clear and unambiguous. The devil was speaking in the woman's one-sided appeal to biblical mercy, just as surely as he did when he quoted the Scriptures to Jesus as he tempted the Lord in the wilderness a thousand years later! Satan loves to pose as an angel of light!

6. Her final touch was to flatter David (14:20). David had finally put two and two together, realized the woman had been spinning a yarn, and, if he hadn't seen the error he was being led into, he certainly discerned the source of the woman's petition as **'the hand of Joab'** (14:19). This was, of course, the moment at which David had an opportunity to turn about, denounce the trick and settle the matter justly with Absalom and perhaps also Joab. If David had any such sentiments, the woman countered them by a combination of honesty about her mission and sheer flattery of

David's wisdom and discernment: **'My lord has wisdom like that of an angel of God — he knows everything that happens in the land'** (14:20). The truth, confirmed to her when David recalled Absalom, was that her 'wisdom' had prevailed over whatever wisdom he had exercised in this matter, and neither was thereby serving the will of the Lord. David had wanted to be convinced — Joab had seen that — and the woman had delivered David his excuse on a platter. The die was cast. Absalom would be recalled. David failed again.

Return [14:21-27]

On receiving the order to bring back Absalom, Joab expressed his gratitude with the usual outward oriental obsequiousness and, no doubt, with a large measure of secret self-satisfaction (14:22). He then **'went to Geshur and brought Absalom back to Jerusalem'** — surely in the most magnificent of processions (14:23).

David then made another mistake. He refused to receive Absalom at court (14:24). He was like the boy who stole apples but felt so guilty about what he had done that he couldn't look at them or eat them — so they just rotted. David couldn't face the fact that recalling Absalom implied restoring him to his former position. So he refused to go the whole way and kept Absalom at arm's length for two more years. But this was merely compounding the problem, for it set up a polarization of power and influence between them. With every passing day, those who were in any way disaffected from David had a rallying-point in the person of the estranged heir apparent. By making a point of his disapproval of Absalom, by first recalling him and then making a vague show of offence, the king made the political blunder that set Absalom on the road to rebellion and brought the nation to civil war.

The historian informs us of Absalom's **'handsome appearance'**, his remarkable head of hair and his attractive family (14:25-27). The point is that David had put Absalom in the position where he could only do the maximum damage. He was in Jerusalem at the centre of things, he was lionized by an adoring public, he was the heir to the throne and he was vaguely disapproved of by his father, the king. He had all the attributes of a young leader who would lead his followers into the modern world! In this context it is surely significant that there is no mention of any wisdom or personal godliness he might have possessed.

'Reconciliation' [14:28-33]

Absalom was humiliated by his exclusion from the palace. After two years of this, he had had enough. Remembering that Joab had been instrumental in his return, he sought to enlist Joab as his advocate with the king. Joab refused, one suspects because the wily soldier-politician could see nothing but trouble ahead with Absalom and was regretting his part in bringing him back. Absalom was not one to take no for an answer, so he decided, as the saying goes, 'to light a fire under' Joab — and so make sure he got some attention. He sent some servants to set fire to one of Joab's barley fields (14:30).

People may not like terrorism but it always makes them sit up and take notice. Joab duly arrived at Absalom's house, looking for an explanation for his scorched crops. What he got was an impassioned plea to be brought before the king. Absalom's request offers a glimpse of what was in his heart. Everything is manipulative and self-serving. There is hardly a shred of honesty in anything he says (14:32).

First is the pretended self-pity: **'Why have I come from Geshur? It would be better for me if I were still there.'** He knew very well that his two years in the Israelite public eye had served him infinitely better than mouldering in his grandad's distant mini-kingdom. Above all, Absalom knew how to strike a pose and how to use the pressure of his popularity to shift men like Joab and David. The last thing he wanted to do was to go back to Geshur.

Second is the pretended love for the king: **'I want to see the king's face.'** He did, of course, 'want to see the king's face' in the literal sense that this was necessary to his reinstatement as his heir. But his whole carriage and certainly his subsequent behaviour indicate an underlying contempt for his father. There was no personal affection. David was merely a means to Absalom's ends.

Third is his pretended submission to the king's judgement: **'If I am guilty of anything, let him put me to death.'** Since he knew that his father loved him too much to punish him for Amnon's murder, this was no more than a veiled proclamation of his invulnerability.

All this telegraphed to Joab that, sooner or later, Absalom would have his way, just because David didn't have it in him to stop him. Joab therefore had to look to his own long-term interests and could not afford to offend the man who could well become his king some day. We hear no more about the barley field, but we do read that **'Joab went to the king and told him this'** — i.e., all that Absalom had said — with the result that Absalom was formally received by David and his reconciliation sealed by his father's kiss (14:33). The true situation was actually the exact opposite of what appears to the outward view: the king **'summoned Absalom,'** but the reality is that Absalom virtually compelled him to do so; Absalom **'bowed down with his face to the ground,'** but in reality it was the king who was humiliated by the son he was too weak to resist; and the 'reconciliation' effected when the king **'kissed Absalom'** was no more than a charade. Far from being a reconciliation, it was the final seal of David's defeat in the case of God's law versus Absalom over the death of Amnon.

The 'love' of which we must let go

There is nothing more natural than the love of parents for their children and nothing more difficult for parents than assent to the just punishment of their children for crimes of which they are certainly known to be guilty. In this respect, David was very normal indeed and we can surely identify with his feelings in Absalom's case. We may also be inclined to think that he not only was moved by very natural parental protectiveness (which he was) but that his leniency to Absalom was even the godly thing to do. After all, we are supposed to be gracious and forgiving, we say to ourselves, and was this not exactly what moved David to act as he did? Yes, we see his faults. But don't we also see grace in his attitudes and actions? We understand David's having a bad conscience about restoring Absalom to favour immediately; but we also understand his desire to be loving and forgiving and to be reconciled to his son. We see him as a believer (which he was) racked by conflicting impulses and emotions (which is true) and we are perhaps attracted to the thought that offering forgiveness and a fresh start was, so to speak, the

Christian thing to do. But was it? The biblical answer must be 'No!' and this for a number of reasons.

Firstly, while Absalom was a 'prodigal son', unlike the prodigal of Luke 15, he was totally unrepentant of his sins. We have no warrant to forgive the unrepentant. Even our Lord's words from the cross, 'Father, forgive them,' for they do not know what they are doing' (Luke 23:24), do not exclude the necessity of repentance and faith as integral to the reception of forgiveness of sins.

Furthermore, the lordship of Christ requires the subordination of all other earthly relationships to the claims of his holy and perfect will. Jesus made this clear in Luke 14:26 when he said that discipleship to him could involve breaking with our closest relatives and even the loss of our own lives! David was called by God to be just and in so doing to be blind to relationships of blood or sentiment. He had placed his son above his God.

Finally, we must be careful to distinguish our love for the Lord and a true regard for the best interests of our loved ones in relation to God's revealed will from inordinate affection and false sentimentality. If God's love for his people is the 'love that will not let me go', it is also true that a blind partisan affection is the love of which we must let go. Otherwise, we make a god of our love — a false god, which will inevitably let us down. David allowed his 'love' for Absalom to compromise his love for his Father-God.

None of us is likely to be in exactly the same shoes as David — that is to say, as a chief magistrate confronted with the decision to execute justice against our murderer-son. Nevertheless, in principle and in many practical situations, we are faced with similar tensions. Like David, we may be seriously compromised by our own failings and by problems arising from our personal relationships. The false reconciliation of Absalom points us to the positive blessing of keeping our eye upon the Lord and his Word so that we may be spared the evil of winking at the sins of our beloved children, our friends and ourselves! When the psalmist praised the Lord for taking to his bosom the child of God who had been thrown out by his parents, he gave voice to the glorious promise that for the redeemed of the Lord, there will always be a family of faith, sharing a holy and untainted love, rooted and grounded in our adoption as the children of our heavenly Father.

16.
Conspiracy and rebellion

Please read 2 Samuel 15:1-37
'The hearts of the men of Israel are with Absalom' (2 Samuel 15:13).

The story of David and Absalom demonstrates that 'Sin, though forgiven [as it had been in David's case], rarely passes unpunished in the world.' David, through his adultery with Bathsheba, 'had dishonoured God in the face of the whole world...'[1] and now was about to be 'driven with scorn and infamy from his throne'.[1] And yet, the same writer can say that 'At no period of his life was grace more in exercise within him, as appears from the spirit which he manifested under his afflictions.'[2] The Lord often makes 'the Valley of Achor' (literally, 'trouble') 'a door of hope' for his people (Hosea 2:15). 'After a bitter pill,' writes Thomas Watson, 'God gives sugar. Paul had his prison songs. God's rod has honey at the end of it. The saints in affliction have had such sweet raptures of joy that they thought themselves in the borders of the heavenly Canaan.'[3] This paradox in the lives of the Lord's people is certainly the key to understanding David's experience during the rebellion of Absalom. The fact that this is the nadir of David's career as king must not be allowed to obscure the reality of the rekindling of a love for the Lord which had been dampened by his sinful indulgence of his reprobate son.

The chapter begins with Absalom's successful effort to win the hearts of the people (15:1-6), goes on to recount his conspiracy to topple David from the throne (15:7-12) and concludes with the first phase of David's flight from Jerusalem (15:13-37).

Campaigning for hearts and minds [15:1-6]

Absalom was a man with deep-seated resentment against his father.

Five years of paternal disapproval and banishment from the royal
court had not been wiped away by his father's kiss of restoration
(14:33). However much David may have been convinced that he
and his son were reconciled, there is not the slightest doubt that
Absalom was entirely unrepentant and utterly contemptuous of his
father. After all, he had killed his brother and, apart from five years
of frustration, had been let off scot-free. Indeed, he had advanced
to first place in the succession to the throne! What reason did he
have to respect David? David had let Amnon escape justice for his
rape of Tamar. The same supine response to Absalom's despatch of
that wretched rapist was not only what he expected, from experience, but a further confirmation that the old man was a wash-out as
a king for Israel. Why should he wait for David to die, when he could
be a better king now? Why waste more years on the sidelines? The
logic of it fired his malevolent spirit and he hatched a plan to depose
his father — a plan conceived and executed with a discipline all the
more impressive and chilling in a man of passion and action.

Absalom therefore, far from helping his father to govern the
realm, set himself to undermining David's authority. Long before
our media age, with its obsessive attention to the 'image' projected
by celebrities, Absalom carefully cultivated his public image — the
persona through which he could foster the perception that, were he
the king, the people would be better off and justice in the nation
would be better served. He realized that if he were to supplant his
father, his prestige would need to command the support of a large
proportion of the public. He needed to win the hearts and minds of
the people and he was willing to say and do whatever was necessary
to achieve that end. The parallels with modern political life are
striking. Here is a clever and unscrupulous politician at work —
projecting a messianic image of himself as the only saviour of his
country by a combination of glamour, self-serving criticism, campaign promises and folksy charm. This public relations work would
succeed in bringing him to power and it has remained a standard
method for politicians 'on the make' to this day.

First of all, Absalom created for himself the image of the king he
wished to become (15:1). This is one of the most basic techniques
of self-advancement in modern society: project yourself with
confidence in terms of your personal goals in such a way as to
impress those who can be the means of your advancement. When
style dominates or, worse, obscures substance (or the lack of it), the

result is wholly illusory and ultimately self-destructive. In an age of superficiality, style rather than substance significantly affects public opinion. Absalom's **'chariot and horses'**, allied to his handsome appearance, made him look every inch a king — a criterion, you may recall, which persuaded Israel to call for Saul to become their king (1 Samuel 9:1-2; cf. 8:5-20). Absalom understood the mystique of monarchy. He gave the people a glittering parade whenever he went out in public.

Secondly, he found a way to criticize his father, without seeming to be merely carping, but always appearing to be holding the moral high ground (15:2-3). He found a cause through which he could in time exalt himself at the expense of his father. Absalom got up early and stood at the approach to the city gate — the place where justice was dispensed by the elders — and made capital out of the fact that none of the king's servants was there to hear the cases that people brought for adjudication. Absalom would say to them, **'Look, your claims are valid and proper, but there is no representative of the king to hear you.'** There is no reason to believe that this allegation had substance and that there was indeed no provision of justice at that gate or in the land as a whole. Perhaps the judges were late in taking their seats. Justice ought to have been administered 'every morning' (Jeremiah 21:12). Morning is, however, a longish time and what is clear is that Absalom made a point of being up early enough to intercept the first petitioners (before the judges arrived?). He also made no effort to assist them in finding a proper judge but had no difficulty in dispensing his own opinions of their cases — always in favour of the petitioners, of course, even though he had only heard one side of the dispute! It is impossible to avoid the conclusion that Absalom was acting as an *agent provocateur* in his own interest by deliberately creating the false impression that there was a fundamental deficiency in the criminal justice system of David's Israel.

Thirdly, he dropped the strongest hint that it would be far better for the country were he to be responsible for justice: **'If only I were appointed judge... I would see that [everyone] receives justice'** (15:4). He was 'electioneering' and this was a 'campaign promise', except that it was a *coup d'état* he had in mind and the promise was a bare-faced lie to secure willing supporters. What is disturbing is that the people were so undiscerning that they could not see through Absalom's charade. The choice of judges in Israel was to be

governed by certain rules: they were to be 'capable men... men who
fear God, trustworthy men who hate dishonest gain' (Exodus
18:21). Not only was Absalom not qualified, but his stated views
and intentions on these early morning outings gave little evidence
of a real interest in justice and a large indication of his true
ambitions. Yet he judged the mood of his hearers correctly and
played on their attitudes to the outcome of their cases. And so his
self-interest and theirs met and found some common ground. This
is how men become accomplices in pursuit of wicked goals.

Finally, he impressed the petitioners with his approachableness
and personal charm (15:6). He was accessible to people. He was a
charismatic character and **'he stole the hearts of the men of Israel'**
(15:6). No one has better assessed Absalom's achievement than
Matthew Henry when he wrote, 'No man's conduct could be more
condescending, while his heart was as proud as Lucifer's.'[4] It was
false humility (Colossians 2:23).

Absalom's was the face of godless ambition and, like so many
of his ilk, his thirst for power was not matched by any great interest
in the real responsibilities and duties of such power. This is sadly
true in politics, civil and ecclesiastical, in our own day. The 'golden
boys' with smiles, flattery, a well-groomed image and large promises are able to sway large numbers of people. This is a perennial
challenge to the spiritual discernment of the Lord's people and a
cause for being earnestly prayerful for the welfare of church and
nation.

Coup d'état in Hebron [15:7-12]

For **'four years'** Absalom quietly and with intelligent cunning
plotted the downfall of his own father. He sought and obtained
David's permission to go to Hebron, ostensibly to fulfil a religious
vow. The vow itself was in the nature of making a bargain with God:
**'If the Lord takes me back to Jerusalem, I will worship the Lord
in Hebron'** (15:7-9). We cannot assume that any such vow was
made, for both the tenor of Absalom's character and the oh-so-
convenient way in which this seven or eight-year-old vow fitted
into his bid for the throne suggest it to be a stratagem rather than an
exercise in personal piety. David appears to have suspected

nothing. He granted Absalom his request readily enough and so, unwittingly, made the first move in the *coup* by which Absalom intended to become king in his place. The die was cast. Absalom then moved swiftly to implement his planned revolt.

1. He sent **'secret messengers'** to his supporters throughout the country instructing them to proclaim him **'king in Hebron'** as soon as they heard **'the sound of the trumpets,'** i.e., upon receiving the appropriate notice (15:10; cf. 1 Samuel 13:3; 1 Kings 1:34).

2. He then mustered an imposing cavalcade of 200 **'men from Jerusalem'**, who **'had been invited as guests,'** i.e., they were prominent people. These men had no idea that Absalom was planning a rebellion and went **'quite innocently'** (15:11). They had, however unwittingly, been enlisted in Absalom's cause, because they provided him with an appearance of strong support in Jerusalem which could only impress the people in Hebron. They were in effect hostages, for if they opposed Absalom, they risked his ire. On the other hand, if they supported him they would be guilty of treason, should the rebellion fail. Whatever they did, David could only reasonably assume that they had gone with the purpose of supporting Absalom. They were pawns in a masterly scheme of disinformation.

3. Once in Hebron, and while offering his hypocritical sacrifices, he sent for **'Ahithophel the Gilonite, David's counsellor'** (15:12). Ahithophel was, as it would turn out, the man upon whose counsel the outcome of the rebellion would hinge. He was a 'political thinking man, and one that had a clear head and a great compass of thought'.[5] He may well have been the man David had in mind in Psalm 41:9, when he said that

'Even my close friend, whom I trusted,
    he who shared my bread,
    has lifted up his heel against me.'

The conspiracy **'gained strength'** and, although the actual moment remains unrecorded in the Scripture narrative (surely a deliberate omission to remove all sense of drama and legitimacy), Absalom sounded his trumpets and raised his rebellion against the Lord's anointed king.

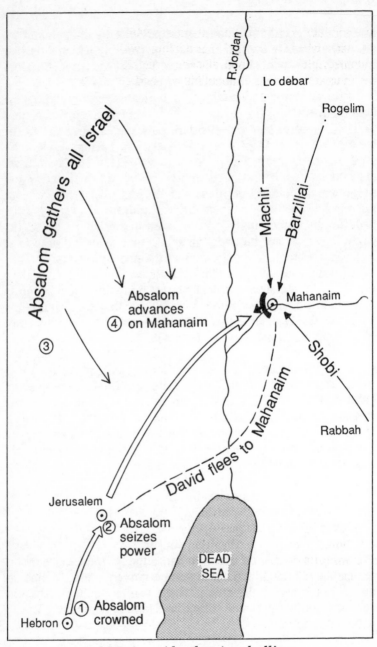

MAP 6 — Absalom's rebellion

David's flight from Jerusalem [15:13-37]

On hearing the news, David fled from Jerusalem — as much to spare the city as to save his own life. Subsequent events would seem to suggest that he overestimated the extent to which **'the hearts of the men of Israel [were] with Absalom'** (15:13). There is, however, no reason to portray David as a pathetic, beaten old man fleeing for dear life, as does A.W. Pink.[6] David had certainly been fooled by Absalom. He was completely unprepared. He had no reliable intelligence on the strength of the rebellion and could not simply assume that all his soldiers would fight for him. Absalom had the initiative and to stay put in such circumstances would be equivalent to capitulation, for even if he stood and fought, Jerusalem could only become a colossal hecatomb and he would go down with the city. David's decision to withdraw and, in effect, declare Jerusalem an open city, was strategically sound and a tactical necessity (15:14). It was not only right, but in his interest, to spare Jerusalem from ruin. And it was absolutely imperative that he trade space for time in order to gather his forces for the inevitable clash with Absalom. David was no doubt crushed by his son's defection and profoundly humbled by the realization that this was the kind of thing which Nathan had long ago said would come upon him because of his sin over Bathsheba. But he had not lost his touch as a military leader. His flight to the east began his march to secure his throne afresh!

Strategic withdrawal (15:15-23)

David set out with his **'entire household'**, which had already declared its loyalty towards him. He left **'ten concubines'** to look after the palace — perhaps an indication of his expectation of returning soon, but, thanks to Absalom's depraved sense of self-exaltation, they were to become grist for the mill of fulfilled prophecy (15:16; cf. 12:11-12; 16:22). The withdrawal was disciplined and unrushed. They halted at **'a place'** (literally 'the last house' — probably on the edge of the city) and the regiments of loyal soldiers marched past the king.[7] The loyalty of Ittai and his men, even when David released them from his service, is an indicator of what was good in David's relationships with people over the years. Ittai was to be rewarded with the command of the third division of David's army for the final battle with Absalom (18:2). David's mention of **'King Absalom'** to Ittai 'does not imply that he recognized Absalom as king,'[8] but simply encourages Ittai to serve whoever was king in Jerusalem. It may be that he had in mind placing Ittai near Absalom as a 'fifth column' against the future day of reckoning. The arrangements for the line of march having been made, they crossed the Kidron Valley to the east, to the accompaniment of the loud weeping of the countryside.

Repentant humility (15:24-30)

The king's departure was also marked by the presence of the ark and the priests, who offered sacrifices to the Lord until the king's people had left the city. David then ordered the priests to return the ark to the city, trusting them to keep him informed of future events at the base he intended to establish at **'the fords in the desert'** — the crossing-points of the Jordan (15:28). It is at this point that David publicly threw himself on the mercy of God: **'Let him do to me whatever seems good to him'** (15:25-26). He, and his people with him, **'continued up the Mount of Olives, weeping as he went; his head was covered and he was barefoot'** (15:30). 'He never wept thus when Saul hunted him,' observed Matthew Henry, 'but a wounded conscience makes troubles lie heavily, Ps. 38:4.'[9]

3. Prayerful preparation (15:31-37)

David had previously been informed of the defection of his most able counsellor, Ahithophel. Knowing how dangerous this would be to his cause, David prayed that the Lord would **'turn Ahithophel's counsel into foolishness'**. His prayer was answered immediately, for another of his counsellors, Hushai the Arkite,[10] approached with **'his robe torn and dust on his head'**. David then sent him back to be a 'mole' in Absalom's court, by pretending to be his servant. He was to gather intelligence and relay it to David through the priests and their sons. His admission to Absalom's war council gave the rebellion the kiss of death'.[11] The question as to the ethics of spying — specifically Hushai's lying to Absalom about his allegiance — is not easily resolved and cannot be discussed in this context. The flow of the text would suggest that Hushai was God's answer to David's prayer, and so it was to turn out, as far as the results were concerned. There is no hint of criticism of either man's motives, any more than Rahab of Jericho is criticized for protecting the Israelite spies (Joshua 2:4-7). This does not exhaust all that Scripture says about the ethics involved, but there is no doubt that David had good reason to thank God for Hushai's work as a 'mole' and this should give us pause before we affect a more tender conscience on the subject than that of the inspired historian. If anything, such cases indicate the limits of our capacity to reduce all problems to straightforward answers.

Learning from David

Throughout our study we have seen many points at which basic biblical principles touch our lives. In drawing these threads together and setting them in the overall context of redemptive history as recorded in the whole of Scripture, we should notice two main themes which clothe the lessons of David's life as a child of God with an immediacy and relevance of vital significance for ourselves today.

We can discern what God is doing in our lives

David was specifically the subject of prophecy (12:10-12). When Absalom so unexpectedly rebelled, he immediately realized that God was dealing with him according to his word through Nathan. Absalom was the evil from his own household and Ahithophel, whom he trusted, was Bathsheba's grandfather (23:34, 39; 11:3). Did he secretly resent David's seduction of his granddaughter? David could see the consequences of his sin in the troubles that came upon him. And he saw that it was God's doing to humble him and bring him to a deeper trust in the Lord.

But how does this apply to us? Surely to reinforce within us a conviction that the sovereign God is holy, that his Word is the truth for faith and life, that he is faithful and loving in his dealings with his believing people, and that we are to learn from his Word and our circumstances so as to humble ourselves under his hand and pray for the blessings of his grace, which he has promised to us by his everlasting covenant.

We are pointed to faith in Jesus Christ

If we are to make sense of Old Testament teaching in our own time (the New Testament era), we must grasp that, rightly understood, it all points us to Jesus Christ and the good news of salvation in him. Without undue spiritualization of the passage, we can surely allow David's humbling experience to remind us of 'another King' who left Jerusalem one evening with a few followers and crossed the Kidron to ascend the Mount of Olives, his soul agitated and his heart turning to prayer. If we learn anything from David, let it be that we must humble ourselves, cast ourselves in repentance on God's mercy and earnestly give ourselves to prayer — and all explicitly in Christ our Saviour, as it was in type and shadow for David. David truly trusted in Christ for his salvation, but it was at a distance, behind the veil of an as yet incomplete revelation of the Messiah (Acts 2:30-31). But David points us to the New Testament fulness that is now a reality for the human race — to a New Testament holiness in a faith-relationship to God through the blood of Jesus Christ, the one who crossed the Kidron, ascended Olivet and died on Calvary's cross for his people.

In this perspective, it becomes easy for us to see the gospel meaning of the psalm David wrote about this time:

'O Lord, how many are my foes!
    How many rise up against me!
Many are saying of me,
    "God will not deliver him."
But you are a shield around me, O Lord;
    You bestow glory on me and lift up my head.
To the Lord I cry aloud,
    and he answers me from his holy hill.
I lie down and sleep;
    I wake again, because the Lord sustains me.
I will not fear the tens of thousands
    drawn up against me on every side.
Arise, O Lord!
    Deliver me, O my God!
Strike all my enemies on the jaw;

        break the teeth of the wicked.
     From the Lord comes deliverance.
      May your blessing be on your people'

                                        (Psalm 3).

Here is a living faith in the Lord of hosts, a holy confidence in the Son of Man! Here is the Christian's only boast — the glory of God and the enjoyment of him for ever, in and through Christ Jesus our Lord!

17.
A false friend and an honest foe

Please read 2 Samuel 16:1-14
'Let him curse, for the Lord has told him to' (2 Samuel 16:11).

When we left David, he was on the summit of the Mount of Olives, first praying and then plotting with Hushai towards the overthrow of the counsel of Ahithophel, now in the service of Absalom. As he continued his march to the Jordan valley down the eastern side of the mountain he met **'Ziba, the steward of Mephibosheth'** (16:1) and, further on, at Bahurim in the territory of Benjamin, he encountered **'Shimei son of Gera'** (16:5). Both men had been servants of the late king, Saul, and represent something of the residual hostility, or at least ambivalence, which must have been stirred up by Absalom's rebellion in the segment of the population which had supported Saul — perhaps most of all in the tribe of Benjamin, through whose territory David was about to pass. David had enemies from of old and we are reminded that resentments die hard.

What is most instructive about these encounters, however, is the dual contrast which we find in them both. There is a contrast of *approach*. Here were two wicked men getting what they wanted from David by means of two entirely different methods — one by flattery and the other by cursing. But there is, on David's part, a contrast of *response*. He reacts quite differently in each case — one in an improper, unspiritual way, the other with a genuinely gracious spirituality. And in the process we are afforded some further insights into human nature and what Christian character ought to be like.

Flattery and failure [16:1-4]

It is said that 'Flattery will get you nowhere.' If this is true in the experience of flatterers, it has surely had little impact on the flow of recruits to that brotherhood! Ziba evidently believed that flattery would get him everything he wanted — and it almost did! Ziba had formerly been a servant of King Saul and was now steward to the household of Mephibosheth, the son of Jonathan and grandson of Saul (9:7). He appeared along the road with donkeys and provisions for David's journey (16:1-2). David, naturally, enquired about Mephibosheth and received the reply that he was **'staying in Jerusalem, because he thinks, "Today the house of Israel will give me back my grandfather's kingdom"'** (16:3). David apparently accepted this highly self-serving answer as the truth and rewarded Ziba on the spot with **'all that belonged to Mephibosheth'**. Ziba bowed with appropriate gratitude (16:4).

This straightforward story is replete with lessons about discernment and personal ethics.

1. Most obvious is the truth that flattery in all its forms is one of the great and effective instruments of human wickedness. It is sin; it is sheer hypocrisy; it is pure deceit; and it is, alas, as common as dirt. Christians are to avoid it like the plague that it is, and must die to the temptation to 'butter up' people for the sake of some supposed advantage. Ziba set out to ingratiate himself with David. He must have had a genuine interest in David's eventual triumph, since his coming into possession of Mephibosheth's property certainly depended on David's success, but his motives were less than worthy.

2. We are also reminded of our Lord's principle not to judge by appearances but to 'make a right judgement' (John 7:24). David was no doubt impressed by Ziba's generosity, especially in view of the risk he was running of reprisals, should Absalom hear of his visit to David. This was impressive by any standard, since David's return was by no means a foregone conclusion. We should certainly take such kindnesses at face value. But when that gratitude is carried over into an entirely different area — such as, in Ziba's case, giving credence to unsupported allegations about someone else — our gratitude has been made the basis of partiality and false judgement. The 'mere appearance' factor has determined the verdict of the case!

3. Closely related is the biblical requirement for the evidence of two or more witnesses (Deuteronomy 19:15; Matthew 18:15-16; 1 Timothy 5:19; Hebrews 10:28).[1] David did not need to disbelieve Ziba's word, but the law of God required him to reserve his judgement until there was corroboration or refutation of Ziba's allegation. Even if our most trustworthy friend tells us something, we have no business judging the other person on that basis. It is not a matter of distrusting our friend and his information — it is a matter of God-honouring justice to the other party in the case. How much pain and strife would be avoided in our churches, were we to take this biblical principle seriously! There is a fine dividing line between some forms of information — 'sharing' is the 'in' word among Christians today — and gossip. Gossip is often just 'sharing' translated into one-sided, prejudicial judgements about others. And gossip does not need to be false to be gossip. Indeed, the juiciest gossip is often the truest. Ziba appears to have been lying about Mephibosheth, or at least not to have told the whole truth (19:24-30). But even if he had been truthful, David should still have deferred thinking worse of Mephibosheth until he heard the other side of the story.

4. David allowed himself to jump to conclusions and that was wrong. We must always be careful and biblically controlled in our assessments of others. This is especially true when weighing a person's motives or discerning where others stand with respect to their personal faith in the Lord. God never calls upon us to judge the hearts of men and women. Their words and deeds are the proper field for judgement and it is true that the church, in the proper exercise of discipline may declare, on the basis of these same words and deeds, that this or that person is or is not a true Christian — i.e., is saved or lost, as the case may be. Nevertheless, it is God alone who actually judges hearts; at best, we only judge outward actions. this emphasizes our limitations as judges of others and calls us to a cautious, compassionate and charitable spirit in such matters.

Cursing and contrition [16:5-14]

'David bore Shimei's curses much better than Ziba's flatteries. By the latter he was brought to pass a wrong judgement on another, by the former to pass a right judgement on himself.' Therefore,

concludes Matthew Henry, 'The world's smiles are more dangerous than its frowns.'[2]

Shimei was at least honest. He hated David and he made no
bones about it. He cursed David and pelted him with stones,
notwithstanding the fact that David had soldiers all around him who
could have snuffed out his abuse with one sword-stroke. Shimei
was completely consumed with bitterness against David. The basis
of this was his accusation that David was receiving his just reward
for **'all the blood [he] shed in the household of Saul'**. **'You have
come to ruin,'** screamed Shimei, **'because you are a man of
blood'** (16:7-8). As it happened, this accusation was entirely false.
David had not killed off the house of Saul and David maintained his
consistency by preventing Abishai from summarily decapitating
the reviler.

David nevertheless recognized that though Shimei's charges
were inaccurate he was not completely innocent of censurable
activities. David above all knew his true guilt before God and,
unlike Shimei, knew that God had predicted his humiliation for
these sins. To vindicate himself against Shimei's charges, though
very easy to accomplish, would not remove the stains of his real
faults. The execution of Shimei for what was little more than
misguided rudeness would have been a hollow affirmation of the
royal integrity. He felt humbled by Shimei's curses and knew he
deserved to be so humbled, even if Shimei was muddled as to the
reasons. In rebuking Abishai, David advanced three reasons for a
lenient attitude to Shimei.

He first reasoned that it might well be the Lord's doing. **'If he
is cursing because the Lord said to him, "Curse David," who
can ask, "Why do you do this?"'** (16:10). The question does not
imply that God was the author of Shimei's misinformation or mean-
spiritedness, just that it was possible that God purposed to use
Shimei, sins, bad motives and all, to humble David. And why
should David be righteously angry about Shimei's sins against him,
when he himself was guilty of far greater sins? This was God's way
of putting David's problems in their true perspective, for God had
certainly not punished him as his iniquities deserved, for all the
difficulties he was going through!

David's second thought was that Shimei's hatred was understandable in the circumstances, however unjustified in itself. David
noted that since his own son was out to take his life, it was small

wonder that a kinsman of Saul should be so opposed to him. Therefore, **'Let him curse, for the Lord has told him to'** (16:11).

Finally, on a more hopeful note, David surmised that the Lord might perhaps bless him, even by means of Shimei's cursing: **'It may be that the Lord will see my distress and repay me with good for the cursing I am receiving today'** (16:12). The thought is simply that the Lord who sent the humbling curses of Shimei is also the God of all grace, who answers repentance with the blessings of his grace. David suffered the insults and let Shimei rave on unhindered. Only when the column reached their destination at the River Jordan did David experience any relief from this 'strife of tongues' and some refreshment for his physical exhaustion (16:13-14).

We have already noted the 'heaviest' doctrinal point in this episode, namely, that Shimei was used by God to humble David before the world's watching eyes. This is to say that God channelled the wilful sin of Shimei to achieve his own redemptive purposes in David's life. It is not to say that God inspired these sinful acts or in some way forced the sinner to commit them. God is never the author of sin, although sin, like everything else, falls within the scope of his eternal decree. The Scriptures clearly teach the fact of the over-arching absolute sovereignty of God and indicate this to be in his very nature as God. The Scriptures also teach the responsibility of men and women for their actions. Perhaps the classic case illustrating this point is that of Judas Iscariot. Judas was an essential component in the eternally laid plan of redemption. He was even the subject of prophecy. And yet he freely decided to betray Christ and was completely responsible for his actions! There is a profound mystery in the relationship between divine sovereignty and human responsibility and it is inherent in the most fundamental mystery of all, which is the infinite, eternal and unchangeable character of God, in his being, wisdom, power, holiness, justice, goodness and truth, and the consequent distinction between the Creator and his creatures. It is curious how so many Christians think they understand the difference between God and man and yet cannot conceive how God can be absolutely sovereign (i.e. predestination and election) and at the same time man fully responsible (i.e. human free agency). In defining man's free agency, it is often insisted that simple human logic must exhaustively explain and even confine the sovereign will of God, i.e., if we are free, then predestination is impossible; if God predestines, we have no real choices. On the other hand, in defining God's sovereignty (or, rather, delimiting it in terms of the foregoing notion of human freedom), the nature of God is understood more as a kind of superhumanity, as opposed to self-existent supernatural divinity. The essential attributes of God imply an absolute sovereignty which not only cannot be contradicted or denied by the fact of human freedom, but is in reality the very sovereign power and will that made man, in his own image, with a calling and a responsibility, in terms of which he would exercise his freedom, yet within the unseen orbit of the hidden purposes of God's eternal decree. Shimei was free, within the constraints of his own sin-bent mind, to do as he pleased. He could have cursed David at home or not cursed him at all, as he chose. But he chose to curse him to his face. He chose, incidentally, to do so against the known teaching of God's law (Exodus 22:28). Nevertheless, he did what he did within the all-encompassing scope of the eternal decree. The reason is that the finite is always comprehended within the infinite and is never autonomous from it; the creature is always enveloped by the secret will of the Creator. This is joy for the believer, but a threatening 'grey eminence' to those who are determined to live their lives their own way rather than God's way.

The behaviour of Shimei and David also affords considerable insight into human character and the difference that the grace of God can make. You need not go far in this life to meet a Shimei. His personal characteristics are all too common, even if they do not all appear in the same person at the same time. Here is an unbridled tongue, fulminating in the foulest language and pointing to an untamed heart (James 3:5-6). Here, also is the capacity to combine a monolithic sense of being in the right with a readiness to indulge a sinful, judgemental attitude to another person (James 3:9). Allied to this is a lack of interest in solving whatever problem exists, or of extending the slightest hint of a willingness to forgive a perceived wrong, and a vicious enthusiasm to see the wrath of God poured out on that person. The Shimeis of this world are driven by a burning desire for revenge. They don't want any repentance, reconciliation, or restitution. They want to see the other fellow 'get his deserts', as the saying goes. Bitterness consumes those who, far from not letting the sun go down on their anger and so leaving everything in the hands of a just Father-God, wallow in unholy anger, self-pity or vengefulness. Shimei is a melancholy proof of the fact that 'Man's anger does not bring about the righteous life that God desires' (James 1:20).

David exemplifies the converse: that personal godliness is a wonderful antidote to unholy anger and its often grim after-effects. David could have risen up against Shimei's unjust abuse. One nod and Abishai would have shut that mouth for ever. But he didn't. Why? Because, as we have already seen, he was as sensitive to his real sins as Shimei was obsessed with his imagined sins. In view of what he really deserved, what did Shimei's rantings really matter? David was listening to another voice! And the Lord was persuading him of his guilt and, not least, pointing him to the hope of deliverance. This teaches us at least two practical lessons.

The first is that experiencing injustice may not be as bad for us as it always feels at the time. It may, after all, be God's means of turning us around to his way of blessing. The psalmist notes that until he was afflicted, he went astray, but 'now I obey your word' (Psalm 119:67). The ultimate fall-back position of the Christian who is confronted with bad things happening to him is the bedrock truth that 'In all things God works for the good of those who love him, who have been called according to his purpose,' and that good purpose is that they might be 'conformed to the likeness of his Son' (Romans 8:28-29).

Another lesson is that we are never required to exact vindication for all personal wrongs done us. Humble acceptance of these and a forgiving spirit towards the perpetrator is an option. A wife does not have to divorce an adulterous husband. Indeed, healing ought to be the first goal in all such problems. Grace, repentance, renewal, forgiveness, restoration and healing must always be better than a bald exaction of justice through 'prosecution to the maximum extent of the law'. We are so filled with our 'rights' and our sense of justice that we are ready to draw our swords, like Abishai and Peter (when Jesus was arrested), and exact our 'pound of flesh' without mercy. But as David's humble spirit restrained Abishai and Jesus' perfect righteousness rebuked the impetuous Peter, so we are called away from self-vindication to the humble exercise of a grace-filled heart that looks to the Lord as the one who saves sinners without allowing his justice to be thwarted. If this chapter in David's life began with sour notes, it closes on a sweet one. He had learned afresh a penitent humility and found it to be the handmaid of a rising hope in God his heavenly Father. So it must be for all God's children.

18.
The downfall of Ahithophel

Please read 2 Samuel 16:15-17:23
'Ahithophel...put his house in order and then hanged himself' (2 Samuel 17:23).

One of the more amazing facts of life in this world is how frequently wickedness is restrained and even overthrown. Christian people, with good reason, rightly mourn the evils that perennially afflict human society. It is, nevertheless, only too easy to dwell on these miseries to the extent that we lose sight of the reality that they invariably fail to keep their grip on people — in individuals or nations — unbroken and indefinitely. Evil is always around, but specific manifestations of evil only last so long and tend to self-destruct under their own weight. A true grieving for the lost and their plight, therefore, need not be shrivelled into woebegone defeatism about the work of God or doubt about the Lord's final victory.

Even the greatest depths of human sin must never be used to justify discouragement and despair in the Christian. We may let it get us down, but we need not do so. That we are so easily depressed by sin in others — and, not least, in ourselves — is more a measure of the deficiencies of our discernment and grasp of the scriptural view of things than an expression of some ineluctable psychological necessity of our humanity. The truth which the Lord has spoken to us for us to believe and to feed upon is that the wicked 'have their reward' in the transient enjoyment of their rebellion against God (Matthew 6:2, 5, 16). Their 'reward' is as existential and as fleeting as the sin itself. The 'pleasures of sin', as Moses had learned while a prince in Egypt, are 'for a short time' (Hebrews 11:25). The rewards of evil are ephemeral and the continuing emergence of fresh evils should not blind us to the fact that much of what afflicts us today goes down to destruction before too long.

I believe that this is the perspective which emerges from the Scripture account of the overthrow of the counsel of Ahithophel. The passage tells a dismal story of intrigue and it ends in a suicide's grave. But it teaches that all who love the Lord may look at the vileness of human wickedness with the sure and triumphant conviction that 'The way of transgressors is hard' and 'the end of it like a bitter day' (Proverbs 13:15, AV; Amos 8:10). In spite of all, the Lord really is in control! We need not be afraid of the conspiracies of counsellors in high places, whether in Jerusalem, Moscow, Washington or, closer to home, even in Whitehall! The Ahithophels of the world cannot vanquish the armies of the living God — not by Marxism, materialism or any other 'ism'.

> 'The One enthroned in heaven laughs;
>   the Lord scoffs at them.
> Then he rebukes them in his anger
>   and terrifies them in his wrath, saying,
> "I have installed *my King*
>   on Zion, my holy hill"'
>
> (Psalm 2:4-6, emphasis mine).

The counsel of Ahithophel [16:15-17:4]

'God suffers wicked men to prosper a while in their wicked plots, even beyond their expectation,' wrote Matthew Henry, 'that their disappointment may be the more grievous and disgraceful.'[1] Absalom duly arrived in Jerusalem **'and Ahithophel was with him'** (16:15). Everything was going for Absalom. It had all been so easy. Perhaps he felt that all that remained was a mopping-up operation against David's retreating forces. The irony of the situation must have delighted him, for he, who had been exiled beyond the Jordan by David, had now driven his father into exile in the same direction.

Hushai is placed in Absalom's court (16:16-19)

The inspired historian has set this scene with brilliant dramatic flair. Absalom's 'triumphal entry' into the capital is followed by the appearance of Ahithophel's nemesis, Hushai the Arkite (16:16). David's plan was that Hushai insinuate himself into the counsels of

Absalom and become a 'mole' in the enemy camp. This appears not to have been a foregone conclusion, for Absalom was well aware that Hushai was **'David's friend'** — an expression indicating, not mere personal friendship, but an official role as a loyal adviser to the king. When Hushai acknowledged him as king, Absalom expressed a genuine surprise. R. P. Gordon neatly observes that this surprise was promptly 'smothered by a dole of pious flummery which concentrates divine election, popular acclaim and personal devotion in one compact sentence,' together with the observation that it was not disloyal to serve David's son (16:18-19).[2] This fulsome nonsense evidently satisfied Absalom but was not enough for Hushai's immediate induction into the council of war (see 17:5). He was, however, in position for his services to be sought, should the notion cross Absalom's mind. The question has arisen, of course, as to whether Hushai's conduct constitutes a mandate from God for espionage and the deliberate dissemination of disinformation in aid of a righteous cause. The best answer to that, I believe, is to resist the temptation to develop a formal theory of covert action from the behaviour of one individual who bravely served his master's righteous cause in an ambiguous role. Suffice it to say that God blesses us in our imperfect faithfulness and not in the perfect holiness we do not yet possess (i.e., this side of eternity). The only reason we need blessing from God is precisely because we fall short of his glory in so many ways. If Hushai teaches us anything, let it be that God can use people like us — in spite of our crises of conscience, faulty judgements and even naïve ignorance — to do the work of his kingdom. But let us also remember that there is no reason to believe that David would have lost his kingdom had he simply given himself to prayer and kept Hushai in his camp. The fact that Hushai succeeded is no proof that God could not, or would not, have overthrown Absalom by less deceptive means. The God who honoured Rahab, who lied about the spies (Joshua 2), also blessed Hushai's duplicity with success.

Ahithophel's astute counsel (16:20-17:4)

Ahithophel was an extremely gifted counsellor. His advice was **'like that of one who enquires of God'** (16:23). It is very possible to be highly intelligent and possess great sagacity and yet be a stranger to the love of God and, therefore, his wisdom. 'The people of this world,' said Jesus, 'are more shrewd in dealing with their own kind than are the people of the light' (Luke 16:8). Matthew Henry reminds us: 'God has chosen the foolish things of the world; and the greatest statesmen are rarely the greatest saints.'[3] These facts ought perhaps to be a caution to those Christians who imagine that Christian writers will produce the best literature, or Christian scholars the best research, Christian athletes will be the Olympic medal-winners, and so on. Gospel faith in Jesus Christ is neither an inoculation against natural physical and intellectual limitations, nor a magic bullet conveying instant 'natural abilities'. Becoming a Christian does change lives and the impact can be very wide-ranging. Spiritual wisdom is true Christian intelligence. But it is not the same thing as 'I.Q.'. There will always be Ahithophels in this world — extremely gifted minds that have no love for the Lord in them — and God's people will be as often learning from them as praying for the Lord to overthrow such of their counsel as is inimical to the progress of the gospel of Christ. Ahithophel's counsel to Absalom was intelligent, far-sighted and thoroughly pragmatic. It was entirely without principle and involved as much sin as was deemed necessary to secure Absalom's grip upon the throne. There were two main components in Ahithophel's strategy for defeating David.

First of all, he advised Absalom to sleep with the concubines his father had left to take care of the palace (16:21-22). To sleep with one's 'father's wife' was a capital offence under the law of God (Leviticus 20:11). The apostle Paul later describes such incestuous acts as immorality 'of a kind that does not occur even among pagans' (1 Corinthians 5:1). The idea was that, in this way, Absalom would become so odious to David that reconciliation would be all but inconceivable. This would strengthen the resolve of those of Absalom's supporters who entertained the fear that if David and Absalom were reconciled they might lose out in the settlement, even if their leader did not. Ahithophel gave these men a reason to believe that Absalom was totally committed to rebellion and would not let his own men down by making a deal with David. Thus was fulfilled Nathan's prophecy as to the consequences of David's sin with Bathsheba (12:11-12).

Secondly, he counselled a swift search-and-destroy expedition, which would relentlessly pursue David while he was still **'weary and weak'**, taking care to minimize loss of life, while ensuring that

the king was killed (17:1-3). This was only good sense for a
rebellion led by the heir to the throne: if the king is dead, what can
people say to his heir but 'Long live the king!'? Absalom must strike
while the iron was hot. We are told that the plan **'seemed good to
Absalom and to all the elders of Israel'** (17:4). These elders,
drawn from the northern tribes,[4] had set their face against the
lordship of God. They were proving that where the Word of God
ceases to guide human behaviour, 'the people cast off restraint'
(Proverbs 29:18). The body politic had embraced the moral evil
which was ultimately to issue in its demise.

The triumph of Hushai [17:5-22]

Absalom stood at the threshold of complete success. And then he
made the decision that was to turn it all to ashes. He sought a second
opinion on Ahithophel's plan of action. He called for Hushai,
David's 'mole' at the palace. We are not told why Absalom did this.
It may well be significant, however, that whereas he very swiftly
followed Ahithophel's advice to sleep with his father's concubines,
he was less inclined to lead his men off at the gallop in pursuit of a
decisive battle with David. The image of the handsome prince with
the long flowing locks and a penchant for conspiracy is the dominant one. Absalom was more 'style' than 'substance' — more a
voluptuary and less a warrior. Sex and licentiousness he relished,
while war and hardship held less appeal. Consequently, he failed
the first true test of his leadership. He hesitated. And that was to be
fatal.

The key to the whole episode is stated in verse 14: **'The Lord
had determined to frustrate the good advice of Ahithophel in
order to bring disaster on Absalom.'** The means by which this
was accomplished was the intervention of Hushai. Hushai knew full
well that Ahithophel's strategy was almost bound to succeed if
executed with despatch. Speed was of the essence and therefore
Hushai's strategy was to buy time for David to marshal his forces.
Without delay he proceeded to subvert Ahithophel's plan.

1. *He boldly contradicted Ahithophel:* **'The advice
Ahithophel has given is not good at this time'** (17:7). There is
something to the (bad) joke about the preacher who wrote in the
margin of his sermon: 'Weak point; shout louder'! Boldness in such

circumstances has considerable shock value. It said to Absalom, 'This man is really convinced about this — maybe he has something. Maybe Ahithophel is mistaken.' Absalom's single-mindedness dissolved into a nagging uncertainty.

2. *He exaggerated the strength of the opposition* and raised the spectre of catastrophe, if precipitate moves were made against David. Hushai realized that since the real David could not, at this point, defeat Absalom in the field, the legendary David of Israel's rise as a nation must defeat the rebel in his mind. He therefore painted a picture of David as the peerless guerrilla fighter who would never put himself in a position to be easily captured and who might well ambush Absalom's troops and, even with a limited victory, spread fear throughout Israel (17:8-10). This was the David who killed Goliath, successfully eluded Saul and conducted lightning campaigns against the Philistines and the Amalekites — the David of song and story — not the tired and chastened David who was beating a retreat across the Jordan! Hushai thereby converted David's lustrous reputation into an army that never was and sent a bolt of fear through Absalom's heart!

3. *He promised certain victory*, providing Absalom adopted a strategy based on the mustering of overwhelming force (17:11-13). He held out the lure of 'the sure thing', and what he succeeded in doing was to persuade Absalom to adopt what, in effect, was David's strategy — take time, gather strength and attack when you have a reasonable expectation of victory. What Absalom failed to see was that rebels cannot afford to be too cautious, because time is very often on the side of the regime, especially if the apparatus of government is intact. Absalom had his supporters up and down the land, but there is little to indicate that his writ as yet extended much beyond the reach of his army. The weeping populace along David's escape route (notwithstanding the cursing of Shimei) suggests that there was a groundswell of support for David, which, given time and some discoveries of Absalom's true colours, would provide the basis for his return. This was to be the case, but Absalom appears not to have seen it coming.

4. Above all, *he appealed to Absalom's vanity* by attributing the coming victory to his leadership (17:11). The inclusion of an element of flattery was not accidental. Hushai knew his man. And men like Absalom are driven by the desire for recognition, because they are essentially worshippers of themselves. The thought of a

glorious victory at the head of his troops was much more appealing
to Absalom than a hit-and-run raid in the dark to kill the king while
he slept! This clinched things for Absalom. The counsel of
Ahithophel was dead! (17:14).

5. Hushai then wasted no time in sending word to David
through Zadok and Abiathar and their sons, Jonathan and Ahimaaz,
advising that he cross over Jordan, in case Absalom should change
his mind and send a force to surprise him (17:15-22).

If this great reversal was a testimony to the power of God to
deliver his people from the most desperate of circumstances, it is
also a witness to what can be achieved for the Lord through
courageous action. 'The king's heart is in the hand of the Lord; he
directs it like a watercourse wherever he pleases' (Proverbs 21:1).
And so very often the means by which the Lord effects these
changes of direction is the practical influence of those people who
are committed to spreading his Word and seeing his will done in the
world. If Hushai had not been willing to risk his neck for David's
sake, who can say that Ahithophel's advice would ever have been
challenged? We may be justified in believing that deliverance for
David would have arisen 'from another place' (Esther 4:14). The
fact is, however, that God's means of thwarting Absalom was that
one brave man with his subtle mind and facile tongue. In a sense this
is the calling of every one of God's people: we are here to be his
instruments, his ambassadors, spreading his Word so that lives
should be changed. His unseen hand is at work, both in us and in
others, but what we do and say matters. We are not incidental to the
work of God in the world. We are, in fact, the chosen channels of
his ministry to save. This is the privileged calling of all who believe
in the Lord.

Another, not unrelated, practical dimension of effective Christian living suggested by this passage is the element of speed in
taking the opportunities God gives us to work for him. In his wicked
way, Ahithophel knew this: it is a universal principle in war that
'getting there the fastest with the mostest' will win victories.
Absalom faltered and that delay would kill his cause. Hushai moved
as quickly as he could. He may have counselled caution, but he
himself acted with the greatest sense of urgency, even though he
was thoroughly controlled in his approach. This is what the spiritual
warfare requires in us all — a sense of controlled haste and of serene

urgency. This is true in witnessing for Christ to people outside the church and it is true in seeking to heal soured personal relationships within the church. Had Hushai hesitated to attack the problem raised by Ahithophel's good advice, all might not have been lost, but things would have been a great deal more complicated for David.

Death by suicide [17:23]

The death of Ahithophel is the final conclusion and application of the account of the overthrow of his counsel. The text states the facts with a bald, even flat, deliberation. There is nothing about Ahithophel's motives, thoughts or psychological struggles. He is simply portrayed as giving up. The moment he heard that Hushai had prevailed, he knew that Absalom was doomed and therefore that he too was finished. And so he became his own executioner, the second of only four suicides in the Bible.[5]

The downfall of Ahithophel signalizes the inevitable and essentially self-destructive end of wickedness. The logic of suicide is itself a dreadful proof of this fact. A man who cannot face the earthly consequences of his failures 'escapes' into death and 'ends it all' — end of story. But the truth is that this only brings him face to face, all the sooner and beyond all possibility of repentance and reconciliation to the Lord, with the eternal consequences of what led in the first place to his suicide — his fundamental hatred for the Lord and his unwillingness to keep his righteous commands. The wages of sin will always be death.

Ahithophel's suicide is also an epitaph for man's best efforts to overthrow the righteousness of God. Sometimes the power of wicked men appears unassailable. We easily rush into irrational fears about all-powerful conspiracies in high places. To be sure, conspiracies are arising all the time (Psalm 2:1-2). But even a sober reading of our secularist history books will show us that they never last long. The psalmist attributes this to the kingly rule of the risen Christ, who is ruling the nations with 'an iron sceptre' and dashing them 'to pieces like pottery'. 'Therefore,' God says to human rulers, 'Kiss the Son, lest he be angry and you be destroyed in your way' (Psalm 2:12). The Lord will always vindicate his cause, establish his will and bless his believing people with deliverance from their enemies and the enjoyment of a life within the encircling care of divine love.

Ahithophel's defeat was an answer to prayer, for David had prayed, 'O Lord, turn Ahithophel's counsel into foolishness' (15:31). The Lord never left David to himself. He stirred him to pray and he answered in grace and in power. It is thought that Psalm 55 — and also Psalms 42 and 43 — may have been written by David during this dark period in his life. There he penned a word for God's people for all time, as they stand amidst the clamour of a world that ruthlessly schemes, plots and fights to gain its own ends, encouraging their trust in the Saviour who will never let them down:

> 'Cast your cares on the Lord
>   and he will sustain you;
>   he will never let the righteous fall.
> But you, O God, will bring down the wicked
>   into the pit of corruption;
> bloodthirsty and deceitful men
>   will not live out half their days.
> But as for me, I trust in you'
>
> (Psalm 55:22-23).

19.
O my son Absalom!

Please read 2 Samuel 17:24-19:8
'The king covered his face and cried aloud, "O my son Absalom!"'
(2 Samuel 19:4).

Absalom was one of those men in this world who owe their prominence to a privileged birth and/or a handsome appearance and who squander their advantages through a mixture of small-mindedness, limited abilities and even sheer venality. He was the 'Bonnie Prince Charlie'[1] of his generation — popular with some, if not all, of the masses, but essentially a trivial character. He was one of those whose position and ambition placed him where he could bring misery not merely to himself but to untold thousands, even to a whole nation. Throughout the whole Scripture record of Absalom's life, there is a decided air of inevitable disaster. A pall of moral turpitude hangs over the man's every recorded action. Even his comforting of his violated sister was self-centred — he was more concerned about his future revenge than her immediate vindication. The central thread is, of course, a moral one: or, we should say, an amoral one, for Absalom operates without any discernible moral standard. Like all such men, he was pragmatic and conspiratorial but above all — and here was his fatal flaw — he was driven primarily by his own vainglorious ambition. When he accepted Hushai's challenge to lead the massed levies of Israel in the decisive defeat of David, he perhaps began to see himself as the hero-king who would surpass his father's accomplishments! But he did not reckon with the Lord, and his fantasies were soon to perish in the forest of Ephraim.

The biblical record of the end of Absalom's rebellion is, however, less about ambition thwarted by death in battle than about a father's sorrow. This grief, as we shall see, was overdone and rightly drew forth a rebuke from Joab. It was, as Thomas Manton put it, a 'peevish, doting love',[2] but that ought not to obscure the reality of the tragedy. And part of David's sorrow was, no doubt, in the fact that all of it was a direct consequence of his adultery with Bathsheba and the death of her husband Uriah (12:11-12).

The death of Absalom [17:24-18:18]

Events moved swiftly to a conclusion. Absalom knew that he would never be secure as long as David was alive. The abandonment of Ahithophel's plan set his course for him. He had no alternative but to amass as large a force as he could and proceed cautiously to the inevitable confrontation with what he could expect to be a sizeable and well-led army.

Opening moves (17:24-29)

The narrative see-saws between the opposing forces, building our anticipation of the impending clash of arms. David moved far to the north-east to Mahanaim, a leading town of Gilead, which, after the death of Saul, had been the capital of the interim kingdom of Ish-Bosheth, Saul's son (17:24).

Absalom, on Hushai's advice, assembled a large host and, confident of victory, he led his army across the Jordan. His commanding general was Amasa, a cousin of Joab, David's commander (17:24-26).

David meanwhile received help from three men, whose loyalty stands in pointed contrast to the treason of Absalom's cohorts (17:27-29). **'Shobi son of Nahash'** was a scion of the Ammonite royal house and may have ruled the now subject kingdom of Ammon by David's appointment (cf. 12:26-31);[3] **'Makir'** had been a friend to Saul's crippled grandson, Mephibosheth, when the latter had been destitute (cf. 9:4) and **'Barzillai the Gileadite'** was a doughty octogenarian whose open-handed generosity so impressed David that he later invited the old man to stay with him in Jerusalem at the royal expense (cf. 19:31-39).

Battle is joined (18:1-8)

David organized his troops in three divisions under Joab, Abishai and Ittai. Joab, as on former occasions, would have been the supreme commander. Just two things are mentioned in connection with the march of David's army.

Firstly, David, unlike Absalom, did not accompany his troops. He had wanted to go with them, but was dissuaded on the grounds that whereas a live David was worth 10,000 men, a dead David would mean utter defeat. The latter had, of course, been Ahithophel's now thwarted strategy and this decision indicates the sound tactical sense with which David's supporters were conducting the campaign. So David **'stood beside the gate, while all the men marched out in units...'** (18:1-4).

Secondly, David ordered his commanders to **'be gentle'** (AV, 'deal gently') with Absalom (18:5). The text records that **'all the troops'** heard David say this. Gracious though it was for David to wish no harm towards his son, it remains a fact that his love for Absalom was obtruding on the situation in an unhealthy way. It caused him to forget that it does nothing for a soldier's morale to know that his leader does not want his enemy to be hurt! This would rear its head after the battle, when Joab, quite correctly, rebuked David for grieving over the death of Absalom when he should be thankful for the soldiers who fought and died to save his life (19:5-8).

The rival armies collided in **'the forest of Ephraim'**, which was in Gilead, not Ephraim, and was so called because it was the place where the tribe of Ephraim had been defeated by Jephthah (Judges 12:5). David's men were victorious. It appears that the terrain claimed more casualties than the battle. 20,000 men paid for Absalom's unhallowed ambition that day! (18:6-8).

Absalom is killed (18:9-15)

Absalom himself was first a victim of the forest before he fell to Joab's javelins. Somehow caught in a tree — tradition, via the first-century historian, Josephus, attributes this to his famous head of hair — he was an easy target. The soldiers, however, had heard the king's order that they 'be gentle' with Absalom (i.e., take him alive) and refused to strike him. Joab had no such scruples and, unlike ordinary soldiers, little fear of punishment for disobedience. He promptly despatched the helpless usurper (18:14). Joab, as usual, served himself as he served the national interest. At one stroke, he

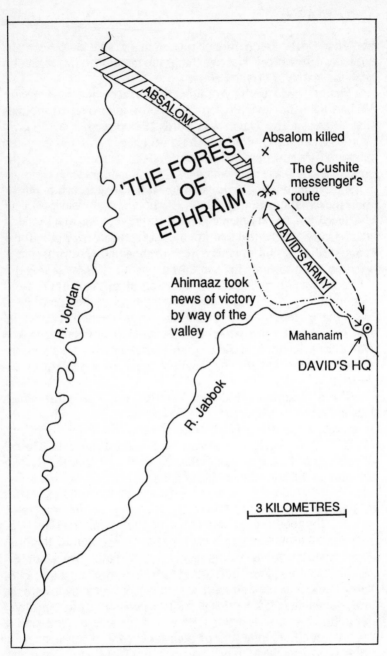

MAP 7 — Absalom's defeat

destroyed the monster he had partly created (it was Joab who had brought back Absalom from Geshur) and overthrew David's maudlin sentiment to spare the young man's life. He knew full well that a live Absalom would be endless trouble and, indeed, could be a legal king one day with a long memory about those who had resisted his earlier seizure of the throne.

Epitaph for a rebel prince (18:16-18)

With Absalom's death, the rebellion was over, so Joab sounded an end to hostilities. He then had Absalom's body buried in an unmarked grave. Perhaps he wanted to prevent the royal rebel's corpse from being enshrined in a grand tomb and made the focal point of future rebellion. In any event, the result was that Absalom's only monument was to be one he had himself put up while alive, because he had no son to carry on the memory of his name (18:18).[4] This sad memorial thereby commemorated the emptiness of a life with neither positive accomplishment nor a viable posterity. How true it is that 'The mirth of the wicked is brief, the joy of the godless lasts but a moment'! (Job 20:5).

David's inordinate sorrow [18:19-19:8]

David heard news of the battle in stages: first, from Ahimaaz the son of Zadok, the good news of the victory, and then from the official despatch-runner (a 'Cushite', from Nubia, south of Egypt) the bad news of the death of Absalom (18:19-33). Joab had not wanted to send Ahimaaz at all — perhaps, speculates R. P. Gordon, because of 'David's poor record where the receiving of the bearers of purportedly good tidings was concerned (cf. v.22; 1:11-16; 4:5-12).'[5] His reasoning appears to have been: 'The son of the high priest must not be risked — a foreign underling, "the Cushite", would be no loss, should David kill a messenger again.' If this was so, Joab had not judged correctly the earlier incidents, both of which involved openly confessed regicide. In the event, Ahimaaz made better time than the Cushite, arrived first and carefully evaded telling of Absalom's death! This may well have prepared David for the news when it did come shortly after. The messenger was unharmed, but David was **'shaken'**.

Far from rejoicing over the victory, David was consumed with grief for his dead son. He went to his room and wept: **'As he went, he said, "O my son Absalom! If only I had died instead of you — O Absalom, my son, my son!"'** (18:33). As a result, the return of the army to Mahanaim was less a victory parade than a wake! (19:1-4). Again the rough-and-ready Joab, who had wisely, if irregularly, put Absalom to death against the king's orders, came to the rescue of his royal master and, also wisely if irregularly, roundly rebuked him and told him to pull himself together and go out to greet his victorious army. Quite rightly, Joab told David that his self-pity was as good as saying that he would have been happier had Absalom lived and they died, and predicted that any unwillingness to honour his soldiers' efforts would lead to revolt and desertion (19:5-7).

David had every reason to feel grief over Absalom's death. What father would not sorrow for a dead son? And in such circumstances — on just receiving the bad news — what parent would not find it difficult to control his emotions? That is precisely why the emotionally distraught need the support of those who are more detached and can take a cooler view of the whole picture. True, Joab had actually been Absalom's killer. He did not share one iota of David's sense of loss. Joab was not a sympathetic comforter. But he was needed — yes! — as the Lord's counter-balance to David's own excessive grief. Joab was at that point God's instrument to keep David on an even keel and preserve him from throwing away all the fruits of victory because of a disproportionate sorrow for his reprobate son — a son who would not have thought twice about murdering his own father! When you find yourself immersed in the sadness of some trouble — maybe bereavement, separation or divorce — be thankful for the cool heads around you who are able to give the wise advice that you find so difficult to grapple with in the maelstrom of your emotional trauma. You will probably say to your counsellor, 'It's easy for you to say! You're not going through what I am facing!' The truth is that it is not always so easy for the counsellor, because the peculiar difficulty he has to face is that of saying the hard things to you that you need to hear, when he knows you want to hear something else. Joab could understand a father's sorrow, but he also understood the necessity of proportion and, not least, of statecraft. David realized that Joab was right, composed himself and went out to receive the army (19:8).

Perhaps the most instructive element in the record of Absalom's death — apart from the obvious, namely, that the wages of sin is always death — is the way in which the Lord, through Joab, rebuked the unbalanced emotionalism in David. Absalom's character was the moral equivalent of the small boy's scowl, of which it was said, 'He had a face that only a mother could love!' David was a father who loved his son. But his love was blind and obsessive. He crossed the line from emotion to emotionalism, from sentiment to sentimentalism, and so denied all rationality, and even righteousness, in his attitude to Absalom and his sins. David had no lack of information; he knew the facts. He had no lack of intelligence; he was a clever man. But his spiritual discernment just evaporated before his affection for his wicked son. His self-possession and self-control crumbled before his grief. Now while there may be some people in this world who can suppress their emotions, so as never to weep and never to lose control to the slightest degree, the Scripture recognizes that the more common human problem is emotionalism and loss of control in stressful situations. Therefore, we are urged to guard our heart (Proverbs 4:23) and reminded that 'Better a patient man than a warrior, a man who controls his temper than one who takes a city' (Proverbs 16:32). And with respect to those matters which so often absorb our interest and blight our lives, we are told to 'set [our] minds on things above, not on earthly things' (Colossians 3:2). Again, in the face of a concern for those Christian loved ones who have died, we grieve, but not 'like the rest of men, who have no hope' (1 Thessalonians 4:13). The point is that David really went to pieces over Absalom and that we too will fall apart whenever our emotions are not moulded by the disciplines of biblical spirituality — that is to say, a spirituality rooted in a saving knowledge of Jesus Christ, a conscientious submission to the teaching of the infallible Word of God and a peace wrought by the indwelling power of the Holy Spirit in the soul. 'How is this to be achieved?' you may ask. The answer: by holding fast to the very words of God, over against the racing of your heart and the agonized moanings of your troubled emotions. You must learn, by the grace of God, to stop the swelling of your passions and concentrate prayerfully upon the appropriate word from the Scriptures. In the case of anger, let it be 'Do not let the sun go down while you are still angry' (Ephesians 4:26); if the problem is lust, 'I made a covenant with my eyes...' (Job 31:1); if we are mourning, we do not 'grieve like the rest of men, who have no hope' (1 Thessalonians 4:13).

We also see some of the fruits of God's grace even in the midst of David's turmoil. That he could take rebuke from an inferior character like Joab, whom he knew to be a law unto himself, indicates a discernment of his sin and the realization that God was telling him what he needed to hear, even if it was through Joab. And in his desire that his men 'be gentle' with Absalom, David did seek to return good for evil — and that cannot but be regarded as a gracious attitude, even if marred by his later inordinate sorrow. Matthew Henry exclaims: 'How does he render good for evil! Absalom would have David only smitten. David would have Absalom only spared. What foils are these to each other! Never was unnatural hatred to a father more strong than in Absalom; nor was ever natural affection to a child more strong than in David. Each did his utmost, and showed what man is capable of doing, how bad it is possible for a child to be to the best of fathers, and how good it is possible for a father to be to the worst of children; as if it were designed to be a resemblance of man's wickedness toward God and God's mercy toward man, of which it is hard to say which is more amazing.'[6] David was, if anything, gracious to a fault. He wanted God's best for his evil son. His fault was to have shrunk from his duty as a father and as a king to deal justly with Absalom.

When Jesus wept for Jerusalem over its rejection of him and when he prayed from the dying agonies of the cross, 'Father, forgive them, for they do not know what they are doing,' he was gripped by that compassion which aches over the hell-bent wilfulness of human sin. But, unlike David, the sinless Saviour's compassion blends perfectly with his eternal purpose of redemption and his passing by of those who steadfastly reject him. The Lord wept for Jerusalem, but his justice was to leave it desolate in due time. If David is a type or foreshadowing of Jesus, it is through his imperfect love for Absalom that we are pointed to the perfect love of Christ for sinners such as ourselves. The God who 'does not leave the guilty unpunished' is 'compassionate and gracious...slow to anger, abounding in love and faithfulness' and maintains 'love to thousands...forgiving wickedness, rebellion and sin' (Exodus 34:6-7). There is hope. There is good news for sinners. Jesus saves!

PART IV
Restoration — David's return

20.
Return and restoration

Please read 2 Samuel 19:9-39
'Then the king returned and went as far as the Jordan' (2 Samuel 19:15).

Civil wars are born in confusion and when they die that confusion is often worse confounded. Israel did not instantly reunite upon the death of Absalom. Notwithstanding his victory, David knew that only the military phase of the rebellion was over. The discontent which had attracted men to his son's colours represented a measure of political ill-will which had to be overcome, or at least substantially mollified, for any return to the reins of government to be effective. It was important for David to be restored as the Lord's choice of king, with the recognition of the people, rather than merely to reimpose himself as a conqueror at the head of his army. This is not to say that the voice of the people is the voice of God — which is to make 'democracy' into a god — but it shows that even among God's covenant people, no king ought to expect to govern without the consent of the governed. The institution of monarchy in Israel was theocratic but constitutional (1 Samuel 10:25). The God-given constitution limited the powers of the king, because the Lord knew that kings were sinners, and as powerful sinners were in the tempting position where they could wield their authority to the severe detriment of their subjects (1 Samuel 8:10-18). This is why absolutism — whether of the 'right' or the 'left' — is the inevitable tendency of all human governments. Since, however, people are also very fiercely attached to their own individualist absolutism — their personal freedom to do as they please — dictatorships tend to rise and fall with a frequency that is not unrelated to the rigour with which they tyrannize their own people. David was no tyrant. He loved the Lord and was aware of the Lord's revealed will for the government of his people. He did not march on Jerusalem and attempt to stamp out the opposition with the sword. He waited for the recall which he knew must come in time, and circumstances that would signal something of the healing of the breach which had lead to the disaster of Absalom's rebellion.

The narrative of David's return and restoration falls into two parts: first, his waiting for the recall (19:9-15), followed by an account of a number of meetings at the Jordan, which parallel the encounters he had on the way to exile (19:16-40).

Waiting for recall [19:9-15]

There is irony in the fact that the men of Israel — the northern tribes — asked for David's recall before the king's own tribe of Judah (19:9-10). This was, however, to strain relations between these two main sections of the nation and contribute to the growing rift which would divide the kingdom on the death of Solomon.

In the meantime, David took two actions to stimulate the process. He first sent a message to the elders of Judah asking them why they — his own flesh and blood — should lag behind the others and be **'the last to bring back the king'** (19:11-12). This was understandable but unwise, since it could only have tended to exacerbate the already existing tensions between the tribes. His second action was to take steps to replace Joab as army commander by Amasa, who had commanded Absalom's forces (19:13). This would serve the dual purpose of placating the losing side and punishing Joab for killing Absalom. Joab was never one to be denied for long, however, and David's reshuffle of his high command would later be undone by the assassin's dagger (20:9-10). In the short term, these efforts succeeded in winning the hearts of **'all the men of Judah as though they were one man'**, and they **'sent word to the king, "Return, you and all your men"'** (19:14). David duly came down to the Jordan, in preparation for the formal celebration of his return, which would take place at Gilgal on the west bank (19:15, 40).

The choice of Gilgal was heavy with spiritual significance for God's people. Here, centuries before, God's covenant with his people had been renewed after the Sinai wanderings and in the mass circumcision that day, had 'rolled away the reproach' (Joshua 5:2-9). The kingdom had been renewed there in Samuel's day (1 Samuel

11:14). Gilgal symbolized God's free grace towards his people and, like all the formal events in Israel's national life, David's return was to be a theological event, attended by the overtones of forgiveness of sin, reconciliation and revival for the people of God. If in practice it fell somewhat short of these lofty motifs, it nevertheless did mark something of a national healing after the schism of the rebellion. In terms of the providential dealings of God with David, it does tell us that if God's children fall, he will raise them up again. Even though the restoration of David was a limited exhibition of reconciliation and healing, it does speak to us of the goodness of God and reminds us that, in the last analysis, every iota of healing and restoration flows from his sovereign grace — in New Testament terms, in Jesus Christ — and sweeps away the notion that our self-generated actions accomplish our own deliverance. David had to know that it was God who had saved him. He knew that his restoration was entirely unmerited and rested wholly on the covenant promises of God (7:5-16). This is the very nature of Christian salvation. It is all of grace in the Lord Jesus Christ, the one and only Saviour of sinners. All of David's blessings point to this truth. This is the Christian's joyous testimony. One of the most marvellous witnesses to this glorious reality of Christian experience is the sixteenth-century Italian Reformer, Aonio Paleario, in his answer to his Roman Catholic inquisitor regarding salvation by good works: 'Cotta [Otho Melius Cotta] asserts that, if I am allowed to live, there will not be a vestige of religion left in the city. Why? Because being asked one day what was the first ground on which men should rest their salvation, I replied, "Christ!" Being asked what was the second, I replied, "Christ!" and being asked the third, I still replied, "Christ!"'[1]

Building bridges [19:16-39]

David waited on Jordan's east bank in preparation for his triumphal entry to Gilgal. He was soon greeted by a succession of visitors, some of whom had good reason to seek personal reconciliation with him, before he resumed his exercise of the reins of power in Jerusalem. These encounters are almost 'a mirror image of his departure',[2] in which Hushai (15:32-37), Ziba (16:1-4) and Shimei (16:5-13) had severally punctuated his flight to the east. This time

the men were successively Shimei, Ziba, Mephibosheth and
Barzillai.

Shimei (19:16, 18-23)

This kinsman of the late king, Saul, had the most cause to tremble
at the restoration of David. He had loudly vilified the king to his face
and only the gracious intervention of the humbled David had spared
him from death at the hand of Abishai (16:9-10). He accordingly
'hurried down with the men of Judah to meet King David' so as
to confess his sin and beg the forgiveness of the king. David duly
granted Shimei an amnesty, once again over the protestations of
Abishai that he be put to death: **'Should anyone be put to death in
Israel today?'** (19:22). David knew that 'Acts of severity are rarely
acts of policy'[3] and that none of the rebels would be sure of keeping
their lives if Shimei were deprived of his. It was not only an act of
mercy towards Shimei, but a signal to the followers of Absalom that
there would be healing rather than revenge. David sealed this with
an oath and Shimei did outlive him. Nevertheless, it was largely a
political reprieve, for David advised Solomon not to consider
Shimei innocent and to 'bring his grey head down to the grave in
blood' — which is what happened after Shimei had demonstrated
his unwillingness to deal faithfully with the new king (1 Kings 2:8-
9, 36-46).

Ziba (19:17-18, 26-27, 29)

All that is said of **'the steward of Saul's household'** is that he and
his sons and servants were present with Shimei and that they
'rushed to the Jordan' and **'crossed at the ford to take the king's
household over and to do whatever he wished'**. Ziba had done
David a service in his flight from Absalom, not without risk to
himself. In the process he had rather self-servingly told the king that
his master Mephibosheth had gone over to Absalom. David, without hearing Mephibosheth's side of the story, had then awarded
Ziba all of Mephibosheth's property. David would shortly hear
from Mephibosheth and return the award to the original arrange-
ment that they **'divide the fields'** — i.e., Ziba would farm the land
and they would share the produce in such a way as to provide for the
disabled Mephibosheth (9:10).[4] If Shimei was spared for his sins

that day, it is no wonder that Ziba was spared for his attempt to deprive Mephibosheth of his patrimony.

Mephibosheth (19:24-30)

The grandson of Saul came to David with all the evidence of one who had not been disloyal, as Ziba had said (16:3), but was genuinely devoted to David. He was unkempt in the style of oriental expressions of grief. It rings true when he denies any disloyalty and declares that Ziba betrayed him by deliberately preventing him from joining the king and then denouncing him for disloyalty. Mephibosheth humbly cast himself on the mercy of David. The king responded with the restoration of his lands. In keeping with the spirit of the general amnesty attending David's return, Mephibosheth extravagantly, but surely with the utmost sincerity, declared himself ready to see Ziba take all — so great was his joy at David's return!

Barzillai the Gileadite (19:31-39)

This grand old man had steadfastly helped David in his exile and was to be rewarded with an invitation to stay in Jerusalem with David at the king's expense. Barzillai begged off, preferring to live out his remaining years at home, but he did send Kimham — one of his sons[5] — in order that he receive the kindness of the king in his place. J. A. Thompson notes that a place near Bethlehem mentioned in Jeremiah 41:17, called Geruth Kimham, was very likely the fief given by David to Kimham centuries earlier.[6]

These various encounters combine to provide a picture of how the grace of God can be channelled through a man's life and touch the lives of others in significant ways. Those who have received forgiveness, as David had, are impelled to show forgiveness to those who have wronged them. If David could be forgiven adultery and complicity in murder, he could be merciful to the likes of Shimei and Ziba. What happens more often is the kind of treatment dished out by the unmerciful servant of the parable in Matthew 18:21-35. You will recall that the king in the story forgave his servant's debt of 10,000 talents, only for the servant to turn around and persecute a fellow-servant for the relatively trivial debt of 100 denarii. The former was the spirit of David, the latter, the attitude of Abishai. Those who are strangers to the grace of God invariably regard forgiveness as a weakness. It is sadly true that many a professing Christian has been very unforgiving and full of the kind of legalistic anger that wants its pound of flesh from the wrongdoer. But these things ought not to be in the heart of one whose sins have been forgiven in the Saviour who taught us to pray, 'Forgive us our debts, as we also have forgiven our debtors,' and who emphasized that 'If you forgive men when they sin against you, your heavenly Father will also forgive you. But if you do not forgive men their sins, your Father will not forgive your sins' (Matthew 6:12, 14-15).

The most glorious thought of all arising from these events is that as we look at David, our gaze is led beyond him to the Lord Jesus Christ, whom he foreshadowed. There is a picture of the nature of the gospel here: especially in the approach of Shimei to the king and in the reception David gave him. How amazing that Jesus receives sinners at all! Yet this is precisely why he came and why he died on the cross and rose again from the dead. There is reason to believe that Shimei did not truly repent and that David did not truly forgive him (1 Kings 2:8). This picture, like the offering of animal sacrifices annually in the temple, only finds its true realization in Christ. Christ is the mercy of God for all who trust in him by faith. Jesus saves! Those who come to him, he will in no way cast out, for all who believe in him will have everlasting life.

21.
The way of the wicked

Please read 2 Samuel 19:40-20:26
'They cut off the head of Sheba son of Bicri...' (2 Samuel 20:22).

Everything we do is a kind of investment in our future — an investment which may give us a good yield or issue in serious losses, depending on what we have done and how we have done it. As we noted already in connection with Absalom's abortive rebellion, wicked actions tend, like Macbeth's 'vaulting ambition', to overleap themselves and fall into self-destruction. When we indulge any kind of evil, it grows like a cancer until it is crushed and devoured by its own internal rot. In contrast, acts of genuine goodness reproduce according to their kind. Personal holiness broadens our vista of fellowship with the Lord and motivates us to an ever more practical discipleship in service to Jesus Christ.

There is no starker example of the self-destructive powers of wickedness than in the chapter now before us. Here are the repulsive fruits of unrestrained sin in the hearts and lives of men. The entire narrative is a litany of evil. And yet, in its negative way, it highlights the positive blessing of a different way of life — a life that can only be lived in the light of God's Word. So it has a certain shock value in that it lays out the consequences of a godless life in the rawest of terms. It says, if misery and death are what you want, you can have them very easily. And by implication we are propelled to the only real alternative: a life enfolded in the everlasting arms of the living God.

The narrative is in three sections, which deal successively with the squabble between Israel and Judah which issued in Sheba's rebellion (19:40-20:2), Joab's murder of Amasa (20:3-13) and the end of the rebellion, with Sheba's summary execution by his own people (20:14-22).

Pride and prejudice [19:40-20:2]

Nothing damages human relationships more than pride. At its most basic it simply means, 'Me first!' — before others, even before God. This is dressed up in 'issues' and 'substantive differences', but has as much, if not more, to do with injured feelings and fears of being disadvantaged in some way. As to real substance, the dispute between Israel and Judah was at the level of an argument in the primary school playground. Yet it had the potential for national suicide. It began with the fact that when David crossed the Jordan to go to Gilgal **'all the troops of Judah'** but only **'half the troops of Israel'** accompanied him (19:40). This was translated by the men of Israel into a conspiracy on the part of Judah to **'steal the king away'**. How this would advantage Judah, in view of the fact that they were all going to end up at Gilgal anyway, they did not say. Of course, there was no conspiracy and no substantive advantage for Judah. The problem was one of pride, of 'image' and suspicion. Israel therefore could not look on the positive side. They could not conceive of Judah being innocent. Did they ask for the reasons for David departing before all of Israel assembled? No, because they had already decided it was all part of a plan by Judah to humble them and make them look less impressive in the victory parade — to make them appear less enthusiastic about getting the king to Gilgal! Notice how the argument develops.

First of all, *Israel accused Judah of bad intentions*, by putting the worst possible construction on Judah's action: Judah, they claimed, wanted to 'steal' the king away! (19:41). There was no willingness to give the benefit of the doubt, no recognition that other factors, including the king's best judgement, might have played a part, no attribution of innocence until proved guilty, not even the slightest interest in an explanation — only naked prejudice, recrimination and accusation! But how sadly true this is to everyday life! When suspicion rules a person's heart, all the evidence just proves the other fellow guilty! The truth is, however, that Israel was only attributing to Judah what it had wanted to do itself — get the glory for bringing back the king! It is easier to attribute our own sins to others than to suspect them of the innocence we do not ourselves possess.

Secondly, *Judah replied defensively* rather than humbly — not only speaking the truth (which was fine), but also saying things that were bound to rub salt in the wound. It was true that Judah was not 'stealing' the king. They were not seeking advantage from him — eating **'the king's provisions'** or **'[taking] anything'** for themselves. It was just that **'the king [was] closely related to [them]'** and it seemed appropriate for them, once they were all there, to escort their kinsman, David, to a meeting-place which was, after all, in their territory (19:42). There is no reason to attribute bad motives to the men of Judah. They were, however, rather insensitive towards the men of Israel. They could have anticipated that not waiting for the other half of Israel's troops to arrive would cause some trouble, however unreasonable it might seem in the circumstances. Matthew Henry is right when he says that 'The men of Judah would have done better if they had taken their brethren's advice and assistance; but since they did not, why should the men of Israel be so greatly offended? If a good work be done, and well done, let us not be displeased, nor the work disparaged, though we had no hand in it.'[1]

Thirdly, *the men of Israel heightened their sense of offence* by claiming that they had the numbers, if not the kinship, that should give them pride of place in bringing back the king: **'We have ten shares in the king'** (Judah, by this method of reckoning had two — herself and Simeon). In any case, adds Israel, **'Were we not the first to speak of bringing back our king?'** (19:43).

Fourthly, we are told that *Judah responded with greater harshness* still, and that in spite of the fact that they had largely been misjudged in the beginning! And, as is almost always the case in squabbles between people and even nations, the original cause of offence became buried under layers of hard words and silly argument. Where a soft answer could have turned away anger, harsh words had engendered deep resentments. 'The perverting of words,' says Matthew Henry, 'is the subverting of peace.'[2]

Finally and almost inevitably, *the dispute escalated into open warfare* when a man named Sheba — **'a troublemaker'** — raised rebellion among the men of the ten tribes (20:1-2). Sheba's case shows how all reason can evaporate when tempers are hot enough. What started with a purely factual, if insensitive, statement from Judah — 'The king is closely related to us' (19:42) — now results in Sheba's declaration: **'We have no share in David'** (20:1). But this is a *non sequitur*, for the fact that David came from Judah does not require, or even suggest, that Israel had no relation to him! But this is how people so easily run to extremes. 'Today "Hosanna", tomorrow "Crucify",' observes Matthew Henry, most aptly.[3] Aroused by Sheba's oratory, the ten tribes changed their minds about bringing David back, while Judah stood fast for the king. Or so it seemed, for as things would turn out, this rebellion was to be something of a storm in a teacup. National reconciliation had, however, received a damaging set-back.

The application to modern life — not least to that of Christians in churches — is plain and ever urgent. The pride of Israel and Judah is still with us. More fellowship between Christians is broken by pride-related personal animosity than by genuine doctrinal disagreements. In fact true fellowship often most wonderfully bridges the latter and brings believers of divergent views together. This is one aspect of what the gospel *must* mean in an imperfect world, for when we do not saturate our relationships with the love of Christ, our differences can soon break out into sores than run with bitterness and rancour. Then true believers in Christ — Baptists and Presbyterians, Episcopalians and Congregationalists, Arminians and Calvinists — begin to view one another as 'the enemy' and go on to multiply damage to the cause of Christ and shrivel their own spiritual life and communion with the Lord. When a very real and serious difference turns to bitterness and angry rivalry, worse still, when trivial distinctions are made into principles and used to flog the 'heretics', or when insensitivity or simple misunderstanding is magnified into a climate of distrust and charges of evil motives — then we have forgotten what it means to have been saved by the free grace of God. Those who feel greatly forgiven *want* to relate to their fellow-believers with love, humility and a forgiving spirit — and desire to reach out with the same attitude even to a hostile or indifferent world. The *personal experience* of the new birth through the saving grace of Jesus Christ can only generate an attitude of grace, in Christ, to all people, but especially to those who also love the Lord.

Murder [20:3-13]

Sheba's rebellion notwithstanding, David returned to Jerusalem at the head of the men of Judah. His first action was to sequester the ten concubines who had been defiled by Absalom in a kind of living widowhood — a constant reminder not merely of Ahithophel's evil counsel and Absalom's lust, but of the long reach of the prophetic word which had predicted these events as elements of the just humiliation of David for his sin with Bathsheba (16:21-22; cf. 12:11). It also was a reminder that God had indeed forgiven him and had in fact punished him for less than his sins had deserved. Why does the Lord allow some of the effects of particular sins to linger in our lives, even after he has forgiven us? Surely to keep us humble and to emphasize that his salvation is *all* of grace and *nothing* of our works. The concubines were a living testimony to David, both of his sin and God's everlasting mercy.

David was not about to allow Sheba the time to gather his strength and thus repeat Absalom's fatal mistake in rejecting the counsel of Ahithophel. He therefore ordered Amasa, his new commander-in-chief, to assemble the levies from Judah and join him in Jerusalem three days later. Amasa failed to keep the rendezvous and David decided to send all his available men against the rebels. He appointed Abishai as commander, thereby reducing Joab to third fiddle behind his brother and Amasa — a further signal of David's displeasure with his role in Absalom's death (20:4-7).

Amasa evidently caught up with them at **'the great rock in Gibeon'** and no doubt prepared to assume the supreme command of the royal army (20:8). Joab, however, had other plans. In a virtual repeat of his murder of Abner, he treacherously despatched Amasa with one blow of his dagger. His leadership so foully reasserted and the bloody corpse of his victim left in a field, discreetly covered with a cloak, Joab led the army off in pursuit of Sheba (20:8-13). Matthew Henry is on target when he remarks that 'David was struck at through the side of Amasa, and was, in effect, told to his face that Joab would be general, in spite of him.'[4] Joab epitomizes the ruthlessness of the amoral attitude that says, 'The end justifies the means.' Throughout his career, he was an intense loyalist for Israel and David — but always on his own terms. He simply disposed of those he regarded as a hindrance to David — and, by the by, to himself. And so, Abner, Absalom and Amasa perished treacherously by his hand and against the specific wishes of his royal master. David, for his part, had compromised with Joab's sins. He had not brought him to justice for the murder of Abner; he had 'helped to harden him in cruelty'[5] by engaging his assistance in the death of Uriah; and he had earned Joab's contempt for his authority by his

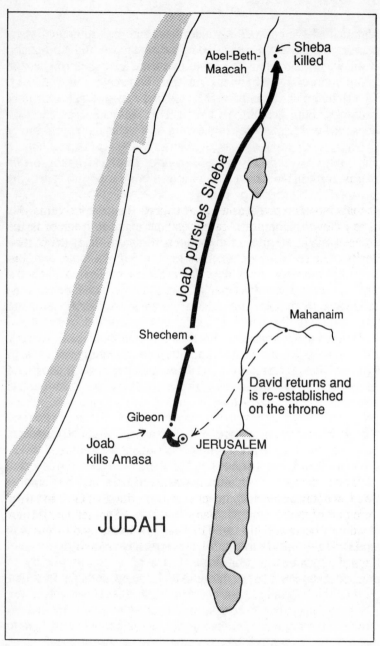

MAP 8 — Sheba's rebellion

pathetic behaviour over Absalom's death. The appointment of Amasa could, Joab reckoned, be swept aside with impunity, for David would do nothing. Joab was in the end like a besetting sin or a thorn in the flesh to David. David paid a price for Joab's talents. Only in dying did David give voice to the claims of justice against the wicked Joab and urge his son not to let 'his grey head go down to the grave in peace' (1 Kings 2:5-6).

Execution [20:14-22]

Sheba's rebellion had all but run its course. He did not command a large following, for all the earlier enthusiasm of the men of Israel to desert David. He appears to have retained only the loyalty of **'the Berites'** (better rendered: 'the Bicrites' — i.e., his own clan of the tribe of Benjamin[6]). Joab brought him to bay in the northern town of Abel Beth Maacah and conducted an orthodox siege of the place, building **'a siege ramp'** and **'battering the wall to bring it down'** (20:15).

While the final preparations for the assault were under way, **'a wise woman called from the city'** and asked to speak to Joab.[7] The ensuing conversation was to end the rebellion (with the death of Sheba) and save the city from sacking. The woman presented a threefold case (20:19).

1. The historic significance of Abel Beth Maacah as **'a city that is a mother in Israel'**. This was a place renowned for wisdom and good counsel. It was a part of the national cultural wealth of Israel. Why should it be destroyed?

2. The theological significance of the people, city and land as **'the Lord's inheritance'**. Israel was the heritage of God and they were part of that heritage (1 Samuel 26:19; 2 Samuel 21:3). How could they be swallowed up? They had title to the land in terms of the Lord's allocation to the tribes when they entered the land of Canaan under Joshua.

3. The unstated but underlying assumption was that Joab had forgotten that God's law prescribed that an offer of peace be made to any besieged city and that the city that accepted terms and opened its gates would be spared destruction (Deuteronomy 20:10-11). The woman would know that explicit rebuke from Scripture would cut

no ice with a man like Joab, but that a combination of lofty ideals and political advantage would influence him powerfully.

And so Joab once more had opportunity to exhibit his political sagacity by trading the city and, not least, the lives of many of his soldiers, for the head of Sheba (20:20-22). Better that one man, and the guilty party at that, die than let loose a blood-letting which would do no one any good for the future. With the sounding of the trumpet, peace was established. The final verses (20:23-26) confirm the re-established stability of David's rule. Significantly, Joab remains as the commander of the army, his position unassailable in spite of all his crimes.

Nevertheless, even in the death of Sheba, a note of grace is sounded. Just as the traitor must be delivered if the city is to be spared, so sin in the sinner must be given up for the whole man to be delivered. In its own way it is a parable of the gospel. The difference is, of course, that Jesus was not himself a rebel or a sinner, but 'became sin' in order to die as the Righteous One in the place of the unrighteous many. The self-destruction of the wicked is simply the wages of sin, but the self-sacrifice of the Son of God paid those wages for all who will believe in him and secured everlasting life for all who love him.

22.
The long arm of God's law

Please read 2 Samuel 21:1-22
'It is on account of Saul and his blood-stained house...' (2 Samuel 21:1).

In the summer of 1977, the United States was rocked by a series of terrible tragedies. California was parched by drought and scorched by forest fires. Floods in central Pennsylvania took many lives and recalled the devastating Johnstown Flood of 1889 that buried a whole city in one night. And the city of New York was terrorized by the 'Son of Sam' murders and the great 'black-out' in which over 2,000 shops were looted in a single night. Many people had cause to ask, 'What do these things mean?' And answers galore flowed from scientists, psychiatrists and sociologists.

Few, if any, of these media pundits had a fraction of the insight on these problems that Pharaoh's magicians had when, 3,500 years ago, they faced the plagues that had descended upon Egypt. The magicians had little conception of the secondary causes which so obsess us in our scientific age. They could not sample the blood-red waters of the Nile and send them to the laboratory for analysis; they had no zoologists to enlighten them about the mass irruptions of frogs and locusts; they had no 'science' with which to provide 'explanations' which are really little more than elaborate naturalistic descriptions of the events. And so, as supernaturalists — albeit heathen supernaturalists — they looked for ultimate answers. They duly put two and two together and arrived at the answer that it was all related to their confrontation with Moses and the Israelites and that, therefore, these calamities were 'the finger of God' (Exodus 8:19). They understood what modern secular man and secular modernist 'Christians' steadfastly refuse to admit — that God acts in history and that, consequently, there is a relationship between human behaviour and the events of history which can only be explained in terms of the interplay, on the one hand, of human sin and, on the other hand, of the long arm of God's law.

This is the issue which is addressed in 2 Samuel 21. It is first applied to the relationship between the Gibeonites, a Canaanite clan still living in Israel, and the Israelites, with particular reference to a past attempt by the late King Saul to apply the 'final solution' of genocide to the ongoing 'problem' of that subject people (21:1-14). It is then shown in action in the destruction of the Philistines and, on one occasion, the saving of David's life in battle (21:15-22). The arm of the Lord reaches out to vindicate his justice and call the guilty to account. But it is the same arm that is not shortened so that it cannot save.

Sin exposed [21:1-2]

The passage records that **'During the reign of David, there was a famine for three successive years.'** It is not clear at what point in David's reign the three-year famine took place. Current scholarship regards 2 Samuel 21-24 as an appendix to the historical narrative — the so-called 'Samuel Appendix'[1] — and therefore probably not in strict chronological order. Whatever the case may be, there is no doubt that the inspired historian recorded the circumstances of the calamity at this point in his narrative in order to focus attention on the same topic as chapters 19 and 20, namely, David's dealings with the supporters and descendants of the house of Saul. You will recall that as David fled from Absalom, Shimei had called him 'a man of blood' on account of his alleged treatment of the house of Saul (16:7-8). The likelihood is that this accusation arose from matters covered by 21:2-14 — the executions of Saul's grandsons.[2] The record of that incident is, accordingly, inserted in the text at this point in order to set the record straight. From the historian's viewpoint, this is an essential component in the account of David's restoration, for it proves him to be the Lord's king over against any residual commitment to the house of Saul, as represented by Shimei, Sheba and the Benjamites. David is held up as the righteous king who is vindicated by the Lord.

The first step towards this implied conclusion is the identification of the three-year famine with the sins of **'Saul and his blood-stained house'**. David had **'sought the face of the Lord'** because he knew that the famine bore a relationship of some kind to the ethical and spiritual condition of Israelite society (Deuteronomy 28:47-48). In modern terms, we might say that so-called natural disasters are never merely 'natural' but are invariably related to the sinful human condition and constitute one component in the dealings of God with the human race. David did not jump to conclusions about this. He did not speculate as to the reasons, or cast around for scapegoats. He enquired of the Lord by the prescribed means and it was revealed to him that the reason was that the late King Saul had **'put the Gibeonites to death'**.

The Gibeonites were an Amorite (Canaanite) people who had been spared annihilation when Israel entered the land. They had secured a treaty of peace with Israel by an ingenious deception (Joshua 9:3-15). When the Israelites discovered that they had been tricked, they nevertheless honoured their oath (cf. Psalm 15:4). This was the covenant which Saul had violated by attempting to annihilate the Gibeonites (21:2). The sin was compounded by the fact that whereas God had commanded Saul to extirpate the Amalekites (1 Samuel 15:3), he had given no such orders with respect to the Gibeonites. Years had passed since the crime, but God had not forgotten it and the famine was the initial impact of his retributive justice.

This remarkable instance of cause and effect and of sin and judgement illustrates three principles of God's dealings with men and nations, and most pointedly with his people, the church — for Israel was the church in the Old Testament period.

1. When Saul attacked the Gibeonites, he almost certainly did it in the conviction that it would be pleasing to God. Yet he had no warrant for so doing. God had told him to deal with the Amalekites, but he had substituted the easier, more convenient task of descending on the hapless Gibeonites. He decided to do what he wanted to do, when he knew very well exactly what God wanted him to do, and he clothed his disobedience in the fraudulent respectability of the notion that he was doing the Lord's work anyway. If you can't just sin boldly, you find a way of redefining it as 'good'! This method can easily be adapted to any aspect of life. Even gross breaches of the Ten Commandments have been justified in this way. Christian martyrs have been murdered under the pretence that it was God who required their deaths, while adulterers have justified themselves by arguing that the new 'relationship' was happier,

more stable and consequently more pleasing to God than the marriage which had been broken by their sin.

2. The troubles and events of history are not haphazard. Calamities are never 'the luck of the draw'. They are all personal providences, falling within the orbit of God's sovereignty — however inscrutable they may appear to be at the time. There is no reason for Christians to be squeamish about this. God is at work in the world and he is telling us something! The world may call it 'bad luck', but let Christians 'employ more God-honouring language' and realize that 'When the smile of God is withdrawn from us, we should at once suspect that something is wrong.'[3] Our first reaction ought to be to go to the Lord in prayer and, with Job, 'say to God: Do not condemn me, but tell me what charges you have against me.' For those who love Jesus Christ, the answer will not be long in coming, for God is a loving Father to his people: like every faithful father he disciplines his children. But as the altogether righteous God, he will crush his enemies and vindicate those they have oppressed. Floods and famines ought to concentrate our minds on the practical — and the ultimate — questions of our life, its meaning and destiny, and the claims of God.

3. It is a myth, although a very popular one, that 'Time' is 'a great healer'. 'Time' is no substitute for repentance and changing our ways. People may forget our past sins and the receding of reproach may seem like healing, but God never forgets because he will perfectly vindicate his law and those who have been wronged. For Israel, the Gibeonite massacre was at most a half-forgotten tragedy; for God, it was a reckoning that only waited for his sounding of the trumpet! This is the very nature of the true justice of the eternal God. No injustice will slip past him. When men seem to get away with things for a certain time, they feel they are in the clear — things have 'blown over' or 'cooled off'. But from the Lord's perspective nothing merely 'blows over'. There is no 'statute of limitations' with the justice of God.[4] He will judge the world with righteousness.

Justice for the Gibeonites [21:2-14]

We should note that the Gibeonites had never complained about Saul's pogrom. Like all oppressed and all-but-overwhelmed minorities, they just wanted to survive. Protest might only draw forth further cruelty and achieve the extinction for which Saul had striven so murderously. The victims kept quiet. It was the Lord who reopened the case with his three-year famine. David therefore approached the Gibeonites in order to redress the long-standing grievance. **'How shall I make amends,'** he asked them, **'so that you will bless the Lord's inheritance?'** (21:3).

The Gibeonite response and request (21:4-6)

The Gibeonite reply was as astute as it was restrained. In the first place, they were careful to observe both the proprieties of God's law and the vulnerability of their own situation as a subject people. They did not ask for monetary damages, because God's Word prohibits trading loss of life through murder for money. The death penalty was — and remains to this day — the proper punishment for murder (Numbers 35:31-33). 'Those over-value money and under-value life,' remarks Matthew Henry, 'that sell the blood of their relations for corruptible things, such as silver and gold.' Neither did they ask to be released from their serfdom under the Israelites, which would be a legitimate implementation of the law of restitution in Exodus 21:26: 'If a man hits a manservant or maidservant in the eye and destroys it, he must let the servant go free to compensate for the eye.'[5] They also recognized that they did not have the right to put anyone to death in Israel. In this way, they wisely laid the entire responsibility for justice upon David's decision as the chief magistrate of Israel. They were not without an idea of what they wanted, but they wanted David to understand that they were responding to him in a humble and genuinely aggrieved way as opposed to a proud and vindictive manner.

When David again asked what he could do, they asked that **'seven of [Saul's] male descendants be given to [them] to be killed and exposed before the Lord at Gibeah of Saul — the Lord's chosen one'** (21:5-6). This request is often regarded today as 'strange and repellent' because it involved the execution of seven supposedly 'innocent men'. It therefore is the current fashion to explain this 'in terms of the culture and attitudes of the age'.[6] This approach, however, casts an aspersion on the Lord, who led David to dispense this justice for the Gibeonites. It suggests that God was himself boxed in by the culture and attitudes of the age and felt compelled to allow this essentially reprehensible deed to be done to accommodate contemporary primitive notions of justice. Meanwhile we can feel good that we are more enlightened! An assessment of this kind, however, ignores the most simple and basic fact of all — a fact that has to be a basic interpretive principle for understanding what was going on in these events — namely that *God* approved of this as a just retribution for the original genocide by Saul. Charles Simeon rightly observes: 'Such a kind of retribution would not be justifiable among *us*; because the children are not to suffer for the parents' crimes [cf., Deuteronomy 24:16]: but, as ordered of God, it was right: and, if the whole truth were known, we would probably find that the sons of Saul had aided and abetted the wicked devices of their father; and that they therefore justly suffered as partners in his crime.'[7] It is significant that 'seven' only of the descendants of Saul were to be killed. This number represented the action of God and the completeness of his action.[8] The Gibeonites asked for the *minimum* number by which the justice so done could be seen to be the work of God rather than the revenge of men. Even in this, the Gibeonites showed a restraint which evidences a profound understanding of and submission to the canons of divine justice. David's response was to grant the request.

The execution of seven (21:7-9)

By the side of Loch Oich, on the road between Fort William and Inverness, in Scotland, there stands a well, called in Gaelic, *Tober n'an ceann'* — the 'well of the heads'. A monument with seven carved heads commemorates the washing there of the severed heads of the murderers of the young sons of Macdonald of Keppoch before they were presented by the executioners to the bereaved clan chief in token of accomplishment of justice, Highland style. When justice is done, it needs to be seen to be done, so that people may understand that God is not mocked. So David chose seven of Saul's house. He handed over the two sons of Saul by Rizpah and five grandsons, the sons of Saul's daughter Merab, taking care to exclude Mephibosheth, because of his covenant **'before the Lord'** with Jonathan, Saul's son (21:7). The seven were executed and their bodies hung up for public display at the time of the barley harvest, in token of the fact that famine had been God's means of bringing the sin of the house of Saul to light. The Scripture says that 'Anyone who is hung on a tree is under God's curse' (Deuteronomy 21:23).[9]

Rizpah's vigil (21:10-14)

The exposure of the bodies was itself an extraordinary exception to
the law of Deuteronomy 21:22-23, which prescribed burial before
nightfall so that 'the land' would not be 'desecrated'. The reason for
this was that 'the land' was God's inheritance and leaving a dead
body unburied was literally and symbolically to pollute that which
God had given.[10] The curse upon the executed evildoer was not to
be transferred to 'the land'. In this case, the opposite was the case.
It was 'the land' which was *already* cursed. The executions were for
the purpose of lifting that curse. Therefore the exposure of the
bodies lasted not only overnight but from the harvest, which was in
April, to the coming of rain, which might well have been the normal
rainy season in October! That is, it lasted until that which guaran-
teed the next harvest, and marked the cessation of God's judgement,
was an accomplished fact.

Rizpah's vigil spanned that period. She grieved over the sin that
had taken her sons from her. She mourned until their remains could
be buried properly. And in the meantime she prevented their
corpses from becoming carrion for wild animals — surely a most
remarkable instance of devotion to her sons (21:10). When David
heard of this, he was moved to gather the bones of Saul and his sons
and, with the remains of the seven, bury them in the tomb of their
father Kish (21:11-14). This marked the definitive settlement of
God's controversy with Israel over the Gibeonite massacre. His
grace once again blessed the crops of his people.

Destruction for the Philistine heroes [21:15-22]

The last section recounts how the long arm of God reached out in
a different direction, in this case to humble the might of the
Philistines. It is not clear at what points in David's reign these
encounters took place. Like the Gibeonite incident, they are recorded here by the inspired historian in order to demonstrate both
justice and mercy in God's dealings with his people: first calling
Israel to account over Saul's genocide of the Gibeonites, and now
showing his grace to David and Israel in destroying the power of

their Philistine enemies. They are a comment on David's life and career as the man after God's own heart. In their significance for us and our time, they are parables of the overthrow of wickedness and the outpouring of God's grace upon his believing people. We are not left to our own devices — neither to sin and get away with it, nor to face the enemy of our soul without the help of the Lord, who loves his own and will not let them go.

The first incident was evidently the last time that David led his men to battle in person and engaged in hand-to-hand combat with the enemy (21:15-16). Abishai rescued David from great danger by killing the Philistine giant Ishbi-Benob. The picture is of a David who, though still as brave as ever, does not have the staying power he once had. The passage need not be seen as out of chronological order, if this is indeed the older David reliving his youth and finding himself unequal to the task. The upshot was that **'David's men swore to him, saying, "Never again will you go out with us to battle, so that the lamp of Israel will not be extinguished"'**(21:17). David's value to the Lord's people was not to be hazarded by his playing foot-soldier in a mêlée. On this occasion the Lord preserved him through the skill and courage of Abishai but it had to become his policy in future to preserve himself from unnecessary danger.

The other three incidents record the killing, in combat, of Saph by Sibbecai the Hushathite (21:18), of 'Lahmi the brother of Goliath' by Elhanan (21:19, footnote, cf., 1 Chronicles 20:5)[11] and of the twelve-fingered and twelve-toed unnamed giant of Gath by Jonathan, David's nephew (21:21). So fell the last giants of the Philistines. 'David began his glory,' writes Matthew Henry, 'with the conquest of one giant, and here concludes it with the conquest of four. Death is a Christian's last enemy, and a son of Anak [i.e., a giant]; but through him that triumphed for us, we hope to be more than conquerors at last, even over that enemy.'[12] John Bunyan gave voice to this imperishable hope in his poetic characterization of the fighting saint:

> No lion can him fright,
> He'll with a giant fight,
> But he will have a right
> To be a pilgrim.

David points us to Christ, who has killed the giant of our sins and death itself. 'Through him who loved us' we 'are more than conquerors' (Romans 8:37).

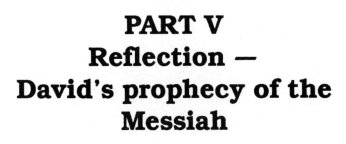

PART V
Reflection —
David's prophecy of the
Messiah

23.
The sufferings of the Messiah

Please read 2 Samuel 22:1-7 and Psalm 18

'In my distress I called to the Lord; I called out to my God' (2 Samuel 22:7).

Have you ever had to eat your words? Strange as it may seem, David was eating some of his own words when he wrote the song recorded in 2 Samuel 22! We are told that he **'sang to the Lord the words of this song when the Lord delivered him from the hand of all his enemies and from the hand of Saul'** (22:1). Yet, not long before, the same man had cried out in despair, 'One of these days I shall be destroyed by the hand of Saul' (1 Samuel 27:1). So he had something to shout about, something for which to praise the Lord, when he saw his deliverance following so swiftly and decisively upon his depression over Saul's relentless persecution. When God saved him from Saul, he was all the more exultant. He also knew that he had been saved from self-pity and the sinful doubt that the Lord would not preserve him as he had promised.

The song in 2 Samuel 22 is a version of Psalm 18. We have here, as C. H. Spurgeon notes, 'another form of this eighteenth Psalm with slight variations and this suggests the idea that it was sung by him on different occasions when he reviewed his own remarkable history, and observed the gracious hand of God in it all.'[1] It may be that the fuller version in the Psalter was David's final version for public use in the worship of God. The differences are fairly numerous, but the teaching is the same. Both are the inspired Word of God: the one set in a historical context, the other in the manual of praise.

A song about Christ?

This song arises from David's personal experience. It also came forth from his lips in the spirit of prophecy and some of its content strongly suggests that this prophecy is about the then promised Messiah, the Lord Jesus Christ. Certain of the psalms are clearly and explicitly messianic and are simply unintelligible apart from Jesus Christ. Whatever they meant to the psalmist, their true meaning is in the person and work of Christ. It is more difficult to establish the messianic status of other psalms, but two basic principles can enable us to identify those songs which speak of Christ.

The first principle is that where the text speaks of perfection of character, depths of suffering, deliverance, glory, or the extent of the kingdom in terms which go far beyond any correspondence with David and other aspects of Hebrew history, it can be taken as referring to Messiah, his sufferings and his kingdom. Jesus himself said there was much in the psalms written about him, which 'must be fulfilled' (Luke 24:44). For example, could David have said 22:21-25 only of himself, or did he utter this as it were in the place of Messiah?

The second principle is that whenever the New Testament quotes a psalm and refers it to Jesus — e.g. Matthew 22:44 (Ps. 110:1); Acts 2:25 (Ps. 16:10) — this is to be taken as the original and proper meaning of the inspired text. If the psalm speaks clearly of that person throughout, then that psalm is messianic. The significance of this for Psalm 18/2 Samuel 22 is Paul's quotation of 2 Samuel 22:50 in Romans 15:9, which, as H. P. Liddon observes, 'prophetically express[es], in the language of Jesus Christ, the praise which He, with His brethren converted from Heathendom, would offer to the Father'.[2] We see a similar usage in Peter's sermon on the Day of Pentecost. There he quotes Psalm 16:10 as fulfilled by the resurrection of Christ and notes that David, when he wrote Psalm 16, spoke as 'a prophet and knew that God had promised him on oath that he would place one of his descendants on his throne. Seeing what was ahead, he spoke of the resurrection of the Christ' (Acts 2:29-31). What this means is that such songs are fully messianic, in that they are ultimately intelligible only in reference to Christ. Christ is their true meaning. Christ has always been their true meaning. We know this because the infallible New Testament interpretation of these particular prophetic songs demonstrates this to be the case. 2 Samuel 22 is a song about the Lord Jesus Christ.

The psalmist speaks the words, as it were, from the mouth of our Lord.[3]

If this song is indeed ultimately about the Messiah who was to come, the question arises as to what it is doing in the context of the history of David nearly a thousand years before the Lord Jesus Christ was born. What was the intention of the inspired historian when he inserted this version of Psalm 18 at this point in his account of David's reign?

1. Whatever awareness David had of the prophetic element in his own utterances — and, for that matter, whatever understanding either he or the historian had of the prophecies involved — it is clear that the song was included because it articulated something of the essential significance of *David's personal experience* as the Lord's king over the Lord's covenant nation. It is a lyrical expression of David's personal relationship with his Lord in the context of his unique calling to rule over Israel in the Lord's name.

2. Equally clearly, this song of praise acknowledges *the unique calling of the people of God* in the world. It is Israel's paean to the Lord for his grace to Israel as the heavenly Autocrat-King who has blessed them through the ministry of his earthly theocrat-king. It asserts the rule of the Lord over all the nations in the interests of his covenant people and looks to the promise of God throughout all future generations.

It is not necessary to posit any comprehensive, or indeed anything more than a rudimentary, awareness on the part of the Old Testament writers of the prophetic goal of their own writing. Much — more — most remained to be revealed in the fulness of time. David had at least a sense of the destiny of God's people and Psalm 18 gives voice to that awareness. We, who read with New Testament hindsight, are shown the riches of both that which was revealed to David and Israel and that which was then veiled but is now revealed in Jesus Christ.

The Lord who is worthy of praise [22:2-4]

The song begins, as all worship must, with the adoration of Yahweh, the living God of the everlasting covenant. God is to be praised for who he is in himself. His essential being calls forth worship. In the 'final form' of the song, Psalm 18, the psalmist declares his love for God: 'I love you, O Lord, my strength' (Psalm 18:1). The focus of this love is in the way the blessings God has given him are used as names for God (22:2-3). He is:

1. **'my rock'** [Heb. *sela*] — the protection of inaccessible height;
2. **'my fortress'** — the armed defence of his servant;
3. **'my deliverer'** — the one who, literally, 'enables me to go forth';
4. **'my God'** — the heavenly Father who is the object of my worship;
5. **'my rock'** [Heb. *sur*] — my defence and defender;
6. **'my shield'** — armoured protection;
7. **'the horn of my salvation'** — a symbolic weapon (?);
8. **'my stronghold'** — a high tower.

Why are these metaphors heaped up in this way? Simply to impress upon us that God delights in doing good things for his people. He opens the windows of heaven and pours out his blessings (Malachi 3:10). Grace flows from the wellsprings of his being. God is love (1 John 4:16). Who God *is* determines what he *does*.

What God has actually done for the psalmist in his past personal experience elicits *prayer* in the face of troubles: **'I call to the Lord, who is worthy of praise'** and this in turn gives way to an *answer* to that prayer: **'I am saved from my enemies'** (22:4). Again, these are David's words in the midst of his affliction but also in prophetic anticipation of Christ in his humiliation, sufferings and death. Jesus was a man of prayer. As the incarnate Son of God he constantly prayed to his Father. The Father says to him, 'Ask of me, and I will make the nations your inheritance' (Psalm 2:8). Jesus' response was to pray, 'Father, I want those you have given me to be with me where I am, and to see my glory, the glory you have given me because you loved me before the creation of the world' (John 17:24). Our Lord's ministry of prayer is described in Hebrews 5:7-9: 'During the days of Jesus' life on earth, he offered up prayers and petitions with loud cries and tears to the one who could save him from death, and he was heard because of his reverent submission. Although he was a son, he learned obedience from what he suffered and, once made perfect, he became the source of eternal salvation for all who obey him.' Later we are told that Jesus 'always lives' to intercede in prayer for those he is saving through his own atoning sacrifice for sin (Hebrews 7:25). John Brown went as far as to say that 'The saving omnipotence of the Saviour is grounded in his intercession.'⁴ This is not to detract from the atonement itself as that which purchased salvation, but to emphasize that the application of redemption in the course of history is accompanied by the heavenly intercession of Christ. This intercession constitutes the ongoing extension of his power to save in the dynamic of the work of redemption in this fallen world.

Praise and intercession come together in the ministry of the Messiah. The Father is worthy to be praised precisely because he is the one who answers prayer. He pours out his saving grace upon believing prayer. He promises to deliver those who call to him in their troubles.

The sufferings of Christ [22:5-6]

These verses are a most evocative account of the sufferings of our Lord. As expressed by David, they arose from his persecution by Saul, but there is a fulness of meaning which can only refer to the Saviour in that humiliation which rose to its crescendo of suffering on Calvary's hill. These sufferings are variously described as **'waves of death...torrents of destruction...the cords of the grave'** and **'the snares of death'**.

Jesus was in a sense bound by 'the cords of death' when he took our human nature and assumed the 'very nature of a servant' (Philippians 2:7), for at his incarnation — from the moment of his conception in the virgin's womb — there was set in motion the process of his mediatorial 'obedien[ce] to death — even on a cross!' (Philippians 2:8; cf. Luke 24:46; Hebrews 2:17). The incarnation was necessary for there to be an atonement for sin. Therefore the whole of Jesus' life on earth was a submission to the 'cords of death'.

Jesus not only lived under the threat or anticipation of death — he did actually and really die! Having suffered unequalled physical and mental anguish upon the cross — the 'torrents of destruction' (i.e., the human evil for which he was taking the punishment) — and having cried out, 'It is finished!' he died. His soul flew to glory and his body was laid in the tomb. During those three days prior to his resurrection, Jesus experienced the state of death — that separation of spirit and flesh occasioned by sin; in Jesus' case, the sin of those for whom he died as substitute, for there was no sin of his own for which he should answer in this way. These also are 'the cords of the grave' and the 'snares of death'. They gripped his body and held it in the grave (Romans 5:12-14).

It is all this that puts in perspective the awful nature of the Lord's sufferings themselves. The reason for his death and the separation of his body and soul is also the reason for his birth to the virgin in the first place: he was to be the sacrifice for other people's sins! 'For death in man,' writes John Brown, 'is the wages of sin — physical evil is the punishment for moral evil.' Brown describes Jesus' sufferings unto death as violent, severe, numerous, fatal and penal — the last being the key to the violence encapsulated in the first four aspects, for Jesus' death was both sacrificial and substitutionary. The 'torrents of destruction' may be understood as the same torrents of evil by which the ungodly were overwhelmed. Jesus bore the effects of the sins of those whose place he was taking, and thus the effects of the wrath of God against that sin were borne in his suffering and death. This is what Jesus' atonement for sin cost!

Christ calls upon his Father-God [22:7]

'There is no such strait,' said David Dickson, 'but God can deliver out of it, no case so desperate as to make prayer needless or useless.'[5] The psalmist cried to God. Christ in his sufferings cried to God: **'In my distress I called to the Lord; I called out to my God.'** How could Jesus call to God, when he knew it was God who had laid upon him the iniquity of us all? Surely only because he accepted his affliction as from God — as just and necessary retribution for sin. That Jesus was no sinner himself makes his sacrifice what it was — a true atonement in which the just dies in place of the unjust to reconcile them to God. Furthermore, Jesus did not pray merely to escape from a terrible experience: he prayed for victorious deliverance in which he would 'see of the travail of his soul and be satisfied' (Isaiah 53:11, AV).

This is the heart of the prayer life of the Lord Jesus Christ. His prayers both 'in the spirit of prophecy' (e.g., Psalm 22; 40:11-17; 69:13-21) and those from 'the days of his flesh' (Matthew 26:39;

John 12:27-28; John 17:1-5) all breathe an air of absolute submission to his great and terrible self-sacrifice. That he is God the Son does not make it any easier. On the contrary, as the incarnate Son with a perfect human nature, his suffering is all the more intense, just because it is his essential sinless perfection which submits to the cords of death and the torrents of destruction for which others were entirely to blame! For God to become man itself implies a humiliation we shall never completely fathom; for the God-man to die for sinners implies a suffering that is utterly beyond our imagining. Jesus reminded us that there is no greater love than that which leads a man to lay down his life for his friends. How much greater the love of God incarnate, when he lays down his life for his enemies — to save them to be his friends!

God answers [22:7]

'From his temple he heard my voice; my cry came to his ears.' Jesus cries to the Lord from the state of death. We recall Jesus' own words about the parallel between himself and Jonah in the belly of the great fish (Matthew 12:39-40). The one great 'sign' given to all the sign-seekers in the New Testament era will be 'the sign of Jonah' — which is that as he was three days in the fish, so Jesus will be three days in the grave, and then — resurrection! But prior to his deliverance Jonah prayed (Jonah 2:1-9). He cried as one who was dead but who was submissive to the Lord in his death. And so it was with Jesus, only with infinitely greater profundity. Jesus cries from beneath the fatal mountain of human corruption, guilt and con-demnation. He cries from a hell of just judgement towards the heavenly temple of his Father. And God hears the beloved Son in whom he is well pleased! Why? Because that prayer is in perfect harmony with his will and because his love for the Son can never be deflected even by the ocean of human sin for which he briefly forsakes him, as he bears it in his body on the cross. The cry of dereliction — 'My God, my God, why have you forsaken me?' (Matthew 27:46) — is a mighty but fleeting echo of a breach soon healed in all the glory of the resurrection, ascension and exaltation of the risen Christ as King of kings and Lord of lords!

What this must mean for us is plain enough. Let me suggest three points of application.

1. *Jesus is the great high priest for lost men and women.* For every believer, he died our death for sin that we might live. He was both priest and sacrifice to mediate our reconciliation to our holy God. In this song which the Holy Spirit gave to David, we are given a glimpse of the cross, of the meaning of the sufferings and death of the Messiah, of the love of Jesus our Saviour in giving himself as the ransom for many (Matthew 20:28).

2. *Consider your personal relationship to Jesus Christ.* His death for sinners calls sinners to live for him. His absolute commitment actually accomplished salvation. It follows that those so saved cannot but feel the pull of practical discipleship to Christ. As the author and finisher of the Christian's faith, Jesus is both Redeemer and Exemplar — he gives new life and shows how new life is lived with fervour and commitment. Why then is there so much holding back, so much luke-warm service to the Lord? Does the love of Christ not draw you all to desire to worship him, to learn from his Word, to pray in secret and in the fellowship of the church, to witness to his grace, to live transparently holy lives?

3. *Learn to call upon the Lord!* There is nothing in the prayer life of Jesus like the spiritualized 'grocery lists' of flatly stated 'items' for prayer that blight so many prayers and prayer meetings. The prayers of Christ are from the depths! They are felt because they are the fruit of agony of soul. There is no reason why the most specific and detailed matters for prayer cannot be expressed with similar holy fervour, except for the influence of shallow trivializing attitudes in prayer. Trivialized prayers arise from trivialized views of Christ and of the meaning of discipleship. Truly and deeply to belong to Christ is the basis of genuine communion with him. 'He will hear us, if we are his,' says John Brown, 'Everything depends on this.'[6]

> 'Out of the depths I cry to you, O Lord;
>   O Lord, hear my voice.
> Let your ears be attentive
>   to my cry for mercy.
> If you, O Lord, kept a record of sins,
>   O Lord, who could stand?

But with you there is forgiveness;
  therefore you are feared.
I wait for the Lord, my soul waits,
  and in his word I put my hope.'

(Psalm 130:1-5)

24.
The deliverance of the Messiah

Please read 2 Samuel 22:8-30
'He brought me out into a spacious place' (2 Samuel 22:20).

The greatest tragedy in many experiences of affliction is not so much the affliction itself, great as that may be, as the inability to gain a measure of spiritual consolation and, indeed, victory in the face of a testing situation. The biblical pattern for facing troubles sets the problem squarely in the arena of a person's walk with God — his relationship with the Lord and his trust in the promises of God. Consequently, the resolution of any difficulty necessarily involves a three-part process in which the afflicted individual seeks help and deliverance from the Lord. The sequence is always: affliction; (believing) prayer; deliverance. The deliverance may or may not be physical, as in the healing of a sickness, but it is always spiritual, in terms of God's strength being perfected in our weakness. The refrain of Psalm 107 stands as a rubric for the Christian method of handling afflictions of all sorts: 'Then they cried out to the Lord in their trouble, and he delivered them from their distress' (vv. 6, 13, 19, 28). We must not stop with the troubles and wallow in self-pity. We must go on to trust the Lord and seek him in prayer as the one who can deliver us.

We have seen so far in 2 Samuel 22/Psalm 18 that Christ, speaking from David's lips as the psalmist spoke in the spirit of prophecy, gave expression to the anguish of his sufferings and **'in [his] distress... called to the Lord'** (22:7). We now turn to the answer to the prayer, which is the deliverance of the Messiah from his sufferings.

The deliverance of Christ [22:8-20]

The description is highly poetic, but must not, on that account, be assumed not to be referring to events in time and space. The literal and the metaphoric are mixed: they find awesome and real fulfilment in actual events. The speaker is Christ and the deliverance is his own, although it also speaks, more distantly, of the salvation of his people. The deliverance is in two phases.

The God who reveals himself (22:8-16)

God manifests himself through the 'preternatural agitation of the elements'.[1] God shows his hand in the so-called 'natural' elements: earthquakes (22:8-9), darkness (22:10-12) and great storms (22:13-16). These fulfil two functions: on the one hand they display the terrible wrath of God against the wickedness of men towards his Son and his people (Romans 1:18-32) and on the other hand, they demonstrate to those with the eyes of faith to behold it, that the same power of God is being exercised to save his people from all their enemies. The way you read these phenomena will, of course, depend on the nature of your relationship with the Lord. There is an analogy here with the preaching of the gospel, which Paul says is an aroma of Christ — to those perishing in unbelief 'the smell of death' and to those who are being saved 'the fragrance of life' (2 Corinthians 2:15-16). This surely touches our personal experience of, say, a thunderstorm. Some people hide under their beds. Others — like our children — glue themselves to the window-pane so as not to miss any of the show. Are the thunder and lightning just another weather phenomenon? The answer is 'Yes and no'. God's created order reflects the one who made it in certain ways. 'His lightning lights up the world; the earth sees and trembles' (Psalm 97:4). Yes, it is 'weather', but no, it is not 'just' weather! God is revealing his eternal power and Godhead for all to see, whether they reject it in unbelief or, by faith, see his hand at work![2] 'Mother Nature' is a pagan fantasy. The world of 'nature' is the world of God's providential hand, upon which we are called to look with a discerning eye. God's dealings with us are cosmic in scope. Man stands at centre stage surrounded by a creation which testifies of God — of the terror he is and will be to his enemies, and the consolation and encouragement he is and will always be to his believing people. The earth belongs to the Lord and all that is in it (Psalm 24:1).

The God who delivers his people (22:17-20)

God delivers his suffering servant(s) from the most difficult of experiences (22:17-20). Four figures are used to describe these afflictions: **'deep waters'** (v.17); a **'powerful enemy'** (v.18); **'the day of... disaster'** (v.19); and, by implication from the text, a place of confinement (v.20). These cover, in very few words, the widest range of human problems. How often do we feel overwhelmed or drowned by some difficulty; or assailed by hostile forces too great for us to handle; or suddenly crushed by some seemingly calamitous event; or simply trapped by circumstances which stifle and limit our freedom, our prospects, even our sense of being a person? Deliverance is freedom from all these stultifying elements of personal failure and oppression. 'Thou hast enlarged me when I was in distress,' says the psalmist, as he expresses the sense of relief he feels when the Lord has overthrown his various disabilities (Psalm 4:1, AV). The glue which binds this deliverance together is God's sovereign grace: **'He rescued me because he delighted in me'** (22:20). The gist of the passage's teaching is that 'The Messiah and his cause should be delivered from degradation and suffering, amid and by events of an extraordinary character, disordering the common course of nature... whether the words are understood literally or metaphorically, this is their meaning.'[3]

The fulfilment of these prophetic words about Christ must be found in the events surrounding the crucifixion and the resurrection of our Lord. There were the three hours of darkness as Jesus hung on the cross, the tearing of the veil in the temple, the shaking of the earth and the resurrection of certain 'holy people who had died' (Matthew 27:45-54). An earthquake also accompanied the resurrection (Matthew 28:1-4). This deliverance of Christ extends in due course to the church, which is his body. The New Testament church is preserved and protected in the general judgement of the reprobate segment of the Old Testament church: this was foretold in the prophets (Isaiah 28:14-18; Joel 2:28-32; Malachi 4:1-3) and fulfilled in the destruction of Jerusalem in A.D. 70 (Matthew 24:1-28).

But the church is also to be brought to completeness through a historical development which culminates in the second coming of Jesus Christ at the end of the age (Haggai 2:6-7; Matthew 24:29-31; Revelation 6:9-17; 8:3-5; 11:13-19; 16:17-21; 20:7-15). This is the eschatological hope of the Christian and the motivating force of his personal holiness and practical discipleship in daily life: because Christ is risen and coming again, every believer is assured of his or her deliverance — of sharing in the ultimate triumph of the Lord Jesus Christ!

The reason why [22:21-25]

Why did God deliver his servant the Messiah? Two reasons are advanced. The first is that Christ is the only perfectly righteous person who was born, lived and died upon this earth. This is clear in this passage. Verses 21 and 25 state the basic doctrine of Christ's perfect righteousness and are the 'book-ends' for verses 22:24, in which the practical obedience of Jesus is detailed as the evidence of the truth of the doctrine. You will notice how these verses focus on the nature of the person of Christ, saying the same things, both positively and negatively, only in slightly different ways.

Positively	*Negatively*
v.22. 'I... kept the ways of the Lord.'	'I have not... turn[ed] from my God.'
v.23. 'All his laws are before me.'	'I have not turned away from his decrees.'
v.24. 'I have been blameless.'	'I have kept myself from sin.'

Now, is this the *man* of Psalm 51? Or is he the Holy One of Israel? Surely we have confirmation in these verses that the speaker is indeed the Messiah, who in prophecy and in fact 'had no sin', but whom God made 'to be sin for us, so that in him we might become the righteousness of God'? This person is none other than 'the light of the world', in whom there is no darkness at all. This is the Lamb, without blemish, slain before the foundation of the world. This is Jesus Christ, the Righteous.[4] Jesus, and only Jesus, was sinlessly perfect in every aspect of his person and work. He took the penalty for sin, but had no sin of his own for which to answer.

A second reason for the deliverance of the Messiah is that he merited deliverance. He was entitled to all the blessings of his

heavenly Father. It is true, even if not stated in this text, that from
eternity to eternity there is an essential delight of the Father towards
the Son and the Son towards the Father. Nevertheless, in the
economy of the plan of redemption, the Father sends the Son, the
Son obeys the Father and the Father receives the sacrifice of the Son
as that which will satisfy his justice and simultaneously release his
loving forgiveness for all for whom the Son is the substitute. The
wrath of God upon the sin of sinners falls upon the incarnate Son,
Jesus Christ. But because Jesus was without sin himself, 'it was
impossible for death to keep its hold on him' (Acts 2:24), and he was
raised from the dead and exalted by his infinite merit to the right
hand of the Father. He merited not only his own deliverance from
death, but also the deliverance of those for whom he died. And in
this we come to the very heart of the gospel of saving grace in Jesus
Christ.

This raises the question as to how this can touch us? How does
the deliverance of Christ tie in with the deliverance of sinners like
you and me?

We must first grasp what Scripture means when it uncompro-
misingly declares that there is 'no one righteous, not even one'
(Romans 3:10; Psalm 14:3). This refers to every child of Adam. But
the one exception is Jesus Christ! He is the *only* righteous human
being (Luke 18:19). His righteousness is the only righteousness.
His good deeds are the only truly good deeds. All other 'righteousness' is 'like filthy rags; we all shrivel up like a leaf, and like the
wind our sins sweep us away' (Isaiah 64:6). Only through cleansing
from sin and the imputation and implantation of *his* righteousness
can we have any righteousness at all that is truly acceptable in the
sight of God.

When we talk about the 'merits of Christ', we are talking about
the basis of salvation itself. It is through faith in the all-sufficient
Saviour — the substitute for sin whose merits purchased redemption — that a person enters upon the experience of salvation. And
one of the first aspects of new-born Christian experience is the
awareness and confession that the believer has no 'merits' of his
own — all is of Jesus Christ. Our personal holiness is never self-
generated, but is the work of God in and through us. And always,
the 'merits of Christ' are the basis of our blessing — past, present
and future. This is why we end our prayers with the words, '... for
Jesus' sake, Amen'. Jesus paid the price and won the victory. For

his sake — the sake of honouring his redeeming work — we ask the
Lord to bless us.

The blessing of the faithful [22:26-30]

In Christ, justice and mercy are on the side of those who put their
trust in the Lord. The goodness of God flows unendingly into the
lives of believers. The very tone of the song becomes more
intensely personal. Hitherto, the psalmist spoke *about* God; now he
speaks directly *to* God. The immediate fruit of deliverance is a
closer communion with the Lord. The Messiah who cried in
dereliction, 'My God, my God, why have you forsaken me?' can
now speak in the confiding tones of unbreakable fellowship. What
is true of him is also the gift of grace to all who believe.

1. The Lord saves **'the humble'** but his **'eyes are on the
haughty to bring them low'** (22:26-28). God is perfectly just in all
his ways; as Paul says, he is 'just and the one who justifies those who
have faith in Jesus' (Romans 3:26).

2. The Lord leads and guides his people: he is their **'lamp'** and
their **'help'** (22:29, 30). 'The Lord is my light and my salvation —
whom shall I fear?' (Psalm 27:1). Three reasons are given here for
the earlier stated fact of God's faithfulness with the righteous and
the wicked alike: the first is that he is the God who *saves* — who
renews the *heart* (v.28); the second, that he is the God who is *light*
to dispel any darkness from his people — he also renews the *mind*
(v. 29); and the third reason is that he is the God who gives *power*
to enable his people to win through against whatever obstacles may
bar their way — he renews our *hands* that we may do great things
for him (v. 30). 'The renewal of heart, head, and hand,' says James
Murphy, 'or of the affections, apprehensions, and powers, is the
restitution of all things in man.'[5] All who love the Lord Jesus Christ
are new creations! (2 Corinthians 5:17).

'It is a delightful truth,' observes John Brown, 'that the Messiah
has not only obtained these blessings for himself by his merciful-
ness, uprightness, and purity, but that he has secured similar
blessings to all his true followers. They are freed from guilt, and
restored to the Divine favour, on the ground of all his perfect surety-
righteousness, which was the price equally of his exaltation and
their salvation, and they are, through the effectual operation of his

Spirit, conformed to his image, and made, like him, merciful and upright and pure. None but such are Messiah's people.'⁶ May the Lord so bless us all with his infinite love and matchless grace.

> And can it be, that I should gain
>   An interest in the Saviour's blood?
> Died he for me, who caused his pain —
>   For me, who him to death pursued?
> Amazing love! how can it be
>   That thou, my God, shouldst die for me?
>
> No condemnation now I dread;
>   Jesus, and all in him, is mine!
> Alive in him, my living Head,
>   And clothed in righteousness divine,
> Bold I approach the eternal throne,
>   And claim the crown, through Christ my own.
>
>   (Charles Wesley, 1707-88)

25.
The kingdom of the Messiah

Please read 2 Samuel 22:31-51
'He gives his king great victories...' (2 Samuel 22:51).

The psalm comes to a conclusion with a ringing acclamation of the kingly rule of the Lord's Anointed over the nations. The apostle Paul, in keeping with the messianic prophetic thrust of the Old Testament revelation in general and the prophetic role of David in particular (Acts 2:30-31), quotes the penultimate verse as fulfilled in the extension of salvation to the nations of the world through the atoning death and resurrection of the Lord Jesus Christ: 'For I tell you that Christ has become a servant of the Jews on behalf of God's truth, to confirm the promises made to the patriarchs so that the Gentiles may glorify God for his mercy, as it is written: "Therefore I will praise you among the Gentiles; I will sing hymns to your name"' (Romans 15:8-9, quoting 2 Samuel 22:50/Psalm 18:49). The only person who can truly praise God 'among the Gentiles' in terms of the fulfilment of the prophecy is Christ himself.[1] Furthermore, when we take into account those sections of the song which appear to transcend any reference to David and can only be fully intelligible in terms of fulfilment in Christ (22:5-7, 21-25, 44-46), the understanding of the song as messianic in nature seems not only consonant with the general thrust of the text but essential to its correct interpretation and application. This is not only a song *about* Christ, but a song *of* Christ — put, to be sure, in the mouth of David, but in the spirit of prophecy as a foretaste of the actual victory and exaltation of Christ. From this perspective, the song expresses Christ's delight in the Father (22:2-4), his distress in dying for sinners (22:5-7), his deliverance from his sufferings (22:8-20), the reasons for this deliverance (22:21-30), the establishment of his kingly rule over the nations (22:31-46) and the praise of Christ the

King as he is exalted in the final triumphant consummation of the everlasting kingdom of God in glory (22:47-51).[2] The triumph of Christ is also the deliverance and victory of the Lord's people. 'Christ's victories are common to him and his followers,' observes David Dickson.[3] David's elevation to the theocratic kingship in Israel and the instatement of New Testament Christians as 'a kingdom and priests to serve his [Christ's] God and Father' (Revelation 1:6) both centre upon the victory of Christ in his death and resurrection. Because he lives, all who believe in him will live; because he reigns as King over all, his people will reign in him!

God is a shield [22:31-37]

The only *source* of justified confidence is in the acts and the word of God. **'As for God, his way is perfect; the word of the Lord is flawless'** (22:31). 'God' is '*the* God' in the Hebrew (*ha-el*), thereby emphasizing his exclusive claims.

The *effect* of this truth is that **'He is a shield for all who take refuge in him'** (22:31). This thought reappears verbatim in one of Agur's sayings (Proverbs 30:5). God's perfection is his people's protection. He is as good as his word. The remainder of the section explains what it means to be surrounded with God's favour as with a shield (Psalm 5:12). Notice the progression of thought, remembering that the psalmist speaks prophetically of Jesus Christ, and, in him, of all the people of God.

1. God is *behind* his servant. He is the eternal underlying support and sustainer. God alone is **'the Rock'** (22:32). All other gods are phantasms — the pseudo-rocks of blinded minds, which in their own way will prove the undoing of their followers. Like an eternal Gibraltar, the Lord stands as the only true refuge and strength for humanity: 'All other ground is sinking sand.' God's sovereignty is the security of believers.

2. God is *with* his servant in his time of testing. God gives the **'strength'** and guidance which are needed to win the victory: **'God makes my way perfect'** (22:33-36). The imagery speaks of speed — **'the feet of a deer'**; unwavering faithfulness — **'to stand on the heights'**; skill — **'hands for battle'**; and strength — **'my arms can bend a bow'.** But most important of all is salvation itself, **'the shield of victory'**, which, in turn, is closely related to the fact that

that the Lord chose in his love to **'stoop down'** (i.e., he was willing to listen to us when we called upon him) and so make us **'great'**.

3. God also goes *ahead* of his servant and prepares the circumstances that lie ahead for us: he **'broadens[s] the path'** we must travel, removing the rougher spots upon which we might turn an ankle (22:37). We are brought full circle: those that love the Lord will not stumble when he is their Rock!

Enemies defeated [22:38-43]

The psalmist 'proclaims in the Spirit the ultimate defeat of all the enemies of the kingdom of God'. 'This Messianic element,' Keil and Delitzsch go on to say, 'cannot be mistaken.'[4] The imagery comes, of course, from the wars in which David had so signally defeated the enemies of God's people. Its meaning cannot stop there, however, for it must point prophetically to the victory of Christ in the subduing of all his enemies. It encompasses the progressive subjugation of sin in all its forms. For the Lord Jesus Christ, and ultimately also for us, this began with his sufferings and death, which his enemies meant to be the end of him and of all he had taught and done in his ministry upon earth. The resurrection signalled their failure to stop him and, just because it was the complete reversal of death, also won salvation for the elect out of every generation, through the efficacy of his death as a sacrifice for sin! From that once-for-all atonement, the saving grace of Christ progressively rolls back the rule of the 'kingdom of darkness' through the binding of Satan (John 12:31; cf. Mark 3:27; Luke 10:17-18; 11:20), the conversion of men and women to Christ in the extension of the church (Acts 2:47), and in his mediatorial kingship over 'everything for the church' (Ephesians 1:22), which restrains and punishes human wickedness and provides for the spreading of the gospel 'from sea to sea and to the uttermost parts of the earth'. Nothing less than the eschatological triumph of Christ and his church is in view!

The language is neither pretty nor gentle. This reminds us that not all God's victories are happy conversions in which his former enemies come to him in repentance and faith. Christ will pursue, crush and destroy his foes. In desperation, but still in unbelief, they will call to their gods for help — and may even call out to the Lord.

But **'there was no one to save them'** (i.e., their gods inevitably fail them). Neither will the Lord answer them, for, it is clearly implied, they are not repentant, only frantic. The totality of Christ's victory and the awful intimation of the 'second death' and the Day of Judgement ring forth in the final verse of this section: **'I beat them as fine as the dust of the earth; I pounded and trampled them like mud in the streets'** (22:43). How solemn it is to reflect on the fact that the consummation of God's kingdom will require the panoply of divine power to crush every vestige of unbelieving resistance to his will!

It is worth pointing out that this militant language is symbolic of the acts of God and does not provide a basis for the militarization of Christian witness in the world. The weapons of the church's warfare are always to be spiritual. The notion that the gospel may be spread by politico-military action has no support in Scripture. Charlemagne's forced 'conversion' of the Saxons, the misnamed 'Crusades' (wars of the cross) to establish Christian kingdoms in the Holy Land and innumerable persecuting attempts to force religious conformity upon free consciences by the sword and the whip are an offence to the gospel of Christ. The victories of the church militant are the triumphs of grace and truth in peaceable submission to the Lord before whatever hindrances the world may offer. *Our* task is to obey Christ; Christ has said that *he* will overcome the world!

The King of the nations [22:44-46]

It is sobering to realize that it was the Lord's people who demanded that Jesus be put to death. Just as he warned his disciples, so it was for himself: 'A man's enemies will be the members of his own household' (Matthew 10:36; cf. Micah 7:6). 'He came to that which was his own, but his own did not receive him' (John 1:11). The words, **'You have delivered me from the attacks of my people'** (22:44), reach beyond the experience of David with Abner, Absalom and Sheba and describe with painful candour the circumstances surrounding Jesus' death and resurrection. Those whom the Lord could call **'my people'** — the church of the Old Testament, the covenant community, the Jews — were the first great obstacle to the gospel. Even Christ's temptation by Satan in the wilderness seems overshadowed by the apostate unbelief of these erstwhile covenant people. The pagan Pilate would have let Christ go; the pious Pharisees and the people of God insisted on his crucifixion! And what has changed in Jesus' treatment at the hands of much of what calls itself the church today? Is it not so-called 'Christian leaders' who insist that Jesus was just a man and not the Son of God, that there is no such thing as a penal substitutionary atonement, that the Bible is a collage of human fables and traditions, that there was no bodily resurrection of our Lord and that there will be no Second Coming and Day of Judgement, that the morals of the Ten Commandments are outmoded and impractical and that God may even be dead? We cannot blame the pagans for the decline of the mainstream denominations of Western Christendom. It has been largely the work of those who *outwardly* were the Lord's people, but who are essentially *inwardly* opposed to the Lord and his gospel! And beginning with the Pharisees and their ilk, they persecuted the true people of God. John Brown points out that Jesus' challenge to the future apostle, Paul, on the Damascus road highlights this fact. Jesus said, 'Saul, Saul, why do you persecute *me*?' (Acts 9:4, my emphasis). To persecute the Christians was to persecute the Messiah and to persecute the Messiah was the last thing a true Jew should have been doing! But that was the sorry state of the latter-day Old Testament church, and was the reason for the destruction of the temple in A.D. 70 and the end of the Jewish theocracy.[5] 'When the Jewish polity was destroyed, the cause of Christ was delivered from the strivings of the people. They had no longer the means of persecuting Christians.'[6]

Reformation and revival in the church is the Lord dealing with this recurring problem and is an essential component in the establishment of his kingship over the nations. He is first the King and Head of Zion (the church) and then head over everything 'for the church' (Ephesians 1:22). The remaining verses (22:44-46) likewise look beyond the terror of the little kingdoms around Israel, who were cowed by the power of David, to the extension of the lordship of Christ among the nations of the world. Christ becomes **'the head of the nations'**. This is true in different ways.

1. Foremost is the way of faith: **'People I did not know'** come to Christ (22:44). Peter reminds New Testament Christians that

they are a 'chosen people' and explains that 'Once you were not a people, but now you are the people of God' (1 Peter 2:10). Christ conquers his elect by sovereign saving grace.

2. The alternative is subjugation through condemnation (22:45-46). Those who steadfastly reject Jesus Christ will eventually acknowledge the truth as the reprobate lost in hell. They **'come cringing'**. They **'obey'**, not with the obedience of faith, but with the grudging resignation of those who dig their own graves. They **'lose heart'** and surrender **'their strongholds'** with the gravest foreboding (Hebrews 10:27).

The everlasting kingdom [22:47-51]

'The Messiah now glories in the perpetuity of his kingdom as secured by the eternity of Jehovah.'[7] Through the words of David we are given a prophetic glimpse of the relationship between Jesus, the incarnate Son, and God the Father. Three points are brought out.

1. Christ praises the Father (22:47). He **'lives'** and is his Messiah's **'Rock'** and **'Saviour,'** worthy of the praise of his servant and his exaltation over all as the living God.

2. Christ gives thanks for the blessings the Father has bestowed upon him (22:48-49). He repeats the earlier points about deliverance from his enemies and exaltation above his foes.

3. Christ rejoices in his everlasting kingdom (22:50-51). We return to the theme of the song, as infallibly interpreted by the apostle Paul in his quotation of 22:50 in Romans 15:9 — namely that it is in Christ that salvation comes to the nations. The focus of this extension of the kingdom of God, **'David and his descendants for ever'**, is not 'David as an individual, but David and his seed for ever, — that is to say, the royal family of David which culminated in Christ'.[8] Only in terms of the kingship of Jesus Christ can we conceive of an everlasting and all-conquering kingdom (Psalm 72:8-11). He is the one to whom all men must answer, because 'all authority' has been given to him in heaven and on earth (Matthew 28:18). God says to men and nations,

'Kiss the Son, lest he be angry
   and you be destroyed in your way,
for his wrath can flare up in a moment.
   Blessed are all who take refuge in him'

(Psalm 2:12).

'How pitiable,' writes John Brown of Edinburgh, 'the situation of men without God, without Christ, in the world. In the day of deep distress God only can help them, but they know not God; Christ only can intercede for them, but they know not Christ. They may cry on God, but if not in faith, in penitence, in dependence on Christ, they cry in vain. It is only in Christ. He is the answerer of prayer. We must come to Christ, that we may be brought to God.'[9]

Part VI
Recessional — David's last days

26.
Last words

Please read 2 Samuel 23:1-7
'These are the last words of David' (2 Samuel 23:1).

The record of David's last days is spread over no fewer than twelve chapters in 2 Samuel (23:24), 1 Kings (1-2) and 1 Chronicles (22:29). These chapters describe both the close of David's reign and life and the commencement of the reign of his son and successor, Solomon. The 2 Samuel account ends without recounting David's death, leaves out everything relating to the succession arrangements and is content to bring us to the threshold of post-Davidic Israel and no more. The emphasis of 2 Samuel 23-24 is on the great themes of the establishment of the Davidic kingdom and the promise of God's everlasting covenant concerning a king of the house of David. The practical details — and the internecine wranglings — attending Solomon's accession are left for other chroniclers and, as it happens, more appropriate settings. 2 Samuel is not concerned with merely logging the facts as they arose, but with a rounded account of the completion of the work of God among his people that began with Samuel, the last of the judges, and ushered in a new era of theocratic rule in the person of David.

The final section of 2 Samuel opens with the 'last words' of David (23:1-7). Since there is a second and entirely different set of 'last words' in 1 Kings 2:1-12 — David's 'charge' to Solomon as he succeeds to the throne of Israel — the question arises as to which are truly the king's last words. Irrespective of the precise chronology of these utterances, there is no reason to see any essential contradiction between them as final statements in their own right and in their own contexts. They cannot be conceived as rival accounts of what David literally said last before departing this life. 2 Samuel 23:1-7 has the character of a prophetic postscript to the preceding psalm (22:1-51) and perhaps to all those inspired songs penned by David in which the kingship of Christ is the focus.[1] This appears to be a prepared public testimony for the entire nation, issued in prospect of the king's passing. In contrast, the 'last words' of 1 Kings 2 are personal words for his son. Since they do seem to be set in the context of the king's imminent death, it may be argued that they are chronologically his last utterance in this life. Even so, it is not impossible that the order is reversed: that since David's charge to Solomon to put Shimei to death cannot be proved to be given immediately before his death, 23:1-7 may well have been his literal last words — written earlier perhaps but now recalled with life's last breath and inserted earlier in the account by the inspired historian in order to make the connection with 22:1-51/Psalm 18 all the clearer. In any event, the chronology is of little concern to the historian for the account as a whole is a kind of recessional — a solemn accompaniment to David's withdrawal from the stage of history — which at the same time restates, as already noted, the continuing promise of God's everlasting covenant with his people, even in the passing of their shepherd-king.

Matthew Henry aptly describes this as 'the last will and testament of King David'.[2] R. P. Gordon calls it 'his enduring legacy to Israel' and notes that it conveys 'both the vitality of the dynastic hope and the idealizing of the Davidic king in inchoately messianic terms'.[3] It reminds us, observes Peter Ackroyd, ' of the last words of blessing pronounced by Jacob on his sons, as representatives of the tribes (Gen. 49), and... that of Moses (Deut. 33)'.[4] These lofty theological themes are vital for our understanding of the significance of David's words in the unfolding of God's redemptive purposes as they have since been revealed in Jesus Christ and the fulness of the gospel of his sovereign grace. There is, however, a more prosaic but no less vital element in David's 'last words'. And it is the fact that these words represent in part David's preparation for his own death. Here is where David's experience touches ours. To be sure, he stood in the stream of redemptive history that led to the advent of the Lord Jesus Christ. His role was unique in the unfolding of God's purposes. But his uniqueness does not obliterate the fact that he was like every other child of God, in that he lived and died. If anything, his role as the Lord's anointed king and the sweet psalmist of Israel lifts him up as a model and exemplar as to how each child of God ought to prepare for death. Every generation, excepting those who are alive at the Lord's return (1 Thessalonians 4:16-17), will have their own 'last days' on this side of eternity. Preparation for death ought never to be seen as a morbid exercise. 'When we find death approaching,' says Matthew Henry, 'we should endeavour both to honour God and edify those about us with our last words. Let those that have had long experience of God's goodness and the pleasantness of wisdom... leave a record of that experience and bear their testimony to the truth of the promise.'[5] The virtual disappearance from Christian literature of death-bed accounts and recorded last words is a sad and significant loss. This is probably a reflection not only of the prevailing squeamishness about death, even among Christians, but also of the fact that, except for those who die suddenly and unexpectedly, we tend to end our days under sedation — and, worse, alone — in a hospital or nursing home. We may thank the Lord for pain-killing drugs, but this must not lead us also to anaesthetize our meditation about, and preparation for, eternity. It is in the face of death that a living faith in Jesus Christ shines most brightly in the depths of the Christian's being.

The thought of David's poem begins with the *proofs of God's blessings* throughout his life, even to the threshold of eternity (23:1-4), goes on to state the *promises of future blessing* in terms of God's everlasting covenant (23:5) and concludes with an implicit *charge to prepare to meet the Lord* who, while he keeps mercy for thousands and forgives 'wickedness, rebellion and sin,' will not 'leave the guilty unpunished' (Exodus 34:7). There is nothing automatic about salvation, for it is all of the free grace of God received in the context of an obedient response to the claims of the Word of God.

Proofs of past and present blessing [23:1-4]

Three evidences of the Lord's blessing hitherto are now adduced. These are David's exaltation by God from shepherd boy to a national prominence, his prophetic role as the vehicle of the inspired Word of God in the psalms and his glorious privilege to serve as the Lord's king over the Lord's people.

'The man exalted by the Most High' (23:1)

The first verse notes both the humble origins of the king, as the **'son of Jesse'**, and the fact that he was raised to high position by the Lord: he was **'exalted by the Most High... anointed by the God of Jacob'** and made **'Israel's singer of songs'**. The last two clauses expand upon the first: David was exalted by God in two major respects — he was anointed *king* and was given to provide *songs* (the psalms) for the praise of God by his people. These were subsequently to be incorporated in the canon of Scripture. The kingly and prophetic offices were combined in him in a most significant measure — a fact presaging the fulness of the threefold office of Jesus Christ, who is King, Prophet and Priest as the Mediator between God and man. The basic point, however, is that David did not make himself great, but was, by the free and sovereign grace of God, elevated to the pinnacle of earthly spiritual and temporal leadership over the covenant people of God. We are surely reminded of the truth that before we came to a saving knowledge of Jesus Christ, we were 'not a people', but now are, in Christ, 'a chosen people, a royal priesthood, a holy nation, a people belonging to God' (1 Peter 1:9-10; cf. 2 Corinthians 1:21-22). The prevailing experimental element in belonging to the Lord through saving faith in Christ is that of a deeply personal love for the Lord for giving his salvation and all his gifts to us, in spite of our not deserving the least of his benefits.

'His word was on my tongue' (23:2)

As Israel's singer of songs, David was given the words by the Holy Spirit. The doctrine of the inspiration of Scripture is embedded in embryo in this verse: **'The Spirit of the Lord spoke through me: his word was on my tongue.'** Before he ever spoke or wrote, David listened to the Lord. The psalms did not originate with the psalmist, for all that they arose in the context of his personal experience. 'For prophecy never had its origin in the will of man,' explains Peter many centuries later, 'but men spoke from God as they were carried along by the Holy Spirit' (2 Peter 1:21). This is 'verbal inspiration' in action, producing the Word of God in written form for all succeeding generations.

'He is like the light of morning at sunrise' (23:3-4)

From what the Lord spoke *through* David, attention moves to what the Lord said *to* his chosen king. Some have seen an intimation of the triunity of God in the successive references to the Spirit of the Lord (23:2), the God of Israel (taken to be the Father, 23:3) and the Rock of Israel (taken to be the Son, 23:3; cf. 1 Corinthians 10:4).[6]

God first describes, almost in passing, the duty of his king to rule **'in righteousness'** and **'in the fear of God'**. This not only applies to David, but to human governments in general. The American 'Pledge of Allegiance,' for example, rightly includes the phrase 'one nation, under God'. All nations and all governments are 'under God', whether or not they admit it. All are called to 'kiss the Son' (Psalm 2:12) — i.e., to serve the Lord Jesus Christ — in terms of God's prescription for the righteousness of nations, namely justice, as defined by biblical norms of righteousness, and the fear of God as the overriding motive for public service.

In the second place, we have a description of the character of the godly king. He is like the morning sun and the bright sun after the rain. The former comes after the darkness of night; the latter produces the richness of a good harvest. On the one hand, the godly king saves his people from the dark experiences of the past, while on the other, he nurtures their growing prosperity. This had indeed been the general experience of Israel in the transition from Saul to David and in the development of the kingship under David. But history and prophecy overlap in David and point to the Son of David, Jesus Christ, the messianic King of kings and Lord of lords. In Psalm 72:6, Solomon uses the language of verses 3-4 with respect to the rule of the godly king and, as with his father's words, the significance transcends any immediate reference to his own rule and kingdom. The messianic implication is inescapable. The coming of Christ is in view. Ultimately, the fruit of the land *is* Jesus Christ, the 'Branch of the Lord' (Isaiah 4:2). He is the ultimate

Davidic king, under whose sceptre his believing people will enjoy the goodness of God both in time and in eternity.

From David's perspective, his life had been filled with the favour of God and he had seen the goodness of God poured out upon Israel. These blessings were proof positive of the love and faithfulness of the Lord towards his people and his servant David. They could not but promise good things for the future.

Promises of future blessing [23:5]

David responds to what the Lord had just said to him about the blessedness of his king with what Matthew Henry rightly describes as 'a most excellent confession of faith and hope in the everlasting covenant'.[7] David goes back to the promise God has made to him earlier in his reign and asks the question: **'Is not my house right with God? Has he not made with me an everlasting covenant, arranged and secured in every part?'** (23:5). Had not God said, 'The Lord declares to you that the Lord himself will establish a house for you: When your days are over and you rest with your fathers, I will raise up your offspring to succeed you, who will come from your own body, and I will establish his kingdom', and 'Your house and your kingdom shall endure for ever before me; your throne shall be established for ever'? (7:11-16). David's house had already seen a great deal of trouble and was to see considerably more in the years ahead. Not everything in David's garden was green and fruitful! Nevertheless, he had been preserved by the Lord, and for all the imperfections of his progress his dynasty was established upon the throne of Israel. But beyond that, as we have already seen in our exposition of 2 Samuel 7, was the promise of the final King, who would be descended from David — 'the Saviour Jesus' (Acts 13:23). Charles Simeon perceptively observes that this means that we are never to conclude that 'this covenant related exclusively to the succession of his [David's] posterity upon the throne of Israel, or even to the advent of the Messiah from his loins, it can be no other than that covenant which God made with his own Son, and with us in him; for no other covenant corresponds with the description here given of it... That covenant relates to the salvation of a ruined world by the blood and righteousness of the Lord Jesus.'[8]

As far as David's personal destiny is concerned, the nature of

God's covenant assures him that the Lord will '**bring to fruition [his] salvation and grant... [his] every desire**'. This verse is not the easiest to translate and it is possible that the last clause may refer, not to David's 'every desire', but to the good pleasure of God.[9] If so, we have a very elegant conjoining of the joy of the one who is saved and the pleasure of the one who does the saving. Either way, the practical point for us is the same: all of our hope and joy ought to centre in God's covenant of grace with us in Jesus Christ. Living faith is covenant relationship. 'Study then the wonders of this covenant,' cries the enraptured Simeon as he concludes his comment on this verse, 'that they may be familiar to your minds in a time of health; and so shall they fill you with unutterable peace and joy, when every other refuge shall fail, and your soul be summoned into the presence of God.'[10]

Prepare to meet your God! [23:6-7]

The botanical allusion to the 'fruition' of David's salvation (v.5) is taken up by way of contrast in the illustration of the judgement of '**evil men**' as the casting aside of '**thorns**'. Just as thorns are handled with the appropriate implements — '**a tool of iron or the shaft of a spear**' — and will ultimately be burned in the fire, so the wicked who reject the Lord will be subjected to the sword of divine justice and be cast into the fire of a lost eternity. 'You will rule them,' says the psalmist of the Lord Jesus Christ, 'with an iron sceptre... his wrath can flare up in a moment' (Psalm 2:9, 12).

If David's song ends on this dismal note, it is only the Lord's way of driving home the point that he alone is able to save his people and that his covenant is no mere option for a more meaningful life, but is the great divide between the saved and the unsaved, in time and for all eternity. There is a window of grace, for the moment, through which the Lord is calling men and women to repent, believe in Christ and receive eternal life. But the time is short and death will make our decision final. The solemnity of the warning against intransigent unbelievers calls us to prepare to meet our God and highlights all the more brilliantly the joy and security of those who love the Lord and are resting upon his everlasting arms. These 'last words' of David may or may not have been the last syllables he uttered on earth, but they do constitute his preparation to meet with his Lord. These are the thoughts that can clothe a dying man's soul with serene assurance and holy confidence.

You will perhaps have noted that the focus of David's meditation is not on morbid introspection and the minute examination of his motives and feelings. It is upon the work of God and his own exercise, by God's grace, of faithfulness and blessing in his calling as a child of God. There is a word for all of us here as we live our lives in prospect of death and eternity. Archibald Alexander, the great theologian of Princeton, New Jersey, puts it better than anyone when he records that he is 'not of the opinion... that the best way to make preparation for death is to sit down and pore over the condition of our own souls, or to confine our exertions to those things which are directly connected with our own salvation. We are kept here to do our Master's work and that relates to others as well as ourselves. We have a stewardship of which we must give account... and it will not do to relinquish the proper work of our calling, upon the pretext of seeking our own salvation.'[11] His point is that active discipleship, while we have the energy and the opportunity, is the best preparation for eternity. And that means the practical living of life in covenant with God. Alexander even anticipates the objection that the aged and infirm can do little or nothing for God. 'They can do much,' he says (he was himself seventy-two years old when he wrote these words), 'and for aught they can tell, more than they ever did in the days of their vigour. It is a beautiful sight to see men laden with fruit, even in old age. Such fruits are generally more mature than those of earlier days; and the aged saint often enjoys a tranquillity and repose of spirit, which is almost peculiar to that age.'[12] David's last words breathe the spirit of active discipleship. He knows his Redeemer. He knows where he is going. He believes the promises of God for the future. He rejoices in his salvation.

27.
Last lessons

Please read 2 Samuel 23:8-24:25
'I have done a very foolish thing' (2 Samuel 24:10).

Anyone who has watched 'the Oscars' being presented each year to the leading film-makers, actors, special-effects artists, and the like, will recall how self-consciously the recipients of that coveted award take time to thank almost everybody they can think of who, in their estimation, contributed to their success — and how thin and unconvincing much of this gratitude seems to sound. It is bad form to take all the glory to oneself, of course, but even where there is sincere gratitude for the help of others, the best of human beings do not naturally find it easy to give away much of the praise for their accomplishments. The greater our achievements in the world's eyes, the greater is the temptation in our own eyes to attribute these achievements to ourselves and to go on to bask in our imagined self-generated glory, as if there were neither a God who gave us life and gifts, nor others whose ministrations, in the good providence of God, were crucial to our development and success. It seems to me that it was to speak to this perennial human frailty that the inspired historian placed side by side at the end of Samuel the list of David's great warrior-heroes (23:8-39) and the account of his sin of counting the number of the fighting men of his kingdom (24:1-25).

No man is an island [23:8-39]

You will notice that this account is clearly out of chronological order, in that it records incidents from the earlier wars against the Philistines along with the roster of the men themselves. The parallel passage in 1 Chronicles contains additional material and, most significant of all, prefaces the account with the statement that 'These are the heads of the mighty men whom David had, who gave him strong support in his kingdom, together with all Israel, to make him king, according to the word of the Lord concerning Israel' (1 Chronicles 11:10-47, NASV). The last clause is the key to interpreting the passage. Here is no mere listing of names, no superfluous detailing of naked facts, but rather an exposition of the core meaning of these events — and, as we shall see, more than a clue to the meaning of David's much later action in numbering his people. These **'mighty men'** were the leading professional soldiers[1] in David's service. They consisted of two groups: the **'Three'** and the **'Thirty'**. Between the two, there were **'thirty-seven in all'** (23:39), so the term 'Thirty' was clearly used as a title for the élite leadership in David's army. Indeed, the Thirty actually included the Three! The thirty-seven members of the Thirty as recorded in this passage would appear to consist of the Three (23:8-12), Abishai and Benaiah (23:18-23), the thirty-one[2] men (23:24-39) and Joab, the commanding general of David's army (23:37).[3]

The main point of this account is to recognize the fact that God provided David with many accomplished and loyal servants, through whose ministrations he was propelled to the throne. No man is an island, as the poet Donne said, and David is no exception. He was surrounded by able men who were willing to die for him — some did — and this was the Lord's gracious provision. The mention of Uriah the Hittite adds a poignancy to this thought, for Uriah's faithfulness to David contrasts graphically with David's betrayal of Uriah by taking his wife and then his life. David repented and received the forgiveness of God, but the practical effects of his sin were to dog him to the grave. David's success did not come from either his sinlessness or his ability to avoid putting a foot wrong! His gifts and abilities were very considerable indeed, but it was all of God's grace that he became king. God's grace was in his personal gifts, his circumstances, his being preserved from disaster through his sins and, not least, his faithful exercise of his calling as God's anointed.

The relevance of the account of the 'mighty men' to David's later sin of numbering his fighting men (24:1-25) is surely in the thought that God had done so much for David in the past with the help of few people. For David to indulge himself in a mere headcount of his potential military strength betrayed an inordinate interest in earthly glory and security over against a simple trust in the Lord who had always proved himself faithful throughout David's long life.

Counting the fighting men [24:1-9]

David's counting of the fighting men of Israel stands as one of the most mysterious of the sins recorded in the Scriptures. It would appear from the passage that the sin lay not so much in the census itself — Moses, after all, had counted the people on two occasions without penalty (Numbers 1;26) — as in the attitude and aim of David in taking this particular census and in the spiritual condition of Israel as a whole. We are told that **'The anger of the Lord burned against Israel, and he incited David against them, saying, "Go and take a census of Israel and Judah"'** (24:1). If anything is clear, it is that there was a deepening problem of national backsliding which the Lord intended to correct. This was presumably some kind of nationalistic pride which robbed the Lord of his glory as the God of Israel. That David shared in this proud and self-sufficient attitude is clear from his overruling the advice of Joab (24:3). The Lord's role confirms this general picture. He did not want such a census. The Chronicler says that 'Satan rose up against Israel and incited David to take a census of Israel' (1 Chronicles 21:1). This puts in perspective the historian's ascription in 2 Samuel of the inciting of David to the Lord and indicates that the Lord adapted the efforts of Satan to further his own purposes for his people. God is not the author of the sin, but he planned to permit that sin to happen. This illustrates the distinction between the preceptive and decretive aspects of the will of God. The former is the positive revealed will of God (his precepts) as to what is right and what is wrong, while the latter is his eternal predestination as to what actually happens in the course of history (his decree). This is often secret until it happens and sometimes, as in predictive prophecy, is revealed as bound to happen according to God's plan.

Light is cast on this event by a passage in the Pentateuch. Exodus 30:11-16 records that the Lord required that any census be accompanied by the levy of a half-shekel tax called 'atonement money' on everyone twenty years of age and older. Plague would then not come on the people when they were counted. This

emphasized that service in the Lord's host — the army of Israel —
required sacrifice, as it was a holy duty.[4] How this ties in with
David's sin is not clear, but it may explain the underlying
presupposition in the advice of Joab and the army commanders that
taking a census was a hazardous business. Beyond this, the text does
not allow us to go, although this has not inhibited Bible
commentators from inventing all sorts of theories to provide the
detail the Lord has chosen not to give us.[5] Matthew Henry hits the
nail on the head in his assessment of the problem: 'It was proud
confidence in his own strength. By publishing among the nations
the number of his people, he thought to appear the more formidable,
and doubted not that, if he should have any war, he should
overpower his enemies with the multitude of his forces, trusting in
an arm of flesh more than he should have done who had written so
much of trusting in God only.'[6]

Whatever the case, an expedition set off to count Israel's
fighting strength. Less than ten months later it returned with the
news that **'In Israel there were eight hundred thousand able-
bodied men who could handle a sword, and in Judah five
hundred thousand'** (24:9). The counting was over and it only
remained to see whether the doubts of Joab and the other commanders would find confirmation in some righteous visitation of God's
holy anger.

Counting heads has long been a snare to God's people. We
always assume that 'bigger' is somehow, or at least somewhat,
'better'. Churches no sooner grow than they begin to drool over
their membership statistics and their burgeoning budgets. And how
often is the first question about your church: 'How many people
attend your services?' In most minds, numbers translate into
security and success. And the evidence we see seems to confirm this
simple correlation, for dying churches all shrink and become
smaller before they disappear, while lively churches tend to have a
measure of growth. David's sin is at least a warning to us not to be
simplistic about numbers in the church, and certainly shows us the
folly of equating mere numbers with the blessing of God. Some of
the largest and fastest growing movements in history have been and
are profoundly opposed to the Lord and his revealed truth. The
continuing mass following of the Roman Catholic Church and the
meteoric rise of cults like Mormonism and the Third World syn-
cretist pseudo-Christian movements demonstrate this fact beyond

all contradiction. Pride and will-worship thrive on the numbers game at the best of times. Those who love the Lord Jesus Christ need constantly to be reminded that true faithfulness and the assurance of the Lord's blessing are rooted in Christ and his Word — the test of truth and of spiritual fruit — as over against the 'head-count' index, which holds in principle that numbers can be a decisive mark of a true church and the blessing of God. It is perhaps significant that the only numbers Jesus mentioned when speaking of his blessing the church with his presence were decidedly small: 'For where two or three come together in my name, there I am with them' (Matthew 18:20). Jesus knew that as large numbers tempt us to pride, so small numbers tempt us to discouragement. He therefore places the emphasis where it is always needed: upon his absolute trustworthiness and unfailing love towards his believing people.

Pangs of conscience [24:10-14]

Like every true believer in the Lord, David had a profound sense of sin which, when stirred by the Spirit of God, made him burn with shame. **'David was conscience-stricken after he had counted the fighting men.'** He confesses to having **'sinned greatly'** and having done **'a very foolish thing'**. We are not told precisely how David defined his sin or what he thought exactly constituted his foolishness. Perhaps he remembered the warning of Exodus 30:11-16. Perhaps he simply faced up to his own secret motives and realized that they were far from honouring to God. In any event, he was not entirely unprepared to hear what the Lord was to say the next morning through the prophet Gad.

The rebuke and its attendant penalties must, nevertheless, have come as quite a shock. The Lord told David 'to choose what rod he will be beaten with'.[7] Three potential chastisements were set before David. Each of them would result in the reduction by death of Israel's numbers and be a clear case of the punishment being made to fit the crime. He was invited to chose from **'three years of famine... or three months of fleeing from [his] enemies... or three days of plague'** (24:13).

There is no mystery about the general significance of this judgement of God upon Israel. Pride in numbers and self-generated glory would be answered with proof of God's sovereignty, the nation's helplessness before him and a reduction in their much-vaunted statistics through the visitation of death. What is not so obvious is why the Lord gave several options and left it to David to make the choice. The heart of the exercise would seem to be responsibility. David, though probably egged on by public opinion, had chosen to sin: he must now choose the penalty. As he was responsible for the former decision, so he would be responsible for the consequences. It was a vivid demonstration of a universal truth, the manifestation of which is more usually obscured by the complexity of circumstances, namely, that all our actions have consequences and that we are responsible for what we do. For the purposes of teaching his people a clear lesson, the Lord arranged for the linkage of cause and effect to be as clear as crystal and also to make clear that those who are responsible face up to the just judgement of the God whom they have premeditatedly and deliberately wronged. Conviction of sin is a most humbling exercise, but it is absolutely necessary to any enjoyment of forgiveness and reconciliation to the Lord. Integral to this process is the willingness to bear the penalty for the transgression. Becoming persuaded that one has made mistakes, being convicted that one is a sinner, expressing sorrow for sin, promising to endeavour not to do it again and asking the Lord for forgiveness, do not *earn* an exemption from all chastisement and discipline. God is a perfect Father and therefore applies his own holy discipline to his own people. Salvation does not imply an end to discipline. Indeed, discipline is *for* our salvation, in that it is designed to issue in the strengthening of our 'feeble arms and weak knees' and the production of a 'harvest of righteousness' (Hebrews 12:7-13; cf. Psalm 89:32-33).

David no doubt saw that the severity of these penalties was inversely proportional to their duration and appears to have opted for the shortest and sharpest, mindful perhaps that three days in the hands of a merciful, if offended, Father-God held less grief than three months in the hands of his less-than-merciful enemies. Some commentators are sure that David did indeed choose the third option — the three days of plague. There is, however, no explicit confirmation of this in the text.[8] All we are told is that David cast himself upon the mercy of the Lord, while expressing the desire that the Lord should not let him **'fall into the hands of men'** (24:14). This suggests fairly strongly that David did not so much make a choice as simply throw himself repentantly on the Lord's sovereign grace, trusting him to do his will, exact his penalty and he hoped, be merciful. There was no cold calculation of percentages, no plea-bargaining in the modern idiom, in which admission of guilt is traded for a lesser charge, and certainly no claim of innocence or diminished responsibility. A holy contrition gripped David's chastened heart.

Punishment inflicted [24:15-17]

The plague duly fell upon Israel for three days **'and seventy thousand of the people from Dan to Beersheba died'**. This was administered by **'the angel of the Lord'**, who was seen by David to be standing on Mount Moriah **'at the threshing-floor of Arau-nah the Jebusite'**. This angel is, as R. P. Gordon notes, 'the same as the "destroyer" of Exodus 12:23 and the "angel of the Lord" of 2 Kings 19:35 (cf. Is. 37:36)'.[9] The death toll amounted to about one in twenty of Israel's manpower — approximately half of the 'decimation' in terms of which punishment was meted out to rebellious soldiery in ancient times. Terrible as this check clearly was to the pride of Israel and her king, the consequences of letting them go on with their self-centred schemes would have been far greater. Indeed, the later degeneration of the Hebrew kingdoms and their final dissolution is an indication of what would have happened much sooner, had not the Lord repeatedly chastised them for their sins and brought them back to a revived faithfulness to his covenant.

This visitation of divine judgement was less lethal that it might have been, for **'When the angel stretched out his hand to destroy Jerusalem, the Lord was grieved because of the calamity and said to the angel who was afflicting the people, "Enough! Withdraw your hand!"'** (24:16). The fact that the angel was standing on the spot on which David would raise an altar and Solomon his great temple is no coincidence. Here was the place where God's mercy would be seen to stretch forth his sovereign grace to his people. The expression 'the Lord was grieved' does not, of course, indicate changeable passions in the Lord, but indicates his compassionate love as it comes to expression in the unfolding of this scenario of divine chastisement.[10]

David, seeing the angel but as yet unaware that the judgement had already ceased, cried out to God and presented himself as the one with primary responsibility for the sin and therefore the one who should bear the penalty. **'I am the one who has sinned and done wrong. These are but sheep. What have they done? Let your hand fall upon me and my family'** (24:17). He is, as Henry remarks, 'severe upon his own faults, while he extenuates theirs'.[11] The shepherd wished to be smitten, that the 'sheep' might be spared — a reminder, surely, to New Testament Christians of the death of Christ, the sinless Shepherd, as the substitute for sinners.

Sacrifice and forgiveness [24:18-25]

Sacrifice and forgiveness are inextricably interwoven into the fabric of biblical redemption. Indeed, 'Without the shedding of blood there is no forgiveness' (Hebrews 9:22). God's acceptance of sacrifice seals the reality of his forgiving and healing mercy. His command to David to **'go up and build an altar to the Lord on the threshing-floor of Araunah the Jebusite'** was an indication that God was reconciling his people to himself. Having observed the repentance of David, and presumably also of the people, he was ready to accept the worship of his servant and stop the plague on Israel.

David duly sought to purchase the threshing-floor of Araunah (24:19-24). Araunah immediately offered to give David the land, together with the materials and animals necessary for the sacrifice.[12] David, however, insisted upon making the proper payment: **'I will not sacrifice to the Lord my God burnt offerings that cost me nothing'** (24:24). There are perhaps two main reasons for David taking this position.

The first is that this was to be the site for the temple (1 Chronicles 22:1). It was important that the property be acquired in a holy way. David specifically says to Araunah, in the Chronicles account, 'I will not take for the Lord what is *yours*' (21:24, my emphasis). Even Jebusites — for Araunah belonged to that con-quered people — had property rights! And it was impossible for the honour of God that he would permit his house to be built on land taken from another without compensation, even if offered as a gift! Cost always implies sacrifice and the erection of the temple was to exemplify the meaning of sacrifice not only in its purpose as the place of the worship of God, but also in its very fabric as the structure upon earth in which God was pleased to manifest his glory.

The second reason flows from the first. As the temple and all to do with it, whether land, materials or services, was to be seen to be set apart as the holy house of the Lord, so all of our service to the Lord must be set apart in holiness as sacrifices of praise and thanksgiving. The Lord is not to be offered the dregs of our lives. True consecration can only be measured in terms of the sacrifices of a life laid upon the altar of living discipleship. David's words encapsulate a principle which applies to all worship, offerings and service to the Lord. The Lord is worthy of the first-fruits — the cream — of our lives. And the reason for this is so clear from the message of God's Word as a whole, for just as God sent his most precious only-begotten Son as the sacrifice for the sins of people like us, so those saved by the blood of his dear Son can only answer from their hearts with the sacrifices of their new lives in Christ. Thus the first day of the week belongs to the Lord and is an earnest of the dedication of the work of the other six days; the first tenth of our income is set aside on that day, in token of the fact that all we are and have is given us by the free grace of our Saviour; and the first priorities of our time, our love and our prayers are set in relation to the love of the Lord Jesus Christ and the glory of his everlasting gospel and kingdom.

The sacrifices were duly offered and we are told with majestic simplicity that **'The Lord answered prayer on behalf of the land, and the plague on Israel was stopped'** (24:25). Jesus Christ is himself the true sacrifice. It is to him that David's sacrifices pointed. He is the substance of which David's offerings were only pictures, emblems and shadows. David knew this. He never imagined that animal blood atoned for sin. David was a prophet who was looking ahead to the risen Christ (Acts 2:30-31). Jesus Christ and the gospel of saving grace are the message and meaning of David's life and ministry as recorded in 2 Samuel.

> 'Save me from bloodguilt, O God,
>   the God who saves me,
>   and my tongue will sing of your righteousness.
> O Lord, open my lips,
>   and my mouth will declare your praise.

You do not delight in sacrifice, or I would bring it;
   you do not take pleasure in burnt offerings.
The sacrifices of God are a broken spirit;
    a broken and contrite heart,
    O God, you will not despise'

                      (Psalm 51:14-17).

Postscript

Please read 1 Kings 1-2 and 1 Chronicles 22-29

There is a certain tidiness about the historical account of David's life as given in 2 Samuel. The last chapter ends with the purchase of the land on Mount Moriah which was to become the site of the temple in Solomon's day. The offering of sacrifices to the Lord on that spot — in connection with God's just judgement on the sin of numbering the warriors of Israel — concludes the history of David on a high, yet humble note. David's 'despotic self-interest' in taking a census of his nation's military potential gives way to his acting as the 'shepherd-king... willing to suffer (die?) for the sake of the sheep (24:17)'.[1] David's life was, however, not over by any means and it is clear from what is recorded elsewhere in Scripture that 2 Samuel studiously avoids the last convolutions of his reign and quite deliberately ends with a redemptive, even messianic note which dovetails beautifully into the tone and tendency of the inspired historian's account, and leaves the reader with a picture of the significance of David as the progenitor of the greater King who would come in the fulness of God's time. In the light of the New Testament, the shadows of prophecy are banished and we see with unmistakable clarity that David was the forerunner of his greater Son, the Lord Jesus Christ.

Given the loftiness of this theme, it may be too easy to forget that many things were still to take place in David's life and, of course, he was still to die. As we noted in our study of 2 Samuel 23, it is significant that these events are taken up in 1 Kings 1-2 and 1 Chronicles 22-29 not as part of a definitive biography of David but almost as a backdrop to the beginning of the reign of Solomon. It is Solomon who is centre stage as 1 Kings begins, while David is consistently in the position of one whose day is done. When David finally departs the scene, it is with the quietly exultant epitaph: 'He died at a good old age, having enjoyed long life, wealth and honour' (1 Chronicles 29:28). He went to be with the Lord, to enter into the quiet rest of the redeemed in heaven. Meanwhile, the promises of God's everlasting covenant remained in the hearts, lives and experience of the Lord's people, awaiting their revelation in fulness with the advent of Jesus, the Son of David, to be the once-and-final Saviour of sinners and the King of kings and Lord of lords.

References

References

Introduction
1. G. J. Keddie, *Dawn of a Kingdom — the message of 1 Samuel* (Evangelical Press, 1988), 274pp.
2. J. Brown, D.D., *The Sufferings and Glories of the Messiah* (Sovereign Grace Pub., 1970). The second half of the book is an exposition of Isaiah 52:13-53:12.
3. *Ibid.*, p. 25.
4. *Ibid.*, p. 35.
5. G. Goldsworthy, *Gospel & Kingdom* (Paternoster, 1981), p.120.

Chapter 1
1. D. F. Payne, *Samuel* (Westminster Press, 1982), p.157.
2. C. F. Keil and F. Delitzsch, *The Books of Samuel* (W. B. Eerdmans), p.286.
3. A. W. Pink, *The Life of David*, 2 volumes in one, (Reiner, 1974), vol. I, p.232.
4. R. P. Gordon, *1 & 2 Samuel* (Paternoster, 1986), pp.209-210. The fact that an Amalekite could be a resident alien (Hebrew: *ger* — 'sojourner') in Israel at that time is further proof of Saul's disobedience to the Lord's command that he expunge that reprobate nation from the face of the earth (cf. Exodus 17:16; 1 Samuel 15:1-35). No Amalekite should have been a 'sojourner' among God's people. See my discussion of this issue of the 'ban' on Amalek in my comments on 1 Samuel 15 (*Dawn of a Kingdom*, pp.141-4). A. W. Pink observes that 'As an Amalekite, he was devoted to destruction (Deut. 25:17-19), and as the elect-king, David was now required to put the sentence into execution' (Pink, p.233).
5. D. F. Payne, p.158.

6.   R. L. Harris (ed) *et al*, *Theological Wordbook of the Old Testament* (Moody Press, 1980), vol. 2, p.798, ref. 2018a (*qina*).

7.   R. P. Gordon, p.211, thinks 'Jashar' may be connected to 'Jeshurun', a name applied to Israel in the Song of Moses (Deuteronomy 32:15).

8.   D. F. Payne, p.161, gives clear and persuasive reasons for rejecting the 'homosexual' interpretation.

9.   Newbolt's poem *'Vitai Lampada'* begins on the cricket field ('There's a deathly hush in the close tonight'), goes on to a desperate battle somewhere in the British Empire ('The sand of the desert is sodden red') and ends back at schools across the land, where the next generation of cricket-playing colonialists was being fed with the philosophy that would get them through life with heroic patriotism — and perhaps to an early death:

> This they all with a joyful mind
> Bear through life like a torch in flame,
> And falling fling to the last behind —
> 'Play up! play up! and play the game!'

Chapter 2

1.   A. W. Pink, vol. I, p.237.

2.   R. P. Gordon, p.213, notes that this was the second of three anointings of David (1 Samuel 16:13; 2 Samuel 2:4; 5:3).

3.   C. F. Keil and F. Delitzsch, p.296. R. P. Gordon, p.214, thinks David and Ish-Bosheth ruled their respective kingdoms for two years after Gilboa, then David ruled all Israel from Hebron for five and a half years before becoming king of all Israel. This is not supported by the natural reading of 5:1-5.

4.   R. P. Gordon, p.216.

5.   J. C. Laney, *First and Second Samuel*, (Moody Press, 1982), p.91, notes: 'In ancient times a concubine was a slave woman who was the legal chattel of her master and often served to raise him an heir. By the time of the monarchy the possession of concubines appears to have been a royal prerogative. Having intercourse with a king's concubine was a serious offence, for it was in essence making a claim for the throne (cf. 16:20-22; 1 Kings 2:13-25).'

6.   R. P. Gordon, p.221.

7.   The NIV renders the Hebrew *nabal* 'lawless' ('Should Abner have died as the lawless die?'). The NASB's 'fool' — the basic meaning of *nabal* — makes more sense here, since the implication is that Abner should have known better than to trust Joab. For another Nabal see 1 Samuel 25:25.

8.   John Balliol, to his credit, rebelled against the English, but was soon deposed and is, curiously, remembered today through his family's foundation of a college at Oxford. His 'toom tabard' was well filled by Robert Bruce who regained Scotland's ancient independence at Bannockburn in 1314.

Chapter 3
1.   G. Goldsworthy, p.73.
2.   R. P. Gordon, pp.49ff.
3.   Zion or Jebus was the southern and highest hill of Jerusalem and not the modern Mount Zion, which is on the lower hills to the north. The northern part of Jerusalem had once been attacked successfully (Judges 1:8), but Jebus held out, a constant reminder of the incompleteness of the Israelite conquest of the promised land.
4.   R. P. Gordon, p.227, discusses this exegetical problem.
5.   J. Murray, *Redemption Accomplished and Applied* (Banner of Truth, 1961), p.93. Murray's treatment of the atonement and the *ordo salutis* is one of the truly great Christian books of the modern era and ought to be read carefully by all who aspire to teach others anything about the gospel.
6.   M. Henry, *A Commentary on the Whole Bible*, (World Bible Publishers), 6 vols, vol. 2, p.469. The reference is to 1 Peter 2:9.
7.   Hailsham quoted this in Latin, not English (*Non nobis, Domine...*) and reminded the reporter of the words of Shakespeare's Henry V on the occasion of the deliverance of the outnumbered English at Agincourt in 1415:

> Let there be sung *'Non nobis'* and *'Te Deum'*,
> The dead with charity enclosed in clay.
> And then to Calais, and to England then,
> Where ne'er from France arrived more happy men
> *(Henry V*, Act IV, Sc. VIII).

8.   This psalm may well commemorate the lifting of the Assyrian siege of Jerusalem in Hezekiah's reign (Isaiah 37). See H. C. Leupold, *Exposition of the Psalms* (Baker, 1972), pp.366-7.

Chapter 4
1.   C. Simeon, *Expository Outlines on the Whole Bible*, 21 vols, (Baker, 1988), 3, p.242.
2.   The English word 'ark' is from the Latin *arca* and translates the Hebrew *aron*, which basically means 'a box' or 'a chest'. Since *aron* is

used 195 times of the ark ('ark of the covenant', 184 of these) and only seven times of a chest or (once) a coffin, it is in effect a technical term. The other 'ark' in English usage is Noah's ark. This translates a different Hebrew word, *teba*, and is also a unique and therefore technical term. Both arks are covenant boxes — in their different ways, they are symbolic of God's covenant faithfulness and his provision of salvation for his people.
3.   W. H. Gispen, *The Bible Student's Commentary — Exodus* (Zondervan, 1982), p.248.
4.   This is why the biblical teaching on the necessity of the atonement is called, in theology, 'consequent absolute necessity'. It was 'consequent' upon God's free and sovereignly gracious purpose to save sinners (the eternal decree). It was an 'absolute necessity' that atonement for sin be made, because, given his purpose to save, sin could not simply be forgotten, but had to be punished perfectly and justly in satisfaction of the perfect holiness of God. The sacrifice of the Son of God arose from the perfections of the very nature of God, Father, Son and Holy Spirit. That is why there can be no salvation apart from Jesus Christ and why those who trust in their own best efforts (Islam, Buddhism, New Age mysticism, Unitarian universalism, Roman Catholic ritualism, etc.) are lost unless they repent and believe in the risen Christ of the Bible!
5.   Arnold Silcock (ed.), *Verse and Worse* (Faber & Faber, 1962), p.217.
6.   R. P. Gordon, p.233, has a helpful discussion on the 'ins and outs' of Obed-Edom's origins and suggests that he may have been a Gittite who moved to Israel as a result of earlier contacts with David in the latter's days in Gath. Even so, it looks as if David dumped the ark as fast as he could, for godly man as Obed-Edom seems to have been, he was not a Levite — so, once again, David failed to observe scriptural order.
7.   C. F. Keil and F. Delitzsch, p. 334.
8.   M. Henry, vol. 2, pp.474-5.
9.   H. Law, *The Gospel in Exodus* (Banner of Truth, 1967), pp.101-2.

Chapter 5
1.   Great occasions are often marked in such a way. In June 1953, every schoolchild in the U.K. was given a coronation mug to mark the accession of Queen Elizabeth II. As I remember, we also received a roll of a now-defunct confection called Merrols. I think it was these 'sweeties', as much as anything else, that convinced us kids that queens were a good thing!
2.   D. F. Payne, p.185.

Chapter 6
1.   A helpful sketch of the covenant context of Scripture may be found in

F. Schaeffer, *Joshua and the Flow of Biblical History* (IVP (US), 1976), pp.49-70, and in W. Hendriksen, *The Covenant of Grace* (Baker, 1978), 76pp.

2.   G. Goldsworthy, *Gospel & Kingdom* (Paternoster Press, 1982), p.74. This little book (124pp.) provides an excellent non-technical overview of the Old Testament theological framework.

3.   We ought to be careful about using language like 'The Lord told me to do...' (as if the Lord was whispering instructions for every detail of life in the ear) or 'I just know this is the Lord's leading...' Quite often, what we tell others is 'the Lord's leading' turns out not to be the Lord's will at all and we leave others with the impression that we use such expressions too easily (and presumptuously) and do so mainly to impress people with our holiness. As a general rule of thumb, we only know something to be the Lord's leading if (1) it is expressly commanded in God's Word, (2) it is a necessary consequence and application of Scripture principle in a given situation and (3) after the event has actually taken place. In all other circumstances, we ought to admit we cannot see the future and confine ourselves to confiding quietly and prayerfully in the Lord, with an 'If the Lord wills, we will do this or that' (see James 4:15).

4.   R. Ganz, *You shall be free indeed!* (GSG Group, 1989), p.33. This is a marvellous treatment of the true freedom of the Christian by Reformed Presbyterian pastor and counselling psychologist, Dr Richard Ganz.

5.   M. Henry, vol. 2, p.480.

6.   G. Goldsworthy, p.74. Goldsworthy suggests that the expression, 'I will be his father, and he will be my son' (7:14) ought to be understood as 'an individualizing of the covenant statement, "I will be your God and you shall be my people".' He adds, 'David's line is thus declared to be representative of God's people or, to put it another way, David's son is the true Israel.'

7.   M. Henry, vol. 2, p.481.

8.   Dispensationalist premillennialism sees this as referring to the church, in Christ (Rev. 19:11-16) and then, after the so-called 'Church Age', to a revived Davidic kingdom of Israel (temple, sacrifices and all) for a literal thousand-year millennium (Revelation 20:1-4). This ignores entirely the repetitive and progressive parallelism in the structure of the book of Revelation (which covers the same history of the New Testament age over and over again) and instead treats Revelation as a strictly serial account of future history. It also ignores the true place of the church as the final temple and interposes an impossible revival of the temple and theocratic Israel.

9.   M. Henry, vol. 2, p.482.

10. C. Simeon, vol. 3, pp.262-3.

11. J. G. Murphy, *A Critical and Exegetical Commentary on the Book of Psalms* (James, 1977[1876]), pp.481-2.

12. I have lost the reference, but believe it originally came from Thomas Scott's *Commentary on the Whole Bible*. Thomas Scott (1747-1821) was an Anglican divine and the successor to John Newton at Olney, having been brought from Unitarianism to Calvinistic evangelicalism through the ministry of the converted slave-ship captain..
13. C. Simeon, vol. 2, pp.263-4.

Chapter 7
1.   R. P. Gordon, p.242, points out that 'Metheg Ammah' in 8:1 is unknown as a place-name and is impossible to interpret as two proper nouns. It may be some alternative and obscure reference to Gath. The clarity of the parallel passage in Chronicles must be taken as the definitive description of the location of David's victory.

Chapter 8
1.   D. F. Payne, p.197. Abimelech (Judges 9:5) and Athaliah, the mother of Ahaziah (2 Chronicles 22:10-11) attempted to wipe out all potential rivals to their rule. David is hardly in the same category as these murderous reprobates.
2.   R. P. Gordon, pp.41-44 (also more thoroughly in his JSOT monograph *1 & 2 Samuel*, (JSOT Press, 1984, pp.81-94) discusses this hypothesis with the air of a man who would rather be doing something else — a distinct point in his favour!
3.   D. F. Payne, p.197, seems to regard loyalty (the covenant with Jonathan) and gracious initiative (reaching out to Mephibosheth) as mutually exclusive motives for what David did. Payne suggests: 'The story, then, is not so much about undeserved charity as about loyalty.' Having effectively cut grace out of the picture, by highlighting obligation almost as little more than a legal duty, Payne goes on to insinuate doubt about the sincerity of even this truncated view of David's motives. As a mirror of the covenant of grace in Christ, the believer's motives in personal relationships are always both covenant and grace: *covenant*, in that we are under God's holy covenant to deal faithfully with others (even where we have made no specific promises to them) and *grace*, in that we are always to give freely of that which we have freely been given by the Lord (Matthew 10:8).
4.   M. Henry, vol. 2, p.488.
5.   *Shorter Catechism*, Question 10: 'How did God create man? *Answer:* God created man male and female, after his own image, in knowledge, righteousness, and holiness, with dominion over the creatures (Gen. 1:26-27; Col. 3:10; Eph. 4:24).'

6.   Andrew Bonar, *Memoirs and Remains of R. M. M' Cheyne* (Banner of Truth, 1966), pp.632-3.

Chapter 9
1.   D. F. Payne, p.201, thinks it may have been a treaty between Ammon and David, when the latter was king over Judah in Hebron, while Abner and Ish-Bosheth still ruled the northern tribes. Maybe, but where's the evidence?
2.   A. W. Pink, vol. II, p.10.
3.   The Church Growth school of thought uses the parable of the sower as a basis for assessing the potential fruitfulness of a mission-field ahead of time — specifically identifying 'good soil' and then sending in workers to harvest souls for Christ. This is decided, in practice, by means of demographics and preliminary surveys supposedly indicating receptivity to the gospel. This is, however, simply unbiblical, for in Scripture, the quality of the soils is known only to God. The field is the world as a whole! We must not read modern agricultural techniques into Jesus' parable. And we must not imagine that sociological analysis is a means of discerning the secret will of God! It is also true that we are not to cast pearls before swine and that the time can come in any evangelistic effort when it is appropriate to shake the dust from off our feet at unresponsiveness. But the point there is that we only know the swine by their reaction to the gospel; we only know who are unresponsive through the experience of the rejection of our mission. God's principle and our calling are that we sow in faith, cultivate it with love and prayer and leave the increase to the Lord.
5.   R. P. Gordon, p.250.
6.   Simon Patrick (1626-1707), Bishop of Ely, was a commentator on many Old Testament books and a co-founder of the S.P.C.K.
7.   M. Henry, vol. 2, p. 491.
8.   R.P. Gordon, p.251, suggests that Joab made a mistake by marching on the city and getting himself 'boxed in' between the two enemy armies. This is a misreading of the military situation and tactics employed. The Ammonite-Aramean forces blundered by being too far apart. Joab, to be sure, found himself between them before he knew what was going on — that is the nature of that most elusive of the elements of battle, the 'fog of war'. There was obviously plenty of room for manœuvre — a clear indication of how separated the enemy contingents were. On the other hand, they must have been close enough together to make it impossible for Joab to dispose of each army one at a time. He realized he must tackle them both at once. So Joab divided his forces unequally: the best troops under his command to smash the Arameans, while Abishai conducted an offensive holding operation against the Ammonites. Joab would reason that the

Ammonites would want to keep their escape route open (into Rabbah) and would be less than enthusiastic about fighting through the whole Israelite army in order to assist their Aramean mercenary allies. With interior lines of communication between his two armies, Joab could retain flexibility and allow for speedy reinforcement between himself and Abishai, should it prove necessary. The evidence is that Joab conducted a brilliant battle. His tactics were impeccable and the conduct of his soldiers magnificent. The Lord was indeed with the armies of Israel that day!

9.   R. P. Gordon, *idem.*, sees this as 'perhaps a sign of desperation' and likens it to the Philistine declaration in 1 Samuel 4:9. It should be noted that *all* such orders before battle are heroic in tone and make no assumptions about easy victory. Joab's is a very conventional declaration, even to the invocation of the Lord's name (the sincerity of which we have no reason to doubt). In contrast, the Philistine order in 1 Samuel 4:9 is an expression of grim and desperate determination, in the face of fear that the coming of the ark of God into the Israelite camp would be a decisive factor in the battle. If 2 Samuel 10:12 represents resolute faith, 1 Samuel 4:9 represents unyielding unbelief! The contrast could not be greater.

10. M. Henry, vol. 2, p.494.

Chapter 10

1.   R. P. Gordon, p. 252.
2.   M. Henry, vol. 2, p. 494.
3.   A. W. Pink, vol. II, p.18.
4.   M. Henry, vol. 2, p. 494.
5.   R. P. Gordon, p. 252.
6.   *Ibid.*
7.   M. Henry, vol. 2, pp. 494-5.
8.   R. J. Rushdoony, *The Institutes of Biblical Law* (Craig Press, 1973), p.395.

Chapter 11

1.   R. P. Gordon, p. 254, notes that 'feet' in this context may be a euphemism for genitalia, as has been suggested is the case in Song of Songs 5:3. A more decorous interpretation sees it as merely referring to 'the comforts of home' as symbolized in the washing of a day's grime from the feet on returning home after work.
2.   The law of God did not prohibit sexual relations between man and wife *at home* at any time, excepting for considerations of ceremonial uncleanness (Exodus 19:15).
3.   The reference to the 'ark [of the covenant]' being with 'Israel and Judah' and 'in tents' appears, on the face if it, to suggest that the ark had accompanied the army, as on the disastrous campaign against the Philis-

tines in Eli's day (1 Samuel 4:3-11). It is possible, however, to understand Uriah's mention of 'the ark' as a reverent reference to Yahweh, the God of the covenant, under the figure of the ark, which would actually have remained in its own tent in Jerusalem. The idea is simply that God himself was with the armies of Israel in the field. In support of this interpretation is the fact that there is no explicit evidence that the ark was taken on campaigns with Israel's armies. Furthermore, in view of the revival associated with the bringing of the ark to Jerusalem, and especially the lessons taught by the loss of the ark at Aphek and its long absence from the centre of Israelite life in consequence of taking it from the tabernacle at Shiloh in the first place, it would seem altogether reasonable to see a figurative reference to the ark in this context.

4.   M. Henry, vol. 2, p.496.
5.   *Ibid.*, p.497.

Chapter 12

1.   M. Henry, vol. 2, p.500.
2.   R. P. Gordon, p.257, notes that some have seen an echo of David's invocation of the fourfold penalty in the deaths of his first four sons: Bathsheba's child, Amnon, Absalom and Adonijah.
3.   *Ibid.*, p.258.
4.   The death penalty was the prescribed penalty for adultery in the law, although there is no record in the Old Testament of any instance of its imposition (Leviticus 20:10; Deuteronomy 22:22; Numbers 5:11-31).
5.   M. Henry, vol.2, p.502.
6.   A. W. Pink, vol. II, p.53.
7.   J. C. Laney, p.109.

Chapter 13

1.   Nathan remained a close adviser of David (1 Kings 1:7-49) and was one of the historians of Israel, whose material must surely have been incorporated in the books of Samuel, Kings and Chronicles (1 Chronicles 29:29-30; 2 Chronicles 9:29).
2.   A. W. Pink, vol. II, p.66.
3.   R. P. Gordon, p.259, points out that David's reply to his officials is 'a short sermon on the futility of prayers for the dead' and adds, 'All that verse 23 is saying is that David would one day go to the same shadowy world that the child had entered, and that there was no hope of the child returning to this life; "but how far this falls short of the Christian hope of the Resurrection of the Body, and the Life Everlasting!" (Kirkpatrick).'

Chapter 14
1. R. P. Gordon, p.53.
2. Tamar's appeal that Amnon ask David for permission to marry her was probably a ploy to cool Amnon down. She would have known that the law of God prohibited half-brothers and half-sisters from marrying (13:13; Leviticus 18:11).
3. M. Henry, vol. 2, p.508.
4. *Ibid.*, p.509.
5. J. C. Laney, p.111.
6. R. P. Gordon, p.264.
7. M. Henry, vol. 2, p.509.
8. W. C. Kaiser, Jr, *Toward Old Testament Ethics* (Academie Books, 1983), p.297. The law against rape (Deuteronomy 22:25-29) required death for the man who raped a betrothed woman, because he had violated not only her integrity but that of the family, which is the basis of stable and God-honouring life in society. In the case of an unmarried, unbetrothed woman, the rapist (assuming no other complications, such as the incest in Amnon's case) was, if acceptable, to marry the girl (with no divorce permitted for any reason whatsoever) and pay a dowry to her father. If he was not acceptable, he was to pay the dowry as a fine (cf., Exodus 22:17). In this way the girl's marriageableness was enhanced by a double dowry — the father's and the rapist/seducer's. See R. J. Rushdoony, pp.396-397.
9. R. P. Gordon, p.264.
10. M. Henry, vol. 2, p.507.

Chapter 15
1. R. P. Gordon, p.268.
2. A. W. Pink, vol. II, p.84.
3. For an illuminating discussion of these provisions of God's law, see R. J. Rushdoony, *The Institutes of Biblical Law*, pp.375-381.

Chapter 16
1. C. Simeon, vol. 3, p.281.
2. *Ibid.*, p.282.
3. T. Watson, *A Divine Cordial*, (Sovereign Grace, 1959[1663]), p.22.
4. M. Henry, vol. 2, p.520.
5. *Ibid.*, p.521.
6. See A. W. Pink, vol. II, pp.102f.
7. David's forces were not inconsiderable, although hardly sufficient to face an enemy whose strength was unknown but could be assumed to be

much greater. David had 'his men' — the royal guard — and two contingents of non-Israelites. The 'Kerethites and Pelethites' were a mercenary force of men drawn, it is thought, from peoples related to the Philistines, while Ittai and his 'six hundred Gittites' were followers from the Philistines of Gath. These foreigners may well have been proselytes.

8.   J. C. Laney, p.114.
9.   M. Henry, vol. 2, p.525.
10. D. F. Payne, p.232, points out that to be called the king's 'friend' indicates the possession of high political office.
11. R. P. Gordon, p.275.

Chapter 17
1.   R. J. Rushdoony, pp.565f.
2.   M. Henry, vol. 2, p.529.

Chapter 18
1.   M. Henry, vol. 2, p.530.
2.   R. P. Gordon, p.278.
3.   M. Henry, vol. 2, p.530.
4.   R. P. Gordon, p.280.
5.   The others are Saul (1 Samuel 31:4), Zimri (1 Kings 16:18) and Judas Iscariot (Matthew 27:5).

Chapter 19
1.   Charles Edward Stuart (d.1788), the last Stuart claimant to the British throne and the leader of the second Jacobite (Catholic) Rebellion in 1745-6.
2.   T. Manton, *Works*, vol. 12, p.457.
3.   R. P. Gordon, p.283.
4.   The sons mentioned in 14:27 must have predeceased him. This pillar no longer exists. The so-called 'Tomb of Absalom' in the Kidron Valley today dates from around the first century A.D.
5.   R. P. Gordon, p.286.
6.   M. Henry, vol. 2, p.537.

Chapter 20
1.   Aonio Paleario, *The Benefits of Christ's Death*, p.8. There is a reference to this very rare work in S. M. Houghton's introduction to his

edition of J. H. Merle D'Aubigné, *The Reformation in England*, (Banner of Truth, 1962), vol. I, pp. 7-8.
2.   R. P. Gordon, p.289.
3.   M. Henry, vol. 2, p.546.
4.   *Ibid.*, p.547.
5.   R. P. Gordon, p.292.
6.   *Ibid.*

Chapter 21
1.   M. Henry, vol. 2, p.550.
2.   *Ibid.*, p.551.
3.   *Ibid.*
4.   *Ibid.*, p.552.
5.   *Ibid.*, p.553.
6.   R. P. Gordon, p.295.
7.   Matthew Henry, rather obviously genuflecting to the sovereign at the time of his writing (1708), Queen Anne, notes that 'This one woman with her wisdom saved the city. Souls know no difference of sexes. Though the man be the head, it does not therefore follow that he has the monopoly of the brains, and therefore he ought not, by any Salic law, to have the monopoly of the crown' (p.554).

Chapter 22
1.   R. P. Gordon, *1 & 2 Samuel [Old Testament Guides]*, (JSOT Press, 1984), pp.95-7. This monograph, published by the (British) Society for Old Testament Study is not to be confused with R. P. Gordon's commentary on 1 and 2 Samuel, to which I have frequently resorted in these studies.
2.   J. C. Laney, p.123.
3.   A. W. Pink, vol. II, p.230.
4.   M. Henry, vol. 2, p.556.
5.   Restitution, directly from the perpetrator to the victim, is integral to biblical justice. The freeing of the slave had to involve a measure of compensation, making his or her release a decided advance on being a slave, and also a commensurate loss for the slave-owner. In modern society, punishment (usually equated with a term in jail) has increasingly been separated from restitution, with the result that the victim remains, in effect, victimized and the criminal avoids the true (biblical) punishment for his action.
6.   D. F. Payne, p.259. Even J. C. Laney, p.124, is willing to say that 'Perhaps David did wrong,' although he goes on to point out that God honoured the action by ending the famine and the reason for the famine had

been the action of Saul 'and his *blood-stained house*' (21:1). There is not the slightest indication in the text that David 'did wrong' and there is no reason for Christians to be defensive or apologetic about these executions. We always underestimate human guilt — including our own individual guilt — and therefore tend to sit in judgement upon God and turn our spurious conception of our 'innocence' into an indictment of the alleged excessive severity of God.

7.   C. Simeon, vol. 3, p.304.

8.   As, for example, in the creation week of six days of creative activity followed by the seventh day (of rest) indicating the completion of the work.

9.   Which is why the death of the Lord Jesus Christ was upon a cross. He took the curse upon himself, that all who believe in him might have everlasting life.

10.   P. C. Craigie, *The Book of Deuteronomy* (Eerdmans [NICOT], 1976), p.285.

11.   R. P. Gordon, pp.303-4, has a good discussion of the difficulties with the text of 21:19 and its parallel in 1 Chronicles 20:5. The solution appears lost in the transmission of the text. I favour taking 1 Chronicles 20:5 at face value, on the supposition that 21:19 has been garbled in transmission: i.e., that (1) since David killed Goliath long before, Elhanan could not kill him later; (2) Elhanan did not kill another Goliath; (3) Elhanan was not another name for David (making this a flashback to 1 Samuel 17).

12.   M. Henry, vol. 2, p.559.

Chapter 23

1.   C. H. Spurgeon, *The Treasury of David* (Guardian Press, 1976), vol. 1, p.226.

2.   H. P. Liddon, *St Paul's Epistle to the Romans* (James & Klock, 1977), p.278. See also W. G. T. Shedd, *A Critical and Doctrinal Commentary on the Epistle of St Paul to the Romans* (Zondervan, 1967), p.410: 'The original speaker is David, who is the type of Christ, who promises to glorify God among the Gentiles.'

3.   Psalms which, on this principle, must be held to speak explicitly of Jesus Christ are Psalms 2, 8, 16, 18, 22, 40, 41, 45, 68, 69, 72, 102, 109, 110 and 118.

4.   J. Brown, *The Sufferings and Glories of the Messiah*, p.59. Brown (1784-1858) wrote many great works of biblical exposition: most notably *The Discourses and Sayings of Our Lord* (in 3 volumes) and his commentaries on *Galatians* and *1 Peter*. A point of 'trivia' — Brown's Broughton Place Church, Edinburgh, was used in the film *'Chariots of Fire'* for the scene in which Eric Liddell (Ian Charleson) reads the Scripture in a service

supposedly on the Lord's Day on which Liddell refused to run in the Paris Olympics.

5.   David Dickson, *Psalms* (Banner of Truth, 1965), p.78. Dickson (1583-1662) was a Covenanting preacher and theologian of the Second Reformation period in Scotland. He was co-author with James Durham of the *Sum of Saving Knowledge*, one of the documents included in Presbyterian doctrinal standards to this day.

6.   J. Brown, p.75.

Chapter 24

1.   J. Brown, p.79.

2.   A. Dallimore, *George Whitefield* (Banner of Truth, 1970), vol. 1, pp.542-3, records a wonderful occasion in Whitefield's ministry in New England when, during a sermon, he used the darkening of the sun by clouds, the crash of thunder, the flash of lightning and the coming of the rainbow after the storm was over, to illustrate the points he was making. This was no mere literary device. It was the Lord's hand accompanying the preaching of the Word with the demonstration of his power.

3.   J. Brown, p.83.

4.   2 Corinthians 5:21; John 8:12; 1 John 1:5; Revelation 13:8; 1 John 2:1.

5.   James G. Murphy, *Commentary on the Psalms* (James, 1977), p.148.

6.   J. Brown, p.121.

Chapter 25

1.   'I will sing hymns...' (NIV), is a misleading rendering of the Greek *psalo* ('I will sing praises'). This is the divinely inspired praise of the Lord Jesus Christ and is not in the same category as even the very best of our hymnology.

2.   I would not conceal from you that a majority of commentators are not persuaded that 2 Samuel 22/Psalm 18 is a messianic psalm in the fullest and incontrovertible sense that, for example, Psalms 2 and 110 clearly are. For the most part, even those who see it as speaking mostly of David's actual experience recognize that it has at least 'a touch of the Messianic' (H. C. Leupold, p.174), or even presents David in the latter part of the psalm as 'a special type of Christ, in his conquest and victories' (D. Dickson, p.84). No one has, however, matched the thorough study of this song by John Brown of Edinburgh in his classic work, *The Sufferings and Glories of the Messiah*. This has proved persuasive to me and will certainly bless your study and meditation, whatever conclusion you may come to in the end.

3.   D. Dickson, p.87.

4.   C. F. Keil and F. Delitzsch, p.481.

5.   Mentioning this event in terms of a date (A.D. 70), a building (the

temple) and a superseded form of church government (Jewish theocracy), should not become a euphemistic evasion of the lamentable fact that well over a million Jews perished in that cataclysm and that this was the judgement of God upon the apostasy of the Old Testament church. Jesus' lament over Jerusalem anticipated this terrible visitation of God's righteous anger (Matthew 23:37-38). See J. Brown, p.150.
6.   J. Brown, pp.153-4.
7.   *Ibid.*, p.157.
8.   C. F. Keil and F. Delitzsch, p.484.
9.   J. Brown, p.160.

Chapter 26
1.   C. F. Keil and F. Delitzsch, p.485. 'And whilst the psalm may be regarded (ch.22) as a great hallelujah, with which David passed away from the stage of life, these "last words" contain the divine seal of all that he has sung and prophesied in several psalms concerning the eternal dominion of his seed, on the strength of the divine promise which he received through the prophet Nathan, that his throne should be established for ever (ch. 7).'
2.   M. Henry, vol. 2, p.564.
3.   R. P. Gordon, p.310. I would prefer to say '*implicitly* messianic terms' (i.e., in view of the developed messianic prophetic elements in others of David's psalms) rather than Gordon's cautious 'inchoately' (undeveloped). It is true that the messianic content is less than explicit in 23:1-7, but that is not to say, in the light of David's undeniable self-perception of his own prophetic role (cf. Acts 2:30-31), that it should not be understood primarily in terms of fulfilment in Jesus Christ.
4.   P. Ackroyd, *The Second Book of Samuel* (Cambridge University Press, 1977), p. 217.
5.   M. Henry, vol. 2, p.564.
6.   A. W. Pink, vol. II, p.290, is persuaded, but Matthew Henry simply reports this interpretation without committing himself. Later commentators say nothing on the subject, no doubt because they understand the God of Israel and the Rock of Israel to be synonymous descriptions of the living God that fall short of an explicit trinitarian differentiation between the persons of the Godhead.
7.   M. Henry, vol. 2, p.566.
8.   C. Simeon, vol. 3, p.309.
9.   C. F. Keil and F. Delitzsch, p.489.
10. C. Simeon, vol. 3, p.313.
11. A. Alexander, *Thoughts on Religious Experience* (Banner of Truth, 1967), p.249. This is a wonderful and very readable treatment of Christian

experience from the cradle to the grave, one of the few Christian books which *every* Christian would profit by reading repeatedly along life's way.
12. *Ibid.*, p.250.

Chapter 27

1. H. W. Herzberg, *I & II Samuel* (Westminster Press, 1964), p.404.
2. From a reading of 23:24-29 in the NIV, you will count twenty-nine names and will wonder how commentators (who tend not to explain such details of their work in their commentaries) can arrive at a figure of thirty-one men. Whence came the two 'extra' names? The answer lies in the unravelling of the corruptions in the text of two verses in particular (23:32, 36). In 23:32 (cf. 1 Chronicles 11:34) the words **'the sons of'** in 'the sons of Jashen' (23:32) appears to be a textual transmission error called a dittograph — a copyist repeated the preceding three consonants by mistake and it subsequently was regarded as a word in its own right in the text. The consonants happened to form the word translated in English 'the sons of'. When this is removed, we are left with Jashen, not as the father of previously mentioned men, but as himself one of the mighty men. Add one name to the list. The other missing name is probably in verse 36, where **'the son of** Hagri (or Haggadi)' is probably a mistranslation of the proper name 'Bani the Gadite'. Now there are thirty-one and the tally of thirty-seven noted in 23:39 is accounted for!
3. J. C. Laney, p.128.
4. J. G. Murphy, *A Critical and Exegetical Commentary on the Book of Exodus* (James, 1976), p.336.
5. Matthew Henry, vol. 2, pp.570-1, unenthusiastically lists five such theories, all of which in the nature of the case have some degree of plausibility. Anything short of comprehensive knowledge seems to be a great frustration to us and perhaps the Lord, knowing this, is deliberately vague just so that we would, by faith, be content with what little we are told. The real point is clear enough, after all.
6. *Ibid.*, p.571.
7. *Ibid.*, p.573.
8. R. P. Gordon, p.319, rests on the doubtful authority of the Septuagint (the Greek version of the Old Testament) which,he says, 'makes good the omission' in the Hebrew text; see also J. C. Laney, p.129.
9. R. P. Gordon, p.320.
10. This subject is discussed more fully in the chapter 'The repentance of God' in my Welwyn Commentary on Jonah, *Preacher on the Run* (Evangelical Press, 1986), pp.95-103.
11. M Henry, vol. 2, p.574.

12. R. P. Gordon, p.321, points out a parallel with Genesis 23:10-20, where Abraham purchased land from Ephron the Hittite, and suggests that the initial offer to give the land, in both these instances, was simply the appropriate opening to what would be serious bargaining over a price, given a context in which a greater and more powerful party is seeking to make a purchase from a lesser and weaker one. This is an interesting if rather speculative interpretation.

Postscript
1. R. P. Gordon, p.322.

ECCLESIASTES & SONG OF SOLOMON
A Life worth Living and a Lord worth Loving
Stuart Olyott
0 85234 173 3 Large paperback,   128pp.

ISAIAH *God Delivers*
Derek Thomas
0 85234 290 X Large paperback, 416pp.

LAMENTATIONS *Great is your Faithfulness*
Richard Brooks
0 85234 257 8 Large paperback, 160pp.

EZEKIEL *God Strengthens*, Derek Thomas
0 85234 310 8 Large paperback, 320pp.

DANIEL *Dare to Stand Alone*
Stuart Olyott
0 85234 163 5 Large paperback, 176pp.

JOEL *Prophet of the Coming Day of the Lord*
O. Palmer Robertson
0 85234 335 3 Large paperback, 112pp.

AMOS *The Lord is his Name*
Gordon J. Keddie
0 85234 224 1 Large paperback,   112pp.

JONAH *Preacher on the Run*
Gordon J. Keddie
0 85234 231 4 Large paperback, 144pp.

MICAH & NAHUM *Balancing the Books*
Michael Bentley
0 85234 324 8 Large paperback, 128pp.

HAGGAI & ZECHARIAH *Building for God's Glory*
Michael Bentley
0 85234 259 4 Large paperback, 240pp.

MALACHI *Losing Touch with the Living God*
John Benton
0 85234 212 8 Large paperback, 140pp.

Welwyn Commentaries on the New Testament

LUKE *Saving a Fallen World*
Michael Bentley
0 85234 300 0 Large paperback, 336pp.

ACTS OF THE APOSTLES *You are my Witnesses*
Gordon J. Keddie
0 85234 307 8 Large paperback, 336pp.

ROMANS *The Gospel as it Really is*
Stuart Olyott
0 85234 125 3 Large paperback, 176pp.

1 CORINTHIANS
Strengthening Christ's Church
Roger Ellsworth
0 85234 333 7 Large paperback, 272pp.

GALATIANS *Free in Christ*
Edgar H. Andrews
0 85234 353 1 Large paperback, 320pp.

EPHESIANS *Alive in Christ*
Stuart Olyott
0 85234 315 9 Large paperback, 144pp.

PHILIPPIANS *Shining in the Darkness*
Michael Bentley
0 85234 403 1 Large paperback, 192pp.

1 & 2 THESSALONIANS *Patience of Hope*
J. Philip Arthur
0 85234 385 X Large paperback, 160pp.

1 & 2 TIMOTHY *Passing on the Truth*
Michael Bentley
0 85234 389 2 Large paperback, 320pp.

TITUS *Straightening out the Self-centred Church*,
John Benton
0 85234 384 1 Large paperback 192pp.

JAMES *The Practical Christian*,
Gordon J. Keddie
0 85234 261 6 Large paperback, 240pp.

JOHN'S EPISTLES *Knowing where we Stand*,
Peter Barnes
0 85234 414 7 Large paperback, 160pp.

1 & 2 PETER *Living for Christ in a Pagan World*
Michael Bentley
0 85234 279 9 Large paperback,   256pp.

JUDE *Slandering the Angels*
John Benton
0 85234 424 4 Large paperback, 192pp.

REVELATION *The Lamb is all the Glory*
Richard Brooks
0 85234 229 2 Large paperback, 224pp.

A wide range of excellent books on spiritual subjects is
available from Evangelical Press. Please write to us for your
free catalogue or contact us by e-mail.

Evangelical Press
Faverdale North Industrial Estate, Darlington, Co. Durham,
DL3 0PH, England

Evangelical Press USA
P. O. Box 84, Auburn, MA 01501, USA

e-mail: sales@evangelical-press.org

web: www.evangelical-press.org